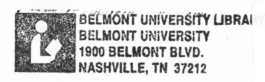BELMONT UNIVERSITY LIBRARY
BELMONT UNIVERSITY
1900 BELMONT BLVD.
NASHVILLE, TN 37212

D1049904

TRANSFORMING DESIRE

TRANSFORMING DESIRE

EROTIC KNOWLEDGE
IN BOOKS III AND IV
OF *THE FAERIE QUEENE*

LAUREN SILBERMAN

University of California Press
Berkeley · Los Angeles · London

University of California Press
Berkeley and Los Angeles, California

University of California Press, Ltd.
London, England

© 1995 by
The Regents of the University of California

Library of Congress Cataloging-in-Publication Data

Silberman, Lauren.
   Transforming desire : erotic knowledge in Books III and IV
   of the Faerie queene / Lauren Silberman.
   Includes bibliographical references and index.
   ISBN 0-520-08486-1 (alk. paper)
   1. Spenser, Edmund, 1552?–1599. Faerie queene. 2. Desire
in literature. 3. Love in literature. 4. Sex in literature.
5. Erotic poetry, English—History and criticism. I. Title.
PR2358.S5 1995
821'.3—dc20   94-13630
                                            CIP

Printed in the United States of America

9 8 7 6 5 4 3 2 1

The paper used in this publication meets the minimum requirements of
American National Standard for Information Sciences—Permanence of
Paper for Printed Library Materials, ANSI Z39.48-1984.

189667

BELMONT UNIVERSITY LIBRARY

PR
2358
.85
1995

ABA-6094

For my mother and the memory of my father

Contents

Acknowledgments

This study began over a decade ago as a dissertation initially directed by A. Bartlett Giamatti and ably seen to completion by Margaret W. Ferguson. I can only begin to acknowledge the numerous individuals who have helped me over the years. Thanks go to Maureen Quilligan, who was a sympathetic reader of the dissertation and has been a supportive and exemplary colleague ever since. The crew of jolly Spenserians, most of whom gather at Kalamazoo each spring, have offered intellectual support and friendship and have listened to my kvetching over many years. I cannot imagine what I would have done without them. Particular thanks are owed Donald Cheney, Anne Lake Prescott, and William Oram for their sensitive and learned reading of this manuscript. Summer grants given by the Professional Staff Congress of the City University of New York and summer seminars subsidized by the National Endowment for the Humanities afforded me time to work on this book. These latter were directed by Thomas P. Roche, Jr., who has given me invaluable professional help and, when summer in New Jersey overcame my sinuses, accompanied me to the Princeton Emergency Room in what must have been at least five out of seven corporal acts of mercy. A year's fellowship leave and course remissions allowed me to complete work on this book. For this, many thanks to Norman Fainstein, Dean of Liberal Arts and Sciences of Baruch College. Professor Harold Brent was my department chair at a crucial time during the work on this book. I owe him a great deal for giving me the support to proceed with this project as I saw fit. Thanks to him, all the errors in this work I can confidently acknowledge as my own.

The library staff of the Yale Club of New York City has been especially helpful during the writing of this book. I should particularly like to thank Louise Jones for her kind interest in my work. I should also like to thank Bill O'Brien for continuing to ask when the book was going to be completed while others would have given up inquiring long ago.

I am very grateful to Doris Kretschmer, the acquisitions editor of the University of California Press, for her interest in the manuscript and to Dore Brown for seeing the project through to its completion. Edith Gladstone, the Platonic ideal of a copy editor, has favored my manuscript with her careful attention. I am grateful for her eagle eye and wonderful ear for style.

Portions of the first three chapters have been published previously. Parts of chapters one and two have appeared in earlier versions in "Spenser and Ariosto: Funny Peril and Comic Chaos," *Comparative Literature Studies* 25 (1988): 23–34, and "Singing Unsung Heroines: Androgynous Discourse in Book III of *The Faerie Queene*" in *Rewriting the Renaissance: The Discourses of Sexual Difference in Early Modern Europe*, ed. Margaret W. Ferguson, Maureen Quilligan, and Nancy Vickers, 259–271 (Chicago: University of Chicago Press, 1986) (© 1986 by the University of Chicago, all rights reserved). Portions of chapter three have appeared in "The Hermaphrodite and the Metamorphosis of Spenserian Allegory," *English Literary Renaissance* 17 (1987): 207–223, and "Mythographic Transformations of Ovid's Hermaphrodite," *The Sixteenth-Century Journal* 19 (1988): 643–652 (© 1988 by the Sixteenth Century Journal Publishers, Inc., Kirksville, Mo., all rights reserved). I am grateful to the editors of the University of Chicago Press, *Comparative Literature Studies*, *English Literary Renaissance*, and *The Sixteenth-Century Journal* for their permission to use this material. Portions of the argument of this book have been presented at meetings of the Modern Language Association, Renaissance Society of America, the Medieval Institute, the Columbia Renaissance Seminar, and the Society for the Study of Women in the Renaissance. My thanks to the audiences for their kind response, even when they disagreed.

Introduction

Literary critics of the 1990s face the problem, eminently predictable for more than a decade, of what to call what comes after postmodernism. Deconstructive criticism of the 1970s has taken us beyond formalism and shown us new ways of paying close attention to texts, particularly to processes of literary signification hitherto taken for granted. Criticism of the 1980s loosely labeled New Historicist has reminded us of the ways in which literary texts are both products and producers of the wider culture of which they are a part. Nevertheless, all of this theoretically conscious attention paid to literary texts has left a very uncertain sense of why a particular work of literature should matter, whether it is worth studying in any capacity other than as a symptom, significant insofar as it illustrates or confirms a given theory of language or history.

Recently, I heard a former president of the Modern Language Association allude to reading Edmund Spenser's *Faerie Queene* as the paradigm of pointless, boring activity. My response to this, once the impulse to throw something subsided, was embarrassment for my chosen profession as I tried to imagine an analogous scene in which, for example, the president of the American Medical Association referred to treating a particular disease with equal contempt because the disease had a funny-sounding name. What is at stake, here, is not blind reverence for short, dead, canonical poets (or the AMA), but some rudimentary sense of engagement with and respect for what one does. With this book, I hope to bear witness to the proposition that reading *The Faerie Queene* is a worthwhile activity. I shall be drawing on theoretical work of the last twenty years—feminist, deconstructionist, and New Historicist—as well as on earlier Spenser scholarship, insofar as that work provides forms of engaged attention to the literary text. My working assumptions are, first, that the intellectual activity involved in thinking about a poem as complex as *The Faerie Queene* is pleasurable and worthwhile for itself but, also,

1

that the poem has something to say to us, even if, indeed, especially if the highly problematic nature of that "saying" is an important part of the message. *The Faerie Queene* has accommodated various critical approaches and inspired diverse critical responses. The one requisite, as far as I am concerned, is to recognize *The Faerie Queene* as the product of a powerful and idiosyncratic intelligence. Miss that and miss everything.

Whether *The Faerie Queene* is a poem for all time we cannot, even as we approach the second millennium, yet know. For good or ill, however, there is still considerable cultural continuity between England in the late sixteenth century and the English-speaking world in the late twentieth. Arguably, these two eras share a peculiar sense of crisis and transition. Then, as now, new philosophy calls all in doubt. And one of the fundamental projects of *The Faerie Queene* is to address that doubt and to explore the role of ideas and ideals in an uncertain world. In this, *The Faerie Queene* anticipates postmodernist concerns with destabilizing language but denies to the distrust of language the status of absolute truth. Spenser was writing in an age that understood faith but saw the beginnings of a great movement of scientific inquiry. Unlike us, who live in the decadence of an Arnoldian age of criticism, Spenser was not apt to mistake faith for theory. Truth is one and given to faith alone, but the mind can construct theories to cope with a world in flux. Spenser directs attention to the nature of linguistic signification not because it is trendy, but because it is important.

Books III and IV of *The Faerie Queene* address the problem of making sense of the sensual world by subjecting conventional discourses of love to critique. Spenser directs a powerful critical intelligence at the sexual ideology of his time while registering the strength of the social forces and philosophical predilections that support that ideology. The poem pursues understanding over social change, and its critique of sexual ideology is ultimately absorbed (if not co-opted) by concerns about epistemology and politics in a society that was historically patriarchal. Nevertheless, ideas have consequences, even if those consequences do not necessarily occur immediately (or bear much resemblance to anyone's intentions). The Spenserian critique of conventional sexual ideology becomes part of a cultural discourse that, several centuries later, produced feminism.[1]

The Faerie Queene is a very long poem. Critics attempting to produce books on *The Faerie Queene* have adjusted their approach to accommodate a poem of over thirty thousand lines.[2] One consequence of these efforts is a distinguished tradition of studies of individual books of *The Faerie Queene* or studies of a limited group of books. Other critics have chosen to focus on a particular theme or motif as it appears in *The Faerie Queene* or to discuss the nature of Spenserian allegory in general terms. Martha Craig's groundbreaking article "The Secret Wit of Spenser's Language" has taught us the necessity of looking closely at the language of *The Faerie Queene*, daunting as that task may be. The rehabilitation of allegory under the influence of postmodernism has also directed attention to *The Faerie Queene* as a complex verbal text.[3]

Nonetheless, most current works of Spenser criticism tend not to sustain close attention to Spenser's text for the duration of an extended argument about large units of *The Faerie Queene*. In contrast, this study bases larger claims about Book III and IV on a detailed and intense reading of major portions of those books, while placing interpretations of individual passages and episodes in the context of an implicit argument about how individual books function in the poem as a whole. I shall be arguing that the individual books of *The Faerie Queene* are in fundamental ways *essays*, as signaled by their subtitles, that is to say, attempts at examining a given subject.[4] Thus, while the books of *The Faerie Queene* contribute severally to a coherent poetic vision, or to a poetic vision as coherent as might be achieved in the sublunary world, each individual book proceeds from a different set of intellectual assumptions in an effort to explore a different intellectual problem. Although Spenser critics have traditionally considered the shift in theme from one book to the next, the extent to which there is a programmatic shift not only in theme, but in allegorical procedure from one book to the next has largely been ignored.[5] Many years ago, A. S. P. Woodhouse pointed out that Books I and II of *The Faerie Queene* presuppose different intellectual contexts—Book I places itself within the order of grace and Book II the order of nature—but little attention has been paid to this shift of framework as a consistent intellectual strategy and an organizing principle of *The Faerie Queene*. Each book has something of the character of a thought experiment as it focuses on a given issue and on its own processes in framing that issue. Each successive book takes up problems left in abeyance by the theoretical focus of previous books as Spenser's allegory shifts to address a new set of issues. Book I develops and explores a typological allegory in which the word of the text is grounded in but not coterminous with the Word of God as part of its exposition of Holiness. Books III and IV address under the rubrics of Love and Friendship respectively the worldly concerns transcended by Holiness and explore how versions of conventional erotic discourse function to shape and express those concerns.

What, then, are the intellectual projects essayed in Books III and IV? They are the construction of a progressive utopian ideal and the unsentimental demonstration of what can happen to a beautiful ideal when it is subjected to a not-so-attractive social reality. Book III develops an ideal of love, of understanding, and of the relationship between individual and world figured by the Hermaphrodite image with which the original version concludes. When *The Faerie Queene* is continued through Book IV and beyond, the Hermaphrodite stanzas are canceled and the ideal represented by that figure is shown to be untenable in the face of conventions and institutions of Spenser's own place and time.

The ideal developed in Book III and shown under attack in Book IV represents a way of addressing the world of the senses. Books III and IV treat issues of understanding initially considered in Book I, but from a different perspective. Book I treats the question of truth from the perspective of Christian eschatology. It presents the mortal world as a sign pointing toward a higher, spiritual reality and presents faith in Christian revelation as the ideal of understanding. Book III shifts perspective from transcending to making sense of the fallen world. It does not deny the truth of revelation but rather addresses that practical concern for the here and now that, at the conclusion of Book I, moves the protective mothers of Eden to pull their children away from the dragon slain apocalyptically by Saint George. Book III develops a model of reading that allows for the uncertainty of knowledge in the fallen world, not as an expression of universal doubt, but as the logical concomitant of the understanding of faith as the evidence of things unseen, as the belief in the truth of revelation. Book I and Books III and IV participate in a coherent vision; however each is a self-contained essay that addresses its own set of concerns.

Having affirmed the truth given to faith alone in Book I, Spenser goes on to register in Books III and IV the provisional nature of temporal understanding. In those central books, dedicated to love and friendship, Spenser examines the role of desire in both moving us to function in an uncertain world and tempting us to foreclose that uncertainty by various strategies that seek to frame knowledge in such a way as to posit total mastery of it. In these two books, Spenser focuses a critical eye, both on the conventions and presuppositions of his own culture and on the aims and limitations of his own practice by examining how the erotic discourses current in Elizabethan literature both facilitate and deform perceptions of and engagement with the world.

In Book III, Spenser develops an allegory that is the shared enterprise of writer and reader who join in the quest to make meaning in order to accommodate epistemological uncertainty in the fallen world, as he seeks to construct a reader fit to cope with this uncertainty. The languages of love become ways of talking about the relationship of self and other, and Spenser's transformation of traditional erotic discourses, represented by the concluding figure of the Hermaphrodite, becomes a way of positing creativity and the growth of knowledge as the ideal model of engagement with the outside world. The heroine Britomart's uncertain quest for Artegall, whose image she has seen in an enchanted mirror, is analogous to the reader's struggle to understand the complexities of Book III. When Britomart fashions herself into the Knight of Chastity as she risks pursuing what might be the delusive shadow of a man, the adventures of Spenser's figure provide a model for the reader, who learns the power of language to construct reality as well as to delude.

In Book IV, Spenser shifts his focus from the construction of an ideal reader to the consequences of addressing a preexisting interpretive community as he shows how the ideal of creative sexual harmony figured by the Hermaphrodite cannot be sustained in a culture of sexual hierarchy. Spenser cancels the Hermaphrodite stanzas as a signal that the erotic ideal embodied in the Hermaphrodite cannot be readily sustained in a culture antagonistic to that ideal. Whereas in Book III, Spenser examines the development of new ideas in a revision of the epistemology of recollection articulated in Plato's *Meno* and *Phaedo*, in Book IV he explores the generation of the text (and of social institutions) and the pressure of what has already been written on the generation of ideas. For this reason, Spenser casts Book IV as the continuation of Chaucer's "Squire's Tale": Spenser inserts his own text self-consciously into one by the earlier poet. He emphasizes issues of narratology as he shows the progress of his own narrative to be a paradoxical attempt to get back to lost precursor texts and to reunite the lovers whose union was given in the canceled conclusion of the first installment of *The Faerie Queene*. At the same time, Spenser shows the process of narrative deferral—that is, the narrative's apparent movement away from itself and its own origin—to be culturally grounded rather than, as modern theorists such as Paul de Man and Jacques Derrida would have it, the inescapable condition of language. Book IV explores how the retrospective stance, the longing for and emphasis on origins figured mythologically by the story of Orpheus and Eurydice, is implicated in the sexual politics of the male point of view, which reduces the female other to an object and occasion for male competition and camaraderie (an issue discussed in various ways by René Girard, Luce Irigaray, and Eve Kosofsky Sedgwick). Moreover, Spenser explores how narrative complications can proceed from and conceal the fundamentally ideological commitment to the notion of sameness, which gives privilege to the masculine over the otherness of the female. Specifically I shall argue that Book IV, nominally the book of friendship, provides a critique of the notion of friendship as the mark of sameness by revealing the sexual politics involved in such a notion.

The first three chapters of this study are devoted to Book III; the last five chapters treat Book IV. Chapter 1 considers the adaptation of quest-romance narrative to construct an epistemological model of limited, temporal knowledge. Book III shows the transformation of Britomart from a love-sick girl into the Knight of Chastity as she pursues a lover she has never met as a paradigm of coping with the uncertainty of the fallen world. The heroine's forward-looking quest presents knowledge as an evolutionary process in which the truth is always more fully but never completely known. This chapter considers Spenser's use of the erotic as an intellectual model that allows him to explore poetic and epistemological issues. In Book III, the sexual relation becomes a model for more general relationships between an individual and what is Out There. Spenser revises and transforms conventional discourses of love, particularly those that figure love as a hunt, in order to explore the problem of achieving some sort of critical perspective on and understanding of a given system when one is part of that system: the universal problem of addressing the fallen world from within the fallen world rather than sub specie aeternitatis. The shift in the basis of Spenser's allegory from the typological evocation of revealed truth (figured by the betrothal of the Redcrosse

Knight to Una) to the pursuit of temporal understanding (figured by Britomart's quest) marks the distinction between faith and theory. Redcrosse is initially parted from Una when he believes the vision of Una's adultery created by Archimago's artifice. He trusts the evidence of his senses over his faith in his lady. The standards of truth and falsehood under which Redcrosse operates are clearly defined in this episode. Truth is the evidence of things unseen, known to faith alone, and falsehood is the illusion received through the senses. Redcrosse and the reader learn to understand the fallen world as a series of signs that point typologically to spiritual truth. The errancy of the Redcrosse Knight's adventures, which proceeds from his initial error in doubting Una, achieves closure insofar as it assumes the pattern of sin and redemption. Britomart's uncertain vision of Artegall, which impels her on her quest, contrasts explicitly with Redcrosse's false vision of Una. Her belief that the image she has seen in Merlin's mirror represents a real knight is provisional. She pursues Artegall without being certain she is not chasing after an illusion, the creation of her own imagination. She has an emotional stake in the object of her quest, but no guarantees of its existence. The truth of her vision is theoretical in terms that would be codified by seventeenth century science as something subject to confirmation. The pattern of her quest, as she pursues her object without prior assurance about what she pursues, is a theoretical model of understanding that contrasts with but does not contradict the spiritual quest after final things enacted by the Redcrosse Knight.

The second chapter focuses specifically on the theme of risk as the concomitant to the epistemology of uncertainty. Chapter 1 shows how Britomart's quest after a man she has seen only in a supernatural vision addresses the problem of epistemological certainty by positing uncertainty as the condition of mortal knowledge. Britomart risks pursuing what is merely an erotic fantasy as she risks physical dangers on her journey. Her wounding, first by Gardante and then by Busirane, represents graphically her spiritual and emotional vulnerability as well as her psychic engagement with the objects of her pursuit. Chapter 2 takes up the theme of risk and the motif of wounding as these are focused in variations of the myth of Adonis. Britomart's quest appears as a creative alternative to the literary convention of love as a chase. The Gardens of Adonis and Timias' wounding by the boar-spear-carrying forester direct attention to the discursive character of erotic metaphor. On the one hand, these episodes insist on the corporeal aspect of erotic desire. On the other, they emphasize the function of discursive structures in enabling or deforming desire. These episodes take Spenser's exploration of risk to a higher level of abstraction by showing how the choice of linguistic terms itself participates in the calculus of risk and benefit.

Chapter 3 examines the Hermaphrodite as a complex image of an ideal romantic love that supplies an alternative to erotic desire represented by the conventional motif of the hunt. The Hermaphrodite figures androgynous reversals of gender roles as a substitute for the fruitless reversals of pursuer and pursued that characterize the erotic chase.[6] The figure of the Hermaphrodite concludes Book III in 1590 and marks Britomart's victory over Busirane, a provisional but not final conclusion to her adventures as the Knight of Chastity. The Ovidian myth of the Hermaphrodite functions as an important subtext of Book III as it examines issues of closure and certainty central to Britomart's quest and to the open-ended prospective orientation represented in that quest. The myth treats the complex interplay of Eros, the body, and linguistic expression crucial to Spenser's construction of an alternative discourse of love.

Chapter 4 treats the cancellation of the Hermaphrodite stanzas in 1596 as the focus of Spenser's shift from the construction of an ideal of creative love and understanding to a critical exploration of the cultural forces that frustrate that ideal. Those forces are specifically identified as the desire for absolute security and an ideology of sexual hierarchy designed to provide guarantees of security and control. As *The Faerie Queene* moves from Book III to Book IV the myth of the Hermaphrodite is replaced by the story of Orpheus and Eurydice as a subtext. The change in subtext reflects a shift in theoretical orientation from a forward-looking emphasis on making sense of things, to the assertion of totalizing control represented by the retrospective gaze in the myth of Orpheus and Eurydice.[7] Similarly, the emphasis in Book III on an open-ended process of finding becomes in Book IV an obsessive concern with a closed circuit of winning and losing, as Scudamore's Orpheus-like quest for Amoret emphasizes winning the lady over finding her. Chapter 4 shows how strategies that seek to assert control over the sexual relation are strategies that ultimately foreclose the satisfaction of desire. In moving its focus from an ideal to how that ideal is thwarted, Book IV shifts attention from the act of reading to the question of textuality. Chapter 4 considers this shift from the Book III construction of ideals as an education in reading to the Book IV examination of institutional force as it is codified textually.

Chapters 5 and 6 concern the joust as a paradigmatic institution. In Book IV recurrent examples of organized combat, the joust between Cambel and Triamond, Satyrane's tournament, the single combat between Britomart and Artegall, the combats by which Scudamore wins Amoret, and many lesser clashes between knights over a lady, become the vehicle for Spenser's exploration of the nature of institutional power. These jousts give concrete form to the binary of winning and losing that in Book IV replaces the open-ended, prospective structure of Book III. Chapter 5 considers the combat between the eponymous heroes Cambel and Triamond as it reflects critically on the apparent authority of social and linguistic constructs. The combat is initially presented as an etiological fable about the development of institutional order: the joust is instituted by Cambel as a means of directing the passions of his sister's suitors into manageable outlets. As the episode proceeds, however, we see a reversal. While the story of the joust first appears to offer an explanatory gesture, a meditation on the nature of institutional order cast as a narrative of origins, what finally emerges is an exploration of the nature of narrative cast as a combat between its conflicting components. The combat of Cambel and Triamond reflects ironically on the project of seeking guarantees from social and textual structures by showing how all structure is provisional.

Chapter 6 considers the erotic symbolism of the joust as it focuses on Satyrane's tournament and the subsequent single combat between Britomart and Artegall. This chapter examines the sexual politics of the joust as a structure of order. While competition between males is ostensibly for the purpose of winning a lady, the joust depends on the lady's remaining aloof and untouched so that the two knights can continue a relationship, the fundamental purpose of which is their own mutual self-assurance and self-definition. In Book IV, the sexual politics of the joust reflect critically on broader issues of representation. As the joust is construed in Book IV, the lady's chastity is appropriated as part of a structure designed to ensure the knights' self-definition. The apparent sexual relationship between knight and lady is something of a red herring, a nominal relationship

the fundamental purpose of which is to occasion the mutual definition of two knights. The joust engages a relationship of male and female only by process of specious extension from a relationship between men. Moreover, the joust is emblematic of broader strategies
of extending structures beyond what they can encompass with certainty in an attempt to assert specious control of what is not totally
amenable to control. The joust depends on the binary of winning and
losing to ensure coherence. The tautology that one party wins if the
other loses makes the joust a signifying structure that is necessarily
true: the winning knight is the winner by definition. The fruitless
proliferation of tournaments and jousts in Book IV tacitly criticizes
the mind-set that expects certainty in all things because one can get
it in some things.[8] In focusing on the erotic aspect of the joust, Chapter 6 treats Spenser's critique of reductive attitudes toward sexuality.
In Book IV, Spenser shows the reduction of the complex virtue of
chastity to a fetishlike prize for the triumphant male as part of a
larger cultural obsession with security.

The single combat between Britomart and Artegall examines
the joust structure from a different perspective. Their private battle
presents the relationship between the erotic and the discursive in
more sympathetic terms. The episode shows the complex interplay
between human emotion and the intellectual structures through
which emotions are expressed and understood. At the same time, the
episode examines critically the Sidnean version of mimesis, which
posits a straightforward, morally charged relationship between textual representations and human behavior. The combat of Britomart
and Artegall shows discursive processes to be much more complex
than the formation of role models.

Chapter 7 focuses more narrowly on Spenser's critique of Sidnean
mimesis as that critique is reflected in the Lust episode. The grotesque representation of sexuality in the allegorical figure of Lust
strains the Sidnean "role model" model of moral fiction so as to reveal its limitations. At the same time, the episode includes an allegorical representation of Elizabeth in the figure of Belphoebe.
Belphoebe's defeat of Lust provides a model for the transaction of
reader and text when the reader has genuine authority.

Although Book IV largely functions as a critique of strategies of literary closure that seek to fix meaning, its conclusion, with the marriage of Thames and Medway, undermines the self-critical stance of

Book IV by showing how limited an ideal of closure and totalizing control seems when compared to a poetic vision of universal fluidity and limitless plenitude. The final chapter of this book considers the conclusion of Book IV, both the set-piece marriage of Thames and Medway and the narrative framework for the river marriage in the reunion of Florimell and Marinell. The river marriage provides a model in which the text and its referents are both partial unfoldings of a fluid whole that escapes being fully circumscribed and fully known. And the story of Florimell and Marinell—by showing the practical advantage of eschewing closure—reflects with gentle irony on the repudiation of closure as a principle in the marriage of Thames and Medway. Florimell and Marinell are brought together through a series of improvisations and spur-of-the-moment shifts in theoretical commitment that recalls Britomart's improvisatory self-fashioning in Book III. This reassertion, at the conclusion of Book IV, of the value of improvisatory change appears, not as challenge from within to dominant ideology and discourse, but as a minority report, a vision of a better alternative.

The marriage of Thames and Medway is triumphantly Spenserian in its celebration of going with the flow. Books III and IV manifest an intellectual flexibility and exuberance and a joy in the protean as well as an uncompromising sense of how many ways the mortal world falls short of its most beautiful ideals.

1

Britomart's Quest
Fashioning Heroine and Reader

In the proem to Book III of *The Faerie Queene,* the poet invites his sovereign and most important reader to see herself in the Legend of Chastity in mirrors more than one. In so doing, Spenser places the book in the medieval and Renaissance tradition of the mirror of princes, which offered rulers exemplary and cautionary representations of rulership in order to encourage them to emulate the exemplary and avoid the blameworthy.[1] Supporting the moral force of these examples is the belief in divine Providence, which manifests itself in human history through the eventual distribution of reward and punishment. Spenser revises the mirror tradition as he adapts it for Book III. Instead of presenting the reflection in human history of the divine will, Book III focuses on the partiality and contingency of the mirrors. Book III does not repudiate divine Providence. Rather, it concerns itself with the limitations of human understanding. Underlying Spenser's adaptation of the mirror tradition is the verse from St. Paul's first Epistle to the Corinthians, "videmus nunc per speculum in enigmate / tunc autem facie ad faciem" (1 Corinthians 13:12) [For now we see through a glass, darkly; but then face to face].[2] Although Book III concerns itself with what is seen imperfectly, the truth of revelation provides the implicit contrast and corrective to the darkness of earthly vision. It is the illusion of seeing in the glass plainly that is stigmatized in Book III as narcissism, understood as being enamored with the objects of one's own perception.

Book III pairs with Book I as both address the issue of truth, Book I from the perspective of Christian eschatology, Book III from the perspective of the fallen world.[3] In order to accommodate this shift in perspective, the allegory shifts focus from transcending the world of the senses and attending to the evidence of things unseen to engaging the world of the senses and accepting the uncertainty of mortal understanding. The shift from transcending to making sense of the sensual world is defined largely in erotic terms. In Book I, the spiritual goal of the Redcrosse Knight is represented allegorically as marriage to Una and his most serious fall from holiness is figured as his liaison with Duessa. In Book III, the sexual relation becomes a paradigm of all relationships between the individual and what is in the world. Spenser makes use of very traditional habits of allegorizing what is worldly and sensual as female to construct an alternate discourse.[4] He revises conventional discourses of love from within in order to explore the problem of addressing the mortal world from within, rather than sub specie aeternitatis. In adapting conventional habits of treating femininity as metaphor, the allegory of Book III remains very conscious of how deceiving and destabilizing that strategy can be.[5]

The conventional erotic discourses revised in Book III figure love as a hunt. Spenser both reveals the narcissism of such conventional configurations and presents Britomart's pursuit of love as a more productive alternative. In conventional versions of the erotic chase, the object of pursuit is the projection of male desire. In contrast, Britomart's pursuit of Artegall figures her engagement with something not wholly dependent on or answerable to her own desires.

SHIFTING ALLEGORY
TO ADDRESS THIS WORLD

Book III opens, as Book II does, with a narrative continuation of the previous book. In canto i, stanza 1 of Book II, Archimago escapes the shackles with which he was bound at the conclusion of Book I and, with the help of a newly accoutred Duessa, proceeds to stir up trouble between Sir Guyon and the Redcrosse Knight. The opening of Book III sees Guyon and Prince Arthur riding out together after having recovered at the House of Alma from the battles that concluded Book II. On the one hand, these transitions from one book to another give narrative continuity to *The Faerie Queene*. On the other, they suggest at the outset of each book how that book is positioned in an intellectual, rather than a strictly narrative, framework.[6] As has long been observed, the Palmer's comment to Redcrosse about "like race to runne" signals that Guyon's quest will be parallel to that of Redcrosse but in a different context.[7] Similarly, Britomart's summary overthrow of Guyon early in Book III announces that the virtue of chastity will supersede temperance.[8]

The insights of A. S. P. Woodhouse ("Nature and Grace"), A. C. Hamilton ("Like Race to Runne"), and others about the continuities and shifts from one book of *The Faerie Queene* to another can be taken much further into a consideration of how each book traces a paradigm shift as it addresses issues deferred by previous books.[9] Indeed, this shift is prefigured in the bifurcated title of each book of *The Faerie Queene*, which signals generic affinities with both the saint's legend and the essay.[10] Each book is in significant ways an essay, a discrete and coherent examination of an intellectual problem. The shift from one book to another involves not just what Spenser says but how he says it, not just themes but allegorical strategies deployed to explore those themes.

The pattern of allegorical paradigm shift is established at the conclusion of Book I. The Redcrosse Knight's battle with the dragon is an allegorical set-piece that reveals Christian eschatology as both fundamental to the allegory of *The Faerie Queene* and necessarily focused beyond the here and now of fallen existence. The climactic dragon fight is a virtual tour-de-force of fourfold Christian allegory.[11] In the literal sense, it is a representation of Saint George's legendary fight with the dragon. Tropologically, Redcrosse imitates Christ and enacts the pattern of every Christian's battle with sin. Allusions to both Genesis and Revelation demonstrate the typological sense. Anagogically, Saint George's dragon figures the dragon of the apocalypse.[12] Nevertheless, despite the textbook completeness of the fourfold allegorical pattern, the episode is curiously dislocated. Spenser's witty comment on the climactic dragon fight, "The ioyous day gan early to appeare" (1.11.51.1)—it is indeed early for Judgment Day—calls attention to the historical gap between the Redcrosse Knight's battle and the Last Battle it figures forth.[13] The actual fallen world, which ostensibly provides a ground for the redemptive dragon fight, teasingly resists redemption. Eden menaced by the dragon is necessarily a fallen Eden. When the dragon falls to the ground in defeat, he becomes one with the unredeemed physical world and "like an heaped mountaine lay" (1.11.54.9). Although the dragon fight points allegorically toward ultimate redemption, the world remains fallen.

In pointing allegorically toward the apocalypse, Spenser evokes a transcendental signified, knowing as an article of faith its full apocalyptic force as the end of signification.[14] Corollary to the belief in an apocalyptic end of the chain of mortal signifiers is conviction of the unrepresentability of that apocalypse. Spenser casts the hermeneutics of skepticism as a kind of folk wisdom.[15] Doubt in the finality of this representation of apocalyptic closure is comically demonstrated by the mother who worries when her child plays too close to the fallen dragon and the townspeople who are not fully convinced that the dragon is really dead. J. R. R. Tolkien observes that when children ask whether stories about dragons are true, what they want to know is, Am I safe in my bed? (Tolkien 63n). Abstract, categorical knowledge is not necessarily what allows children (or others) to sleep soundly. Similarly, believing in ultimate salvation does not obviate having to cope with the fallen world. Spenser shows that although truth is one and given to faith alone, Duessa and Archimago keep making their appearances in the world.

Even after the Redcrosse Knight has slain his dragon, Archimago and Duessa attempt to prevent his promised marriage to Una. The discrediting of Archimago, despite the literal accuracy of his charge of fornication with Duessa, and the postponed consummation of the marriage until Redcrosse fulfills his promise to the Faerie Queene to "serue six yeares in warlike wize, / Gainst that proud Paynim king, that workes her teene" (1.12.18.7–8) establish the terms of the shift from allegory that points toward and is authorized by Christian revelation and allegory that addresses the contingent and interim nature of the world of appearances. Although Redcrosse is forgiven his involvement with Duessa, the accomplishment of his marriage vows is deferred for the hexameral period of six years. Marriage of Holiness and Truth must await the completion of human history.[16] Book I achieves its allegorical vision of spiritual oneness and truth by transcending the sensual world and deferring the problem of actually coping with earthly experience to later books. Throughout Book I, psychosexual issues seem to be raised only to be deferred beyond the conclusion of that book. For example, as Mark Rose points out, the initial flight of Redcrosse and Una into the Wandering Wood to seek refuge from Jove's rainstorm suggests avoidance of sexuality and a childlike misreading of the loving father as an angry father (*Spenser's Art* 5). Granted that, what else are Una and Redcrosse to do but get out of the rain?[17] The allegory raises the issue of sexuality and sexual repression in such a way that the allegorical significance of the episode cannot determine the action of the figures. Although at the conclusion of Book I, Redcrosse is described "swimming in that sea of blisful ioy" (1.12.41.5), he shortly leaves Una "to mourne" while her betrothed completes six years' service to the Faerie Queene.

When the Redcrosse Knight makes a brief appearance in Book III, his loyalty to Una is again being tried, but in a much different register. He is held at bay by Malecasta's six knights: Gardante, Parlante, Iocante, Basciante, Bacchante, and Noctante, representing the *gradus amoris*, or ladder of carnal love.[18] Although their attempt to force him to forsake Una is unsuccessful, Redcrosse needs the intervention of Britomart to break the standoff. Just as it is the role of the Knight of Chastity to defeat the *gradus amoris* figures, so is it the project of the Book of Chastity to address directly issues of eroticism deferred by Book I, to accommodate, rather than to transcend, fallen experience.[19]

Book I demonstrates the ascendancy of faith as the evidence of things unseen over observed truth. Book III takes as its epistemological model Britomart's uncertain quest for the body that corresponds to the image of Artegall seen in Merlin's mirror. Both the faith that is the focus of Book I and the uncertainty that appears in Book III are part of the same epistemological structure.[20] The conviction of transcendent truth saves the concept of uncertainty from being either logical nonsense or programmatic nihilism.[21] Spenser writes in the tradition of Cusanus, as he focuses concomitantly on divine ineffability and the progress of human understanding.

Spenser explores issues of epistemology and poetic process by means of focus on the erotic.[22] In Book III, the sexual relation becomes a primary model of the relationship of the self to something Out There.[23] In moving from a consideration of spiritual truth in Book I to the sensual world in Book III, Spenser shifts his allegory from one that grounds the word of the text in the Word of God to one that reflects critically on its own bases. Book III examines from within extant discourses of love—primarily the Ovidian and Petrarchan—as a way of locating his allegory in a field of contingent understanding and representation.[24]

REWRITING THE LANGUAGE OF LOVE

Spenser announces his project of rewriting erotic discourse from within at the opening of canto ii, with the first of two encomia to unsung heroines, in imitation of Ariosto's *Orlando furioso* (*O.f.* 20.1–3; 37.1–10). Ariosto pays women a rather backhanded compliment. He poses as the honest historian of their achievements while calling attention to his own invention as a poet, since the Martial Maids Marfisa and Bradamante never existed outside his poem.[25] There have been many renowned women, Ariosto assures us; it is just that somehow or other no one has ever heard of them. Ariosto's pose of ironic superiority becomes a more engaged and uncertain stance in Spenser's version. In revising Ariosto, Spenser shifts emphasis from fictitious heroines to the false men who have suppressed the exploits of heroic women as the narrator takes the opportunity to praise Elizabeth and question himself:

> HEre haue I cause, in men iust blame to find,
>   That in their proper prayse too partiall bee,
>   And not indifferent to woman kind,
>   To whom no share in armes and cheualrie
>   They do impart, ne maken memorie
>   Of their braue gestes and prowesse martiall;
>   Scarse do they spare to one or two or three,
>   Rowme in their writs; yet the same writing small
> Does all their deed deface, and dims their glories all.
>
> But by record of antique times I find,
>   That women wont in warres to beare most sway,
>   And to all great exploits them selues inclind:
>   Of which they still the girlond bore away,
>   Till enuious Men fearing their rules decay,
>   Gan coyne streight lawes to curb their liberty;
>   Yet sith they warlike armes haue layd away,
>   They haue exceld in artes and pollicy,
> That now we foolish men that prayse gin eke t'enuy.
>
> Of warlike puissaunce in ages spent,
>   Be thou faire *Britomart*, whose prayse I write,
>   But of all wisedome be thou precedent,
>   O soueraigne Queene, whose prayse I would endite,
>   Endite I would as dewtie doth excite;
>   But ah my rimes too rude and rugged arre,
>   When in so high an obiect they do lite,
>   And striuing, fit to make, I feare do marre:
> Thy selfe thy prayses tell, and make them knowen farre.[26]
>   (3.2.1–3)

Ariosto sets women up as the butt of his ironic humor. Spenser chooses women's excellence as a topic that will allow him to subject his own writing to scrutiny. He addresses his most powerful female reader and his female protagonist directly, while offering to write about a reality for which men have made no room in their writs. Instead of echoing Ariosto's ironic espousal of feminism, Spenser focuses on the male point of view as it engages or fails to engage female experience. The complex pun, that men "in their proper prayse too partiall bee," suggests that the improper partiality that leads men to slight women produces only incomplete, partial praise of themselves. Spenser's treatment of women throughout Book III is often sympathetic, but that sympathy is part of a larger project of reflecting on the processes of his own poetry. This project affirms the intellectual value of imaginative sympathy and the moral importance of critical self-consciousness. Spenser adapts a long-standing tradition of using female figures as a poetic instrument for exploring aspects of the male, but he does so with a great deal of self-consciousness, both about the danger of arbitrarily appropriating the female for male-identified purposes and about the underlying affinity of male and female that enables such appropriation. From the first appearance of Britomart in male disguise to the image of the Hermaphrodite at the conclusion of Book III, the poem maintains critical tension between the poetic representation and appropriation of gender difference and the biological and social reality that they represent and appropriate.

IMPROVISATIONAL FASHIONING

Britomart is both Spenser's fictional creation and the poet's counterpart. This connection is emphasized when we see Britomart engaged in fiction-making herself. She lies to the Redcrosse Knight about her childhood so she can provoke talk about Artegall without betraying her own interest:

> Faire Sir, I let you weete, that from the howre
>   I taken was from nourses tender pap,
>   I haue beene trained vp in warlike stowre,
>   To tossen speare and shield, and to affrap
>   The warlike ryder to his most mishap;
>   Sithence I loathed haue my life to lead,
>   As Ladies wont, in pleasures wanton lap,
>   To finger the fine needle and nyce thread;
> Me leuer were with point of foemans speare be dead.

> All my delight on deedes of armes is set,
>> To hunt out perils and aduentures hard,
>> By sea, by land, where so they may be met,
>> Onely for honour and for high regard,
>> Without respect of richesse or reward.
>> For such intent into these parts I came,
>> Withouten compasse, or withouten card,
>> Far fro my natiue soyle, that is by name
> The greater *Britaine*, here to seeke for prayse and fame.
>> > (3.2.6–7)

Britomart appropriates the childhoods of the epic characters Camilla and Clorinda, just as Spenser adapts his literary predecessors Virgil and Tasso. In the same canto, we see another version of Britomart's early years in an extended flashback that parodies the *enfances* of her literary precursors. Spenser emphasizes the gendered nature of Britomart's growing up, in an ironic commentary on Virgil and Tasso. Virgil's Camilla is given a symbolic, male-identified rebirth when she is bound to her father's spear and cast across the river to safety (*Aeneid* 11.544–566).[27] In contrast, Britomart's formative experience carries connotations of menarche:[28]

> Sithens it hath infixed faster hold
>> Within my bleeding bowels, and so sore
>> Now ranckleth in this same fraile fleshly mould,
>> That all mine entrailes flow with poysnous gore,
>> And th'vlcer groweth daily more and more;
>> Ne can my running sore find remedie,
>> Other then my hard fortune to deplore,
>> > (3.2.39.1–7)

The novel emphasis on the fact of specifically female physiology calls attention to the literariness of literary genealogy. Having accentuated the discrepancy between the literary formation of Britomart as she inherits traits from her literary predecessors and the biological development of a young woman as she achieves maturity, Spenser focuses on the constructedness of his fictional character. By introducing menarche to the literary tradition of the Martial Maid, Spenser calls attention to his rewriting of that tradition in a strategy of emphasizing the feminine. Whereas Virgil and Tasso describe the extraordinary infant diet and childhood training program of their virago to account for her military prowess, Spenser accounts for Britomart's chivalric vocation in a conspicuously improbable piece of *bricolage.*[29] Although magical visions enframe Britomart's career as a Martial Maid—her vision of Artegall in Merlin's mirror and Merlin's prophecy of their dynastic future represent *termini ad quem* and a *quo*—the arrangements Glauce and Britomart make in order to bring the prophesied marriage to pass are, if anything, stranger because they purport to be practical. Britomart's father is conveniently away at a war with a pair of paynim brothers, so Britomart and Glauce can leave the castle as they please. A band of Britons has happened a few days before to capture a hoard of Saxon goods, among which there happily chances to be a suit of ladies' armor, previously belonging to the Saxon queen Angela. Since Britomart is a big, healthy girl, she can simply disguise herself as a knight. As Glauce assures her: "Ne ought ye want, but skill, which practize small / Will bring, and shortly make you a mayd Martiall" (3.3.53.8–9). The string of coincidences suggests that Britomart and Glauce are not the only ones willing to make things up as they go along. Spenser emphasizes improvisation as a principle both of individual self-fashioning and of narrative.[30] Unlike Redcrosse or Guyon, Britomart is not assigned a quest by Gloriana. She puts on armor as a pragmatic means of achieving her desire, much as Spenser adapts the form of quest romance in Book III as a way of reflecting on his own art and on the relationship of art to desire.

THE PROSPECTIVE MODEL
AND THE PERILOUS QUEST FOR MEANING

The carefully orchestrated improvisation that characterizes Britomart's career as the Knight of Chastity directs attention to what will be a major concern of Book III: the shift from an epistemology of authoritarian certitude, which emphasizes origins, to an epistemology of learned ignorance, which de-emphasizes origins and focuses on the growth of knowledge. Having attested to the absolute authority of divine truth, given to faith alone, in Book I, Spenser turns to the question of making sense of the fallen world by opposing to a largely Platonic focus on origins a protoscientific epistemology in the tradition of Cusanus, Erasmus, and Montaigne, which treats knowledge as an evolutionary process and focuses on how a given judgment can be tested.[31] Spenser establishes Platonic authoritarianism as an antithetical position against which he develops an evolutionary model of knowledge in the proem to Book II. There Spenser defends his fiction against the charge that it is the painted forgery of an idle brain rather than matter of just recollection not, as John Guillory suggests, by associating allegory with anamnesis, but by shifting ground away from the Platonic theory of recollection (*Poetic Authority* 37). Spenser defends his allegory by asserting the growth of knowledge as the corollary of human ignorance and cites two areas in which Elizabethan knowledge had grown spectacularly: geographic exploration and astronomy. The narrator asks rhetorically, "Who euer heard of th'Indian *Peru*?" (2.P.2.6) and "What if in euery other starre vnseene / Of other worldes he [Spenser's judge] happily should heare?" (2.P.3.7–8).

The origin of Britomart's desire, which fetches her from Britain to Faerieland and motivates her quest in Book III, is raised as an issue only to be subordinated to the matter of satisfying that desire. Although Merlin's mirror gives a supernatural éclat to the commencement of Britomart's love for Artegall, that love is described as what "lay hidden in the bottome of the pot" (3.2.26.5). The phrase suggests both that love is commonplace and that it comes as an aftereffect. It is not until after she has been wounded by desire that Britomart realizes she is in love. The actual point of origin is occulted.

Merlin's mirror figures an alternative epistemology, prospective in orientation rather than focused on origins, by manipulating categories of subject and object along with the sexual values— male subject and female object—traditionally given those categories. The magic mirror is presented explicitly as an alternative to Ptolemy's tower:

> Who wonders not, that reades so wonderous worke?
>   But who does wonder, that has red the Towre,
>   Wherein th' Ægyptian *Phao* long did lurke
>   From all mens vew, that none might her discoure,
>   Yet she might all men vew out of her bowre?
>   Great *Ptolomæe* it for his lemans sake
>   Ybuilded all of glasse, by Magicke powre,
>   And also it impregnable did make;
> Yet when his loue was false, he with a peaze it brake.
>   (3.2.20)

Unlike the phallic tower, Merlin's mirror "round and hollow shaped was, / Like to the world it selfe, and seem'd a world of glas"

(3.2.19.8–9).[32] Ptolemy's glass tower offers a parody of the traditional pairing of male subject and female object. With his artifice, Ptolemy makes Phao a subject of perception—she can see from within her tower but cannot be seen—in order to make of her a private sexual object. Ptolemy obstructs the give-and-take of social interaction, in which people are objects of others' perception and subjects of their own, in order to exercise power over Phao and ensure her fidelity. But the security sought by means of sequestering the woman, both in the glass tower and in male-defined categories, proves illusory. Ptolemy's phallic model of artistic creation will not stand up against female autonomy. In contrast, when Britomart looks into the world of glass, we see a more complex image of woman-as-subject. In place of the epistemological shell game, whereby mutually exclusive categories of subject and object are switched around to serve the will to power and desire for security, we see a model of subjective participation in the object.[33] In Merlin's looking glass, subject and object are interdependent. Since the categories are not entirely separable, it is impossible to accord one or the other primacy:

> It vertue had, to shew in perfect sight,
>> What euer thing was in the world contaynd,
>> Betwixt the lowest earth and heauens hight,
>> So that it to the looker appertaynd;
>>> (3.2.19.1–4)

The phrase "so that" is deliberately ambiguous. The phrase can be construed as introducing a result clause: the mirror could show sights in such a way that they pertained to the looker. The phrase can also be construed as the equivalent of "provided that": the mirror will reveal any sight, provided that it pertains to the looker. The double meaning keeps unclear to what extent the vision in the mirror is a subjective transformation of the object—that whatever appears in the mirror is distorted in such a way as to pertain to the looker—and to what extent the pertinence of the object to the subject is a necessary precondition for the magic vision—that the observer can see anything provided it pertains to him or her. Spenser questions the ideal of objectivity while refraining from idealizing subjectivity in its place. The epistemology presented by the magic mirror does not permit the reductive confidence in either ideal. Rather, it offers an engaged subjectivity in which admitting the danger of illusion is the price of vision.

Spenser addresses the problem of epistemological uncertainty by positing uncertainty as the condition of mortal knowledge. He uses the image of the mirror, which engages a complex and ambivalent set of traditions as a focus of those epistemological concerns. St. Paul's text 1 Corinthians 13:12 ("videmus nunc per speculum in enigmate / tunc autem facie ad faciem"), one of the most powerful statements in Western culture of the illusion of unmediated earthly vision and the necessity of finding authority for vision in what lies beyond the senses, underlies Britomart's vision of Artegall in the magic looking glass and her quest to encounter him face to face.[34] Although Britomart's vision of Artegall draws on a Pauline sense of the necessary uncertainty of mortal perception, her pursuit of that vision is played out in this world, not the next. Book III focuses on the calculus of risk as its heroine braves uncertainty in her pursuit of the looking-glass image and uses the complex tradition associated with Narcissus in exploring that risk. The initial description of Britomart's encounter with the magic mirror teases us with hints of narcissism:

> One day it fortuned, faire *Britomart*
>   Into her fathers closet to repayre;
>   For nothing he from her reseru'd apart,
>   Being his onely daughter and his hayre:
>   Where when she had espyde that mirrhour fayre,
>   Her selfe a while therein she vewd in vaine;
>   Tho her auizing of the vertues rare,
>   Which thereof spoken were, she gan againe
> Her to bethinke of, that mote to her selfe pertaine.
>   (3.2.22)

The word "vaine" raises the specter that Britomart may be guilty of narcissistic vanity and self-delusion.[35] Britomart does not know whether she has fallen in love with a man or, Narcissus-like, with the image of her own fantasy. Spenser's joke is that vanity or self-love is not the primary connotation of "vaine" in context. As long as Britomart sees her own face in the looking glass, its magic is vain: it does not work. Like any ordinary mirror, Merlin's glass gives back an image of Britomart's own face until she begins to contemplate something that pertains to herself and thinks about her future husband. Britomart cannot be content to be an objective observer with no prior interest in what she sees; that is what is truly vain.

This episode attaches the moral opprobrium habitually associated with self-love to the danger of mistaking appearance for reality. The dialogue between Britomart and Glauce about the moral judgment appropriate to Britomart's new love reproduces traditional schools of interpreting the Narcissus myth. In the mythographic commentaries that Spenser would have inherited, either Narcissus is treated as an icon of moral failure, of self-love, and of materialism, or he is considered the hapless victim of a mistake.[36] Britomart interprets Narcissus' fault to be that he mistakenly loves an empty image, Glauce that he ignobly loves himself. When Glauce cites a list of classic sexual monsters by way of contrast to Britomart's healthy passion, Britomart counters that, worse than any in Glauce's catalogue, she is a decadent version of Narcissus. At least, Britomart argues, Myrrha, Biblis, and Pasiphäe satisfied their desire, however monstrous; she vainly loves a shadow.

The morally charged debate about versions of narcissism allies Book III to the medieval and Renaissance mirror tradition.[37] Books, such as *The Mirror for Magistrates* or *The Steele Glas*, were metaphoric mirrors "to show virtue her own feature, scorn her own image" and to move the reader to recognition and reform. The mirror tradition provides both a focus on the ethical dimension of reading and a concern for the place of reading in the reader's self-fashioning. Britomart's quest draws on the mirror tradition insofar as her adventures often seem to be morally freighted lessons in reading. Identification of the risk against which Britomart's heroism is measured with epistemological uncertainty draws on the Ovidian myth of Narcissus, which ironically opposes security and knowledge. In Ovid's story, Tiresias prophesies that the infant Narcissus will prosper "si se non noverit" (*Metamorphoses* 3.348), if he does not know himself.[38] Ovid exploits the paradox that, although Narcissus' ultimate recognition of himself in the beloved reflection destroys him with the despair of unrequited love, he initially fell victim to that deadly passion because he did not know himself when he encountered his own image. For Narcissus, self-knowledge and self-ignorance are both inescapably deadly. Tiresias' cryptic warning, in fact, doubles the curse of the rejected youth who prays, "sic amet ipse licet, sic non potiatur amato!" (3.405) [So may he himself love, and not gain the thing he loves!].[39]

Britomart's encounter with the narcissistic Marinell affirms the superiority of facing risk to seeking security. The danger Britomart faces as she pursues her quest is identifiable with narcissism insofar as she risks loving a mere image. The question of referentiality is invested with considerable moral seriousness as well as erotic significance. When Britomart high-mindedly condemns herself as worse than Myrrha, Biblis, and Pasiphäe, she tacitly asserts that incest and bestiality are better than nothing. In pursuing the referent to Artegall's image, she seeks a full presence not strictly Platonic. Glauce's response to Britomart's anxiety combines an ingenuous faith in the referentiality of her vision—"No shadow, but a bodie hath in powre" (3.2.45.7)—with a cheerfully forward-looking epistemology. She assures Britomart that "things oft impossible . . . seeme, ere begonne" and promises "to compasse thy desire" and find that loved knight (3.2.36.9; 46.9). Britomart's decision to risk empty narcissism in the pursuit of true love is ratified when she defeats Marinell, whose life embodies the attempt to play it safe.

NARCISSISM AND FALSE SECURITY

Marinell's life story is an elaborate Spenserian revision of Ovid's myth of Narcissus.[40] Tiresias' prophecy that Narcissus will prosper if he does not know himself becomes Proteus' prophecy that "of a woman he should haue much ill, / A virgin strange and stout him should dismay, or kill" (3.4.25.8–9). While Tiresias' warning, apparently contingent on circumstance, conceals Narcissus' inescapable fate, Proteus' prophecy of seemingly inescapable misfortune is transformed into the needless defeat and ensuing salvation of Marinell. As the narrator comments:

> So tickle be the termes of mortall state,
> And full of subtile sophismes, which do play
> With double senses, and with false debate,
> T'approue the vnknowen purpose of eternall fate.
> (3.4.28.6–9)

The false closure of the prophecy plays, with double sense, against the self-fulfilling nature of the sexual fears it secretly embodies: a man who gives himself over to fear of women has not much left to lose to them.[41] Marinell's response to the prophecy, to avoid danger from women by waiving his manhood and refraining from all contact with women, is precisely what makes him vulnerable to Britomart. The narrator's comment, "This was that woman, this that deadly wound" (3.4.28.1), makes it seem that Marinell's doom is both final and inevitable. Yet on the one hand, he has quite a future ahead of him, and, on the other, Marinell is "dismayed" by Britomart's spear precisely because of his virginal refusal to be dismayed in a less bellicose sense.[42] The apparent closure of Marinell's life story, whereby Britomart's attack fulfills Proteus' prophecy, is subverted by the possibility of multiple interpretations. Marinell's mother chooses her interpretation of Proteus' prophecy according to her own self-interested desire to keep her son boy eternal. Her fear—"Least his too haughtie hardines might reare / Some hard mishap, in hazard of his life" (3.4.24.5–6)—seems at least as much a dread of having her son reach sexual maturity as it is a worry about his health and safety. The bad faith of a castrating mother, who wants to reduce her son to the "deare image of [her]selfe" (3.4.36.1), determines Cymoent's interpretation of Proteus' words, which, in turn, affects the fulfillment of his prophecy. As the narrator notes, "So weening to haue arm'd him, she did quite disarme" (3.4.27.9). Marinell's mother has induced him to secure the integrity of his being by fleeing from love, only to discover too late that "they that loue do liue" (3.4.37.5). Marinell is nearly destroyed by Proteus' prophecy because he fails to understand it as a call to courage, both in reading his fate and living his life.

Britomart's encounter with the enchanted mirror concerns the origin of desire and shows that origin subordinated to other considerations. The story of Marinell, as it revises the myth of Narcissus, concerns the origin of gynophobia. Canto iv opens with Spenser's second Ariostan encomium to unsung heroines. The first, which introduces the story of Merlin's mirror, treats female excellence and male partiality. The second, which introduces Marinell's story, concerns women who kill men. The narrator's own reaction to the legends of female-inflicted homicide is emphasized, but the nature of that reaction remains highly ambiguous. Upon hearing the stories of Penthesilea, Deborah, and Camilla, the narrator begins to "burne with enuy sore" and "swell with great disdaine" (3.4.2.3, 9).[43] The reaction to deadly female violence acknowledged by the narrator ranges unstably from arousal to hostility. The story of Marinell is likewise ambiguous in tracing the source of gynophobia. Apparently, the blame falls squarely on Mom. Marinell's jeopardy seems to derive from an originary castration in which Cymoent makes her son the image of her own feminine lack. But as the story goes on, the force of metamorphosis and romance dilation takes precedence over the power of origins.[44] Proteus' prophecy seems to guarantee Marinell's doom from the start, but the fulfillment of the prophecy does not quite kill him. When Cymoent takes her son to her bower in the bottom of the sea, this metaphoric return to the womb becomes the occasion for an extended recuperation, to be followed, in Book IV, by further adventures with women. The impulse to seek the security of a priori knowledge is linked in Marinell's story both to narcissistic self-absorption and to the daemonization of the female as the source of threat. This narcissistic closure is set against the forward movement of narrative change and revisionary interpretation.

WHOSO LIST TO HUNT: LOVE AS THE CHASE

Not only does Marinell's encounter with Britomart provide specious closure to Proteus' prophecy, it disrupts the narrative coherence of Book III. In so doing, Marinell's story calls attention to the major narrative motif of the chase in such a way as to highlight the potentially narcissistic way the pursued can reflect the desires of the pursuer. As has been observed, Britomart defeats Marinell after having seen Florimell riding through Faerieland, although Arthur is later told that Florimell left Gloriana's court to seek Marinell a day after he was wounded:

> Fiue dayes there be, since he (they say) was slaine,
> And foure, since *Florimell* the Court for-went,
> And vowed neuer to returne againe,
> Till him aliue or dead she did inuent.
>
> (3.5.10.1–4)

The repeated time references make the temporal discrepancy quite explicit. Marinell seems to be in a narrative loop in which pursuit circles back on itself. Britomart's own pursuit of love takes place in contradistinction to that closed loop. She rides off in steadfast pursuit of her quest as Arthur and Guyon chase after Florimell in canto i and again after she has unhorsed Marinell in canto iii, a violent intervention that ironically initiates the chase that Britomart has disdained in the earlier canto. Britomart's quest is positioned against a discursive field that comprises traditional constructions of love as pursuit. These traditional discourses are principally, but not exclusively, Ovidian and Petrarchan.[45] The pun on "venery" as the sport of hunting game (*OED* s.v. "venery" 1.1) and as the indulgence of sexual desire (*OED* s.v. "venery" 2.1) has a long itinerary in its derivation from the Latin.[46]

As Harry Berger, Jr., points out, Book III emphasizes the reversibility of such traditional hunts: the male pursuer is goaded by his own desire to chase an object constructed by those desires. He points to the myth of Actaeon, a crucial Petrarchan borrowing from Ovid, as the major subtext of the erotic chases of Book III in which the pursuer becomes the pursued ("Kidnapped Romance" 212–235).[47] As Arthur and Guyon pursue Florimell, they seem, like Actaeon, to be victims, to the extent that they are subject to forces beyond their conscious understanding. Although attempting to rescue Florimell, they irrationally ride after her rather than her persecutor. Indeed, the two seem a bit like horses who break into a gallop simply because they observe other horses galloping. The language describing their motives is highly ambiguous. They are "full of great enuie and fell gealosy" (3.1.18.2) in hopes of winning "most goodly meede, the fairest Dame aliue" (3.1.18.8).[48] The impression is that the knights are at the mercy of discourses beyond their control.

By comparison to both the knights who are impelled to pursue and Florimell who provokes pursuit, Britomart seems to be operating in a much freer discursive field. A critical difference between Arthur and Guyon's pursuit of Florimell and Britomart's quest for Artegall lies in the Neoplatonic underpinnings of each pursuit. The designation "beauties chace" gives a Neoplatonic patina to erotic transactions between the male knights and Florimell that are not self-transcending but are, in a metaphysical sense, going nowhere. In contrast, the Neoplatonic doctrine that the lover is transformed into the beloved[49] authorizes free improvisation, as Britomart readily transforms herself into a knight, after the image of Artegall she has seen in the mirror.

THE CHASE AS INDOOR SPORT
AND MORAL COMEDY

Britomart's adventures in Castle Joyeous complicate the erotic chase as pursuit across the landscape is domesticated and transformed into bedroom farce. The reversibility of hunter and hunted is transformed into the androgynous combination of traits identified with Britomart:

For she was full of amiable grace,
  And manly terrour mixed therewithall,
  That as the one stird vp affections bace,
  So th'other did mens rash desires apall,
  And hold them backe, that would in errour fall;
  As he, that hath espide a vermeill Rose,
  To which sharpe thornes and breres the way forstall,
  Dare not for dread his hardy hand expose,
But wishing it far off, his idle wish doth lose.

(3.1.46)

The Malecasta episode focuses directly on the issue of gender identity, which is both assumed and elided in the discourse of hunter
and hunted. A fundamental strategy of the episode is the defamil-
iarization of heterosexual desire that Spenser achieves throughout Book III by focusing on the female point of view. This episode
goes further. As Spenser adapts the Fiordespina episode from the
Orlando furioso (25.4–70), he suppresses the undercurrent of lesbian-
ism and, in its place, explores the permutations of heterosexuality.
In Ariosto's text, ironic humor is generated by Fiordespina's confusion about her feelings for Bradamante. Although her desire persists
after it has been revealed that the cross-dressed Bradamante is a female knight, Fiordespina dismisses her feelings because she is unaware of the possibility of love between women:

—Quai tormenti (dicea) furon mai tanto
crudel, che più non sian crudeli i miei?
D'ogn'altro amore, o scelerato o santo,
il desiato fin sperar potrei;
saprei partir la rosa da le spine:
solo il mio desiderio è senza fine!

Se pur volevi, Amor, darmi tormento
che t'increscesse il mio felice stato,
d'alcun martìr dovevi star contento,
che fosse ancor negli altri amanti usato.
Né tra gli uomini mai né tra l'armento,
che femina ami femina ho trovato:
non par la donna all'altre donne bella,
né a cervie cervia, né all'agnelle agnella.

In terra, in aria, in mar, sola son io
che patisco da te sì duro scempio;
e questo hai fatto acciò che l'error mio
sia ne l'imperio tuo l'ultimo esempio.

La moglie del re Nino ebbe disio,
il figlio amando, scelerato ed empio,
e Mirra il padre, e la Cretense il toro:
ma gli è più folle il mio, ch'alcun dei loro.
                    (*O.f.* 25.34.3–36)

["Never was any torment so cruel," she lamented, "but mine
is crueller. Were it a question of any other love, evil or virtuous, I could hope to see it consummated, and I should know
how to cull the rose from the briar. My desire alone can have
no fulfillment. / If you wanted to torment me, Love, because
my happy state offended you, why could you not rest content
with those torments which other lovers experience? Neither
among humans nor among beasts have I ever come across a
woman loving a woman; to a woman another woman does not
seem beautiful, nor does a hind to a hind, a ewe to a ewe. / By
land, sea, and air I alone suffer thus cruelly at your hands—
you have done this to make an example of my aberration, the
ultimate one in your power. King Ninus' wife was evil and
profane in her love for her son; so was Mirra, in love with her
father, and Pasiphae with the bull. But my love is greater folly
than any of theirs."][50]

Ariosto titillates us as Fiordespina unwittingly alludes to a love that
cannot speak its name without appropriate terminology. Although
some of the episode's humor comes from Fiordespina's naïveté,
much of it derives from Bradamante's speedy comprehension of the
other woman's intentions, and from their shared viewpoint about
what constitutes masculine honor. As Bradamante's twin brother
Ricciardetto explains when he narrates the story:

La mia sorella avea ben conosciuto
che questa donna in cambio l'avea tolta;
né dar poteale a quel bisogno aiuto,
e si trovava in grande impaccio avvolta.
—Gli è meglio (dicea seco) s'io rifiuto
questa avuta di me credenza stolta
e s'io mi mostro femina gentile,
che lasciar riputarmi un uomo vile.—

E dicea il ver; ch'era viltade espressa,
conveniente a un uom fatto di stucco,
con cui sì bella donna fosse messa,
piena di dolce e di nettareo succo,
e tuttavia stesse a parlar con essa,
tenendo basse l'ale come il cucco.
Con modo accorto ella il parlar ridusse,
che venne a dir come donzella fusse;
                                    (*O.f.* 25.30–31)

[It was clear to my sister that the damsel had illusions about
her; my sister could never have satisfied her need and was
quite perplexed as to what to do. "My best course is to unde-
ceive her," she decided, "and to reveal myself as a member of
the gentle sex rather than to have myself reckoned an ignoble
man." / And she was right. It would have been a sheer dis-
grace, the conduct of a man made of plaster, if he had kept up
a conversation with a damsel as fair as Fiordespina, sweet as
nectar, who had set her cap at him, while like a cuckoo, he just
trailed his wings. So Bradamante tactfully had her know that
she was a maiden.]

After Ricciardetto hears that his twin sister has acquired the affection
of a woman he himself had despaired of winning, he decides to re-
new his attentions disguised as Bradamante. When he takes his twin
sister's place in Fiordespina's bed, he accounts for the difference by
telling her that, while they were apart, he rescued a nymph and was
granted one wish. They enjoy the serendipity until caught at it, at
which point Ricciardetto is sentenced to be burned at the stake.

In the Ariostan episode, dizzying sexual disorientation contrasts
pointedly with an almost cynical determinacy of sexual intention.
Not only has Bradamante "well understood" Fiordespina, despite
the ambiguity of Fiordespina's desire, but Ricciardetto has very carefully calculated the likely outcome of his masquerade before he puts
on his sister's clothes. In Spenser's version, the ambivalence is shifted
from the realm of sexual orientation to that of interpersonal intentions and expectations. Unlike Bradamante, Britomart does not realize the full implications or consequences of her hostess's false impression of her. Consider the description of Malecasta's overtures
and Britomart's response:

And all attonce discouered her desire
  With sighes, and sobs, and plaints, and piteous griefe,
  The outward sparkes of her in burning fire;
  Which spent in vaine, at last she told her briefe,
  That but if she did lend her short reliefe,
  And do her comfort, she mote algates dye.
  But the chaste damzell, that had neuer priefe
  Of such malengine and fine forgerie,
Did easily beleeue her strong extremitie.

(3.1.53)

Britomart is too ingenuous to understand the significance of Malecasta's pleas for "comfort" and "short reliefe." Although she chastely disapproves of Malecasta's seeming lightness, Britomart entertains her advances out of a naive courtesy and wish to please, totally unaware of the unfortunate surprise she thereby prepares for Malecasta.

Spenser writes a comedy of mistaken identity that reaches a point of maximum confusion with the two principals in bed together, each thinking that the other is a man. Ariosto writes a comedy of protean identity, in which sexual difference and sexual preference are virtually arbitrary matters. Ariosto's comedy is thoroughly destabilizing, but the Spenserian comedy puts more at risk. Ricciardetto nearly dies, but that is the result of being found out as a seducer, not of being mistaken for one. There is a sense of moral ambiguity in Britomart's involvement with Malecasta absent from the Ariostan source.[51] Mistaking Malecasta's intentions and being herself mistaken results in Britomart's being wounded by Gardante. The final image of Britomart, with drops of purple blood staining her lily-white smock, is morally indeterminate. The imagery suggests vulnerability, the beginnings of passion, the loss of virginity; it mirrors Britomart's enrapturement at the sight of Artegall and foreshadows her own wounding by the evil Busirane. Britomart's wounding by Gardante, the figure who represents sight, refigures the fate of Actaeon. In place of the erotic chase in which nominally distinct male subject and female object fatally exchange the roles of predator and prey, Britomart pursues a quest in which risk and subjective engagement are necessary conditions for going forth.

2

The Wounds of Adonis
and the Hazards of Desire

Spenser focuses on the theme of risk and the motif of wounding through variations on the myth of Adonis. Timias' pursuit of the boar-spear-carrying forester in canto v and the Gardens of Adonis of canto vi form a diptych, a pairing common to *The Faerie Queene* of an allegorical set-piece with a narrative treatment of analogous issues.[1] The myth of Adonis, first introduced in the tapestries decorating Castle Joyeous, is relevant to Book III as a myth of the hunt. Throughout Book III, we see variations on Eros as a chase; in the middest of Book III, we find the boar.[2] The hunt after the boar, an animal that will turn and fight when cornered, provides a graphic variation on the pattern of erotic reversal in which hunter becomes hunted. The metaphoric dangers of the lady's killing look become the literal threat of a tusk to the groin.

Not only does the myth of Adonis direct renewed—and ironic—attention to the corporeal dimension of erotic desire, it brings to the foreground the function of discursive structures in circumscribing desire. The Venus of Ovid's story is a reductive and trivialized personification of desire. Her love for Adonis transforms her into a parody of the Venus-virago who, disguised and aloof, directs her son Aeneas' entry into Carthage (*Aeneid* 1.314–401).[3] Ovid's Venus dresses up like Diana in order to accompany her new-found love on the chase, but the transformation is cosmetic. She limits her pursuit to timid game such as rabbits and deer and urges Adonis to do likewise:

> 'fortis' que 'fugacibus esto'
> inquit; 'in audaces non est audacia tuta.
> parce meo, iuvenis, temerarius esse periclo,
> neve feras, quibus arma dedit natura, lacesse,
> stet mihi ne magno tua gloria. . . . '
> (*Met.* 10.543–547)

['Be brave against timorous creatures,' she says; 'but against
bold creatures boldness is not safe. Do not be rash, dear boy, at
my risk; and do not provoke those beasts which nature has
well armed, lest your glory be at great cost to me.']⁴

In urging Adonis to forgo hunting fierce beasts in favor of cony-
catching, Ovid's decorative, fearful Venus dooms her lover by her
own inadequacy as a love goddess. The distinction Ovid's Venus
makes between "soft hunts" and "hard hunts" reduces Eros to triv-
ial pursuits. The boar, as well as the rabbit, belongs in the entourage
of the true goddess of love. Having been excluded because of the inadequate scope with which Venus defines her iconographic territory,
the boar returns as the agent of castration. In Adonis' fate, Ovid
suggests that construing the erotic in reductive terms can have violent consequences.

Spenser's principal variations on the Adonis myth are episodes
that focus on their own discourse as well as on ideas of sexual love
and natural generation in order to direct attention to how ideas and
ideals shape and are shaped by discursive structures. We see Timias
attempting to fashion himself after ideals of chivalrous love and being deformed by them. The Gardens of Adonis consider in more abstract fashion the interplay of linguistically constructed models and
the abstract ideas figured by those models. In both instances, the risk
of castration becomes a metaphor used to explore the epistemological uncertainty generated in the attempt to give abstract ideas concrete expression.

THE PERILS OF TIMIAS
AND THE HAZARDS OF IDEALISM

Timias' pursuit of the "griesly foster" and equivocal rescue by the
huntress Belphoebe present a critical examination of various conventional erotic discourses. Timias' misadventures show us what
happens when the ideals presupposed by those discourses are actually acted out. When a Petrarchan lover-from-afar meets an unattainable lady in the woods, the result is bittersweet comedy. A primary source of the special, delicately comic tone is that in Timias and
Belphoebe we see the awkward coexistence of ideal types and recog-
nizably human characters. As Paul Alpers observes, "Timias con-

stantly thinks of Belphoebe as divine, and he bemoans, like a self-conscious Medoro, his lowly estate (3.5.44,47). Belphoebe meanwhile remains the simple country girl: she keeps on applying her medicines and wonders why Timias does not get better (3.5.49–50)" (*Poetry of F.Q.* 188–189).

The strategy Spenser uses to highlight the gap between a character and the conventional role or textual function he or she performs is narrative doubling. Timias and Belphoebe come together because they literally cross paths as each pursues an individual quarry. Although both engage in a chase of one sort or another, their encounter produces discursive dissonance because each acts a role in a slightly different script, or rather each follows a script in which he or she is protagonist. In consequence, we see multiple revisions in the structure of the chase, not simply the reversal of pursuer becoming pursued. Harry Berger, Jr., observes that Belphoebe's inviolability is the construct of male desire: she provokes desire in order to deny it.[5] While Berger's point is well taken, I think that Belphoebe functions in this episode as a relatively independent figure, as the mistress of the hunt, the main figure in a discrete structure, even if that structure is ultimately male-authored. Her relative independence works to disrupt the apparent closure and coherence of the chase structure and thereby reveals the extent to which pursuer and pursued are mutually dependent counterparts.[6] As Belphoebe's guest appearance in an erotic chase reveals, the traditional erotic discourse of the chase accommodates two relatively independent characters uncomfortably at best.

In pursuing Florimell's attacker, Timias enacts a version of knight errantry that reflects ironically on those knights who follow Beauty's chase. He chooses idealistically to defend the lady by defeating her attacker instead of engaging in the more ambiguous pursuit of the lady herself.[7] Although Timias is often considered to be an idealized portrait of Ralegh, he seems here to be an ingenuous Sidnean, who makes himself into the naive embodiment of literary ideals.[8] As with the conventional erotic chase of which it is a complex parody, Timias' pursuit of the lustful forester is subject to reversal. The forester and his two brothers lie in ambush and wound Timias as he fords a stream. Timias' naive attempt to imitate the tropological sense of allegory by enacting an ideal pattern of moral behavior runs into allegorical complications because what he pursues is not just a villain but a figure of lust.[9] At first, Timias seems to be functioning straight-forwardly as an exemplary figure, but the circumstances in which he operates cease to be naively realistic. Ironically, the trouble Timias encounters as his story shifts away from simple moral allegory car-ries with it a moral, namely the peril of treating ideals as a simple model of how to behave.

In many respects, Timias' encounter recalls the Redcrosse Knight's battles with the three paynim brothers: Sans foy, Sans loy, and Sans joy. Book I undermines the apparent otherness of the Redcrosse Knight's opponents. Although the figures riding out of the woods to challenge the Redcrosse Knight seem to be wholly ex-ternal antagonists, we see how Sans foy reflects Redcrosse's faith-lessness to Una and how victory over Sans joy confirms the knight's own joylessness.[10] If the Sans-brothers ride out of the landscape to confront Redcrosse, Timias is literally engulfed by the landscape when the forester and his brothers attack him. He is at the bottom of an erotically suggestive ravine when he is ambushed. Even so altru-istic a male protector as Timias is physically implicated in the sexual chase. Like Britomart, Timias receives a wound as confirmation of his engagement with the object of his pursuit. While Beauty's chase is re-vealed as a pushmi-pullyu construct of the male imagination, Timias' virtuous and altruistic pursuit is also shown to be more complexly engaged with its object than might first appear. Despite his inten-tions, Timias' engagement with women is shown to be more fully sexual than the ideology of chivalrous disinterest admits.

Timias' chase undergoes a second reversal with the appearance of Belphoebe, who, as a figure of Diana, brings to the fore the Actaeon subtext that underlies the whole pattern of pursuit and counter-pursuit.[11] Pursuing the bloody track of a beast she has wounded, Belphoebe comes upon the bleeding Timias. As she ministers to Timias, Belphoebe "heales vp one and makes another wound" (3.5.42.2). However much Belphoebe's inaccessibility may be, as Harry Berger suggests, a construct of male desire, her intervention here, as she both restores and torments Timias, highlights her well-meaning indifference to his desire. The dissonance between versions of the chase inhabited by each of the two figures focuses attention on the play of physical and metaphoric in Timias' wound. If Timias' wounded heart is clearly a conventional metaphor, we can see how that metaphor is grounded physically as Belphoebe applies her salves to his wounded thigh. Conversely, Timias' painful efforts to fit himself into Belphoebe's frame of reference emphasize the potency of linguistic constructs. Timias achieves a kind of *ascesis*, or emptying out, as he manipulates lyric conventions of the Petrarchan poet-lover:

> Vnthankfull wretch (said he) is this the meed,
>   With which her soueraigne mercy thou doest quight?
>   Thy life she saued by her gracious deed,
>   But thou doest weene with villeinous despight,
>   To blot her honour, and her heauenly light.
>   Dye rather, dye, then so disloyally
>   Deeme of her high desert, or seeme so light:
>   Faire death it is to shonne more shame, to dy:
> Dye rather, dy, then euer loue disloyally.
>
> But if to loue disloyalty it bee,
>   Shall I then hate her, that from deathes dore
>   Me brought? ah farre be such reproch fro mee.
>   What can I lesse do, then her loue therefore,
>   Sith I her dew reward cannot restore?
>   Dye rather, dye, and dying do her serue,
>   Dying her serue, and liuing her adore;
>   Thy life she gaue, thy life she doth deserue:
> Dye rather, dye, then euer from her seruice swerue.
>
> But foolish boy, what bootes thy seruice bace
>   To her, to whom the heauens do serue and sew?
>   Thou a meane Squire, of meeke and lowly place,
>   She heauenly borne, and of celestiall hew.
>   How then? of all loue taketh equall vew:
>   And doth not highest God vouchsafe to take
>   The loue and seruice of the basest crew?
>   If she will not, dye meekly for her sake;
> Dye rather, dye, then euer so faire loue forsake.
>   (3.5.45–47)

By shifting the semantic value of reiterated phrases, Timias moves himself from the position that he would rather die than yield to his physical love for Belphoebe to the assertion that he would rather die than forsake a love he conceives as disinterested service to his lady. The repetition of "dye" empties the word of both its literal and metaphoric meaning as Timias looks forward to purely linguistic *jouissance*. In a sense, Timias' effort at enacting conventional erotic discourse is a failed revision. He attempts to revise conventions of chivalry by taking its professed ideals seriously. He seeks to introduce a moral concern into the conventional forms in a naive way, without appreciating what Book III demonstrates as the moral dimension of interpretation. In this he differs from Britomart, whose heroism contains a strong component of reading and writing. She is a *bricoleuse* in the way she adapts fragments of various conventional forms to construct something new. By contrast, Timias loses control of his discourse. Rather than transforming Petrarchan idiom creatively, he is merely feminized by it. For Timias, language seems a more effective instrument of castration than a boar's tusk.

THE REPRESENTATION OF IDEALS
IN THE GARDENS OF ADONIS

The idyll of Timias and Belphoebe achieves its tone of bittersweet comedy through dramatic irony. We see both the conventional roles and the sometimes ill-fated efforts of Spenser's characters to inhabit those roles. The reader enjoys the security of ironic distance: we need not be as serious about ideals as Timias nor as unwitting in our espousal of them as Belphoebe. In a broad sense, the Gardens of Adonis disrupt the security of the reader. The story of Timias and Belphoebe represents the acting out of ideals. The Gardens of Adonis, as part of the reader's education, reflect critically on the representation of ideals. A fundamental issue raised by what C. S. Lewis aptly termed the allegorical core of Book III is the nature of models in allegorical representation and how those models engage the reader. The Gardens of Adonis subject the Sidnean imitation naively essayed by Timias to fuller examination. Significantly, the most fully realized figures in the Gardens of Adonis—Venus and Adonis—seem both to solicit and resist reader identification. The figures Venus and Adonis elicit a certain gender-specific identification, at least in some highly sophisticated readers of *The Faerie Queene*. According to Maureen Quilligan, "the safest vantage point for viewing the cycles of death and creation, and of the cosmic act of sexual intercourse played out in the landscape of the garden, is that of Venus herself—that is, the female perspective" (*Milton's Spenser* 193). In contrast Harry Berger argues for a certain degree of male bonding with Adonis as a Satanic rebel against enforced service.[12] At the same time, the pose of Venus and Adonis recalls Venus and Mars at the opening of *De rerum natura*, invoked by Lucretius as the embodiment of cosmic forces.[13]

The problem of individual identification with models, whether it is cast as Timias' troubles in living out his ideals or reflected in the temptation of the reader to identify with figures that to some extent confound personal identification, is part of an exploration of the larger question of philosophical idealism. With the Gardens of Adonis at the center of Book III, Spenser reexamines the Platonic distinction between intelligible and immutable ideals and the sensible world of impermanence and change. Specifically, Spenser reworks Plato's theory of recollection propounded in the *Meno* and *Phaedo*, the antithesis of the evolutionary model of knowledge developed throughout Book III. The terms of Spenser's revision are set out in the pun that the garden is "the first seminarie / Of all things, that are borne to liue and die" (3.6.30.4–5). "Seminarie" signifies both a seed plot (*OED* s.v. "seminary" 1) and a place of education (*OED* s.v. "seminary" 4). The pun emphasizes the etymological connection between germination and biological growth and learning. Accordingly, the Gardens of Adonis rework Plato's theory of learning as recollection by emphasizing the dimension of fecundity excluded in the Platonic scheme. In the *Meno*, Socrates addresses the question of how we can come to know something we do not already know by asserting that what we call learning is really a process of remembering what the soul has already known, and he demonstrates his assertion by inducing a slave boy to intuit the Pythagorean theorem.[14] The *Phaedo* opposes abstract and concrete, spirit and flesh, immortal and mortal in order to exalt the ideal over the mutable by positing the immutable origin of ideas. Emerging from both dialogues is a denatured and degendered theory of generation. Tropes of birth and death are appropriated in the service of an ascetic denial of carnality. The witty revision of Plato in Book III, canto vi is not a wholesale rejection of otherworldliness. Transcendental concerns are hardly unknown in *The Faerie Queene*, but Spenserian otherworldliness is fundamentally Christian, rather than purely Platonic. Book I locates Spenserian allegory with respect to revealed faith and Christian eschatology. Book III revises Platonic myth in order to call attention to the problem of reconciling abstract ideas with what is sensible, concrete, and mutable in the mortal world.

CHRYSOGONE: INTELLECTUAL INCARNATION
AND NARRATIVE TRANSITION

The story of Chrysogone links the narrative depiction of Timias and Belphoebe attempting to live out ideals with the allegorical meditation on the nature of ideals and their concrete incarnation that comprises the Gardens of Adonis. The Chrysogone story makes for a complex and suggestive transition. It is itself a story of incarnation as well as an etiological fable connecting the two other episodes in a bizarrely retrospective movement that parodies the Platonic search for origins. The narrator launches into the story of Chrysogone by way of explaining the presence of her daughter Belphoebe in the woods:

> WEll may I weene, faire Ladies, all this while
> Ye wonder, how this noble Damozell
> So great perfections did in her compile,
> Sith that in saluage forests she did dwell,
> So farre from court and royall Citadell,
> The great schoolmistresse of all curtesy:
> Seemeth that such wild woods should far expell
> All ciuill vsage and gentility,
> And gentle sprite deforme with rude rusticity.
>
> (3.6.1)

The initial question is how to account for Belphoebe's gentility, to explain why an exemplar of courtesy is to be found so far from the court. This question has resonance beyond the matter of social mobility. The question of how a character "gets into" the text concerns significant issues of representation, of how characters function and contribute to the meaning of texts. In earlier cantos, we see Timias' misguided attempt to insert himself wholesale into courtly and Petrarchan discourse as a failure to construe the relationship between the imitation of an action and the embodiment of an idea. Earlier still, we see that Britomart's presence in Faerieland is a question with rhetorical dimensions, that her being fetched far by love opens up an exploration of how desire is to be figured.[15] In the central episode of Book III, the issue of how figures function in a text, how they are grounded, so to speak, is considered directly. Canto vi traces its answer to the question of Belphoebe's presence back to an image of universal fecundity in the Gardens of Adonis. Through twists and turns of narrative and allegorical representation, the text presents connections between a role model and a cosmic womb. The chase after Cupid that leads Venus and Diana to Chrysogone and her newborn twins Amoret and Belphoebe parodies the larger movement of Spenser's text as it draws together narrative representation and abstract ideas. The absence from the landscape of Cupid, a figure that is a powerfully conventional representation of desire, ironically heralds the reinclusion of the body excluded from Plato's myth of generation.[16]

The miraculous birth of Amoret and Belphoebe, resulting from the spontaneous fructification of Chrysogone's womb, locates Spenser's fable between Platonic myth and Christian revelation.[17] As a parody of the Virgin Birth, the story both points to the ultimate ground of experience in the spiritual realm beyond the senses and suggests the distance between Christian mystery and Spenser's parodic myth. The Gardens of Adonis will work out issues of ideas and ideals with respect to the material world alone, rather than to Christian eschatology (ironically, the resurrection and ultimate disposition of bodies rather than a dualistic rejection of the material). At the same time, the narrator's description of the birth, that Chrysogone "bore withouten paine, that she conceiued / Withouten pleasure" (3.6.27.2–3) delicately echoes Socrates' observations, quoted early in the *Phaedo*, about the curious interconnection of pleasure and pain.[18] In the story of Chrysogone, Spenser takes the Platonic myth of spiritual origins and makes it erotic in order to challenge the Platonic (and unChristian) distinction between abstract ideas and concrete manifestation. Plato's theory of the heavenly origin of ideas is transformed in Spenser's myth to the image of heavenly influence, which combines austere astrophysics with extremely physical eroticism.[19] Belphoebe and Amoret were conceived "through influence of th'heauens fruitfull ray" (3.6.6.2). "Influence" here signifies literal inflowing as well as the infusion of immaterial power or action at a distance (*OED* s.v. "influence" 1, 3, 4). By positing the immutable origins of Ideas, Plato elevates the abstract over the concrete, spirit over flesh, and the ideal over the mutable. In shifting focus from heavenly origins to heavenly influence, Spenser emphasizes process and relationship over permanence. Spenser seeks intellectual stability by examining the principles of mutability and the nature of the relationship between abstract principles and concrete reality. In this episode, Plato's binary opposition of abstract and concrete is transformed into paradox. Heavenly influence ensures the purity of Belphoebe's conception, "vnspotted from all loathly crime, / That is ingenerate in fleshly slime" (3.6.3.4–5). In other words, Belphoebe's conception has the purity of an intellectual idea. At the same time, the entire cosmos is shown to be sexual, which makes spiritual purity and fastidiousness seem a bit beside the point.

CARNAL KNOWLEDGE:
REINTRODUCING SEXUALITY
IN THE GENERATION OF IDEAS

As an allegorical set-piece, the Gardens of Adonis focus on the relation of ideas and ideals to the carnal world of change. The eroticism of the garden functions both as a corrective to Platonic dualism of body and spirit and as pretext for questioning Aristotelian gendering of dualism as male form and female matter. Adonis' role as "Father of all formes" who is "subiect to mortalitie" yet "eterne in mutabilitie," "transformed oft, and chaunged diuerslie" (3.6.47) is ambiguous. Is the "father of all formes" an archi-form? Or is that which is "eterne in mutabilitie" matter?[20] If Adonis' position in the interplay of form and matter is confusing, so is that of his consort. Although, in context, the coupling of the two brings to mind the pairing of form and matter, the description of how Venus "possesseth him, and of his sweetnesse takes her fill" (3.6.46.9) makes it difficult to sort out which figure is supposed to represent which category.

The Gardens of Adonis episode examines critically the gender construction of nature and traces connections between construing nature as female and construing change in gender-specific terms as castration. The *mons Veneris* and the boar that killed Adonis form part of the same icon at the center of the garden. The episode directs attention to the rhetorical use of the feminine as a trope. While the emphasis on femininity in the garden provides a means of including the element of fecundity and physical generation in the representation of nature, there are evident consequences to these rhetorical means. The Gardens of Adonis reveal how conceiving of the body as a metaphor is a strategy for achieving permanence that ironically resists control and threatens security. Ovid's Adonis is destroyed by being implicated in a discursive structure that is flagrantly reductive and inadequate. In Spenser's Gardens of Adonis we see how even so rich and important a metaphor as that of the body carries danger.

The text provides perspective on the issue of constructing nature discursively by presenting the Gardens of Adonis in three contradictory descriptions. As Donald Cheney has observed, the garden appears, first as the womb of the natural world, then as the image of the natural world, and, finally, as "a grove located on top of a 'stately Mount' " (126–130).[21] The first version of the garden as metaphorical womb represents the idea of generation that underlies the appearance of earthly mutability. The second version represents nature as it appears to us. The third version of the garden meditates on the relationship between constructions of nature and the person doing the constructing.

The first version of the Gardens of Adonis offers an allegory of generation in which the principle of earthly generation is expressed in cyclical metaphors of cosmic fecundity.[22] This version represents nature considered in the abstract without provision made for the constructing mind. A generation myth explains the idea of generation and avoids the problem of epistemology. The narrator observes that "ne needs there Gardiner to set, or sow" (3.6.34.1) In effect, this is an Eden without Adam. The principal shortcoming of this version of the garden is that its permanence, dispossessed of human consciousness, degenerates to the bloomin' buzzin' confusion of Chaos. The philosophical system grows more complicated and self-contradictory as the language becomes choked with arid abstractions. The decay, both of the poetry and the cosmology, is embodied in the decay of those curious "formes" that grow in the garden:

> The substance is not chaunged, nor altered,
>   But th'only forme and outward fashion;
>   For euery substance is conditioned
>   To change her hew, and sundry formes to don,
>   Meet for her temper and complexion:
>   For formes are variable and decay,
>   By course of kind, and by occasion;
>   And that faire flowre of beautie fades away,
> As doth the lilly fresh before the sunny ray.
>   (3.6.38)

A number of critics have made extensive efforts to sort out the metaphysical ground of this passage.[23] Spenser's basic strategy seems to be to cross Plato with Aristotle, but the most salient point is poetic rather than philosophical, namely our aesthetic surprise and relief as that flower metaphor springs from the philosophical compost.

The welcome metaphor of the flower makes the transition to the second version of the garden. What follows is the same cycle of decay and regeneration given in the first version, but this time seen from within, from the human perspective, where the pain of mortality accompanies aesthetic pleasure. Lovely things die and this saddens us. The problem with this version is that nature considered strictly as the world of appearances yields nothing of permanence unless, fulfilling the worst suspicions traditionally directed toward poetry, we are prepared to lie about it. The only vision of eternity possible from this perspective is perpetuity, a spurious extension of familiar nature compounded of wishful thinking and rhetorical epanorthosis, or correction:

> Yet pittie often did the gods relent,
>   To see so faire things mard, and spoyled quight:
> And their great mother *Venus* did lament
>   The losse of her deare brood, her deare delight:
>   Her hart was pierst with pittie at the sight,
>   When walking through the Gardin, them she spyde,
>   Yet no'te she find redresse for such despight.
>   For all that liues, is subiect to that law:
> All things decay in time, and to their end do draw.
>
> But were it not, that *Time* their troubler is,
>   All that in this delightfull Gardin growes,
>   Should happie be, and haue immortall blis:
>   For here all plentie, and all pleasure flowes,
>   And sweet loue gentle fits emongst them throwes,
>   Without fell rancor, or fond gealosie;
>   Franckly each paramour his leman knowes,
>   Each bird his mate, ne any does enuie
> Their goodly meriment, and gay felicitie.
>
> There is continuall spring, and haruest there
>   Continuall, both meeting at one time:
>   (3.6.40–42.2)

Plenty is unproblematically linked with pleasure, and the mutability that underlies the earthly process of generation is wished away.

The final version, the "stately Mount" accommodates permanence and change as it emphasizes the reader's position in the construction of nature. The image of the garden as a *mons Veneris* presents the idea of generation in the guise of physiology, of geography, and of cosmology.[24] The coexistence in one image of multiple paradigms bespeaks the intellectual freedom and flexibility necessary to register and assimilate the distinct versions of generation presented. At the same time, Spenser's image glories in viscous materiality:

> Right in the middest of that Paradise,
>> There stood a stately Mount, on whose round top
>> A gloomy groue of mirtle trees did rise,
>> Whose shadie boughes sharpe steele did neuer lop,
>> Nor wicked beasts their tender buds did crop,
>> But like a girlond compassed the hight,
>> And from their fruitfull sides sweet gum did drop,
>> That all the ground with precious deaw bedight,
> Threw forth most dainty odours, and most sweet delight.
>> (3.6.43)

In admitting simultaneous ignorance and knowledge of the garden's geography, the narrator points to the paradoxical combination of familiarity and estrangement produced by sexual metaphor. The narrator pretends to be uncertain whether Venus' particular pied-à-terre is Paphos, Cythera, or Gnidus while admitting, "But well I wote by tryall, that this same / All other pleasant places doth excell" (3.6.29.6–7).[25] This admission of carnal knowledge trades on a humor bred of familiarity. The sexual terms are certainly commonplace enough; however seeing those terms as metaphor does indeed lead to terra incognita, as it brings us to understand the full implications of troping the body.

The climactic image of the boar imprisoned within the garden presents and anatomizes the epistemology of risk. The image is explicitly offered as evidence of Adonis' security:

> There now he liueth in eternall blis,
>> Ioying his goddesse, and of her enioyd:
>> Ne feareth he henceforth that foe of his,
>> Which with his cruell tuske him deadly cloyd:
>> For that wilde Bore, the which him once annoyd,
>> She firmely hath emprisoned for ay,
>> That her sweet loue his malice mote auoyd,
>> In a strong rocky Caue, which is they say,
> Hewen vnderneath that Mount, that none him losen may.
>> (3.6.48)

At the same time that it promises Adonis' safety, the image of the tusked boar within the *mons Veneris* suggests the *vagina dentata*,[26] an icon of fearsome venereal power. The desire for permanence and security in the material realm leads to conceiving of the body as metaphor, but such physically grounded tropes elude control. The boar, excluded in the interest of security, returns in context. The dualism of spirit and matter, permanence and change, male and female is resolved in an unsettling image of inclusiveness.[27] If readers are free to consider from a safe distance the comedy of Timias and Belphoebe acting out irreconcilable ideas, we are not given that security here. The Gardens of Adonis present the enterprise of incorporating ideals as one that ultimately collapses aesthetic distance. The risk involved is the risk of subjective engagement that Britomart faces in her quest. Like Britomart, readers are denied certainty: the Gardens of Adonis are presented in a series of contradictory and provisional allegorical constructs. At the same time, the physiological aspect of the allegory threatens the security of purely intellectual, aesthetic disengagement.

3

The Hermaphrodite
Making Sense of the Sensual

Although the motif of the chase underlies much of Book III, the book—and the entire poem—in 1590 closes with a clinch rather than a kill. The Hermaphrodite image that concludes the 1590 *Faerie Queene* represents a version of closure different from the alternating circuit of pursuer and pursued that Book III explores in detail.[1] The Hermaphrodite image draws to conclusion a subtext different from those underlying the erotic chases prevalent in Book III. The myths of Diana and Actaeon and of Venus and Adonis are myths of the hunt; the Hermaphrodite figures the union of opposites. If the myth of Actaeon is the subtext of the ironic reversals of pursuer and pursued throughout Book III, the Hermaphrodite underlies the gender reversals (Berger, "Kidnapped Romance" 222–230). Moreover, the alternative subtexts evoke different versions of desire. Beauty's chase is a parodic version of the Neoplatonic pursuit of the Beautiful from its embodiment in mortal exemplars to its transcendent state. Spenser's knights errant, however, are drawn by a projection of their own desire into a thoroughly earthbound pursuit. The alternative version of desire has the lover transformed, after the Neoplatonic image of the Hermaphrodite, into the beloved, as Britomart fashions herself after the image of Artegall, and Amoret and Scudamore exchange attributes in a climactic embrace.[2]

The image of the Hermaphrodite concludes the entire 1590 *Faerie Queene*, as well as the original version of Book III. Ovid's story of the Hermaphrodite is the subtext that underwrites the shift from Christian eschatology in Book I to the project of making sense of the mortal world in Book III. Direct allusions to the Hermaphrodite function as a kind of structural marker that points up the shift. An allusion to Ovid's story of the Hermaphrodite occurs at the center of Book I and at the conclusion of Book III. At the center of Book I, the Redcrosse

Knight is "pourd out in loosenesse" in a failure to submit his physical desires to the control of his rational faculties. Redcrosse's failure of physical control is symptomatic of larger, theological issues. His loss of faith in Una and the Gospel has him whoring after Duessa and Roman Catholic rite. His consequent punishment and rescue provide an object lesson in the primacy of the soul over the body.[3] At the conclusion of Book III, Amoret "pourd out her sprite" in Scudamore's embrace. A central concern of Book III is how to engage and express what is resistant to hierarchical control. As a subtext of Books I and III, Ovid's Hermaphrodite provides focus on the body. In Book I, the body is conceived as a sign pointing beyond itself to spiritual truths. In Book III, the body is central, literally so in the Gardens of Adonis. Book III constructs a revisionary discourse designed to address directly the sensual experience transcended by the typological allegory of Book I.

THE OVIDIAN MYTH:
DISCURSIVE CONSTRUCTION VS.
BIOLOGICAL RESISTANCE

Not only does the Hermaphrodite image figure forth the climactic embrace of long separated lovers, but the Ovidian myth to which that image alludes focuses explicitly on the issue of closure. The myth of the Hermaphrodite is initially presented as an etiological fable that opens with the promise to explain the peculiar properties of the famous fountain of Salmacis and concludes with the curse that gives the fountain the enfeebling properties for which it is known. Ovid tells the story of Hermaphroditus, child of Hermes and Aphrodite, who, out to explore the world for the first time, encounters the nymph Salmacis. The naive youth rejects the nymph's advances but bathes in the pool of which Salmacis is tutelary spirit. The nymph pursues him into the pool and, with the aid of divine intervention, is united to the recalcitrant young man. Hermaphroditus sees himself transformed into half a man [*semimarem*] and curses the fountain, so that anyone drinking from its waters will likewise become effeminate.

The story of the Hermaphrodite functions particularly well as an alternative subtext in Book III because it is a myth of sexual identity and gender formation. Britomart fashions herself into the knight of chastity through open-ended, androgynous improvisation. She dons armor and slips in and out of male-identified modes of behavior, all the while in pursuit of her beloved. Hermaphroditus' adolescent journey of growth and self-discovery is foreclosed in highly ironic ways. His story is a sardonic cautionary tale about taking what one perceives for what is. The Hermaphrodite misperceives his own body and is trapped by his misunderstanding. Ovid offers a myth of sexual identity in which the formal definition of manhood is set in paradoxical opposition to the active experience of it. In Platonic terms, the intelligible meaning of manhood is set in opposition to the sensible meaning. In contemporary terms, an essentialist view of gender plays ironically against one that is constructed.

Ovid's story presents a gap between a character's understanding of his own experience and what the narration of that experience conveys to the reader. Ostensibly, the myth of the Hermaphrodite defines the boundaries of manhood negatively, by Hermaphroditus' loss of shape and by the otherness of the female figure with whom he merges. At the same time, however, the sequence of events composing Hermaphroditus' loss of masculine shape presents an unmistakable, if parodic, representation of sexual intercourse. The potential double meaning of words such as "perstat" [stands firm], "mollita" [soft], and "mollescat" [became soft or effeminate] points up the gap between Hermaphroditus' understanding of his own experience and what his story can signify. Ovid describes Hermaphroditus' vision of his transformation, "fecisse videt mollitaque in illis / membra" (*Met.* 4.381–82), which can be rendered "and he saw that his members had become soft there" (Lewis and Short s.vv. "mollio" 1.2; "membrum" 1) or, following Miller's translation, "that his limbs had become enfeebled there." Although Hermaphroditus gives an implicitly moral interpretation to his physical transformation—he has become weak and effeminate—the physical suggestions of postcoital flaccidity indicate a physiological interpretation of his experience.

In Ovid's myth of the Hermaphrodite, the body is the site of interplay between the epistemic and the structural.[4] The story explores the complex negotiations between experience and the forms consciousness imposes on experience for purposes of understanding. The Hermaphrodite's body does double duty as a model of intelligible form and as an instrument of sensual experience. Hermaphroditus understands his body as a sign of masculinity and interprets changes in his physical shape as the loss of manhood. The youth misreads his body by mistaking what he perceives for all that there is.[5] Ironically, the physical changes he experiences indicate a male sexual function that contradicts Hermaphroditus' interpretation of emasculation and loss. In this case, the intelligible falls short of the sensible.[6]

The ironic limitations of Hermaphroditus' understanding are made clear as the narrator describes the action of the curse on the fountain, "motus uterque parens nati rata verba biformis / fecit et incesto fontem medicamine tinxit" (*Met.* 4.387–88) [His parents heard the prayer of their two-formed son and charged the waters with that uncanny power (the Loeb translation reproduced here of "incesto" as uncanny is probably too weak: "polluting," "unchaste," "incestuous in breaking down boundaries," or the Platonic "pharmakos" might be more appropriate in context)]. Ovid plays "uterque parens . . . rata verba . . . fecit," which can be rendered "each of his parents fulfilled his wish" or, literally "each of his parents made his words fixed" (Lewis and Short s.v. "reor" 2.b.2) against "nati biformis" [of their two-formed son].[7] On the one hand, words have the power to determine Hermaphroditus' form. Insofar as they ratify and make permanent limitations of understanding, words reify the hero's sexual inexperience and thereby create a monster: the Hermaphrodite. On the other, Hermaphroditus is more truly biform than he realizes. He is both an emblem of emasculation and an image of male sexuality. Hermaphroditus understands his transformed shape wholly as a sign of emasculation because he naively considers his body solely as an embodied form and not at all as an instrument of physical experience. He presupposes that he can see himself objectively as he emphasizes the power of one parent—Hermes, god of language—over the other—Aphrodite, goddess of love. From our wider perspective, we can see the Hermaphrodite as a biform sign in which arbitrary semiological difference plays against sexual difference. The "he-she" hermaphrodite is neither genuinely androgynous nor genuinely a boundary figure: it is arbitrarily classed with "she." As far as Hermaphroditus is concerned, the critical difference is not he or she, but he or not-he; not male versus female, but male versus not-male. Although Hermaphroditus exercises arbitrary power of making distinctions, the gendered body provides a reality check. In choosing to draw the boundaries as he does, Hermaphroditus excludes his own sexuality and effectively castrates himself.[8]

The Hermaphrodite is caught between the poles of language and desire. The myth suppresses Hermaphroditus' own desire by assigning it arbitrarily to the female. Hermaphroditus' sexual performance is presented as the object of Salmacis's desire rather than as an attribute of his own. The apparent formal unity of the Hermaphrodite's story excludes the sexual content of his experience. His concluding curse of the waters seems completely to fulfill the opening promise of an etiological explanation of the fountain. When, at Hermaphroditus' prayer, his parents invest the pool with the power to change any man who enters it into half-man, the narrator's initial pledge to tell the hidden cause of the fountain's enfeebling powers seems fully satisfied. Nevertheless, the apparent closure of etiology and curse belies the complications of the story so enframed. In similar fashion, Hermaphroditus' interpretation of the lineaments of gratified desire as an emasculated body forecloses his growth into mature manhood. His final curse, that anyone who enters the pool of Salmacis should emerge half-man, calls for the repetition of Hermaphroditus' emasculation rather than inviting the retrospective understanding of his experience. Nevertheless, in coupling with Salmacis, whatever divine assistance he receives and whatever interpretation he places on the experience, the Hermaphrodite outperforms his own construction of his experience. He is a figure of excess as well as of foreclosure. By naming things in ignorance, Hermaphroditus multiplies entities needlessly and creates monsters. As Hermaphroditus misnames his own desire, he seems to transform the universality of puberty into the anomaly of metamorphosis.

The games Ovid plays with narrative framing, whereby the story of the Hermaphrodite slips in and out of the bounds of the etiological frame, corresponds to shifts back and forth between what now would be called essentialist and constructionist theories of gender.[9] As the monstrous, anomalous Hermaphrodite, the youth seems to be the ironic victim of his own construction of himself. At the same time, we can see his construction as a misconstruction, as a failure to recognize essential manhood and essential sexual difference. Nevertheless, that essential manhood posited by Ovid's story is denied to the protagonist. He is already the Hermaphrodite from the beginning, a figure known for bisexuality at least as early as Diodorus Siculus in the first century B.C. (4.6.5).[10] The hapless Hermaphroditus is a pawn of the narrative; the configuration of his story suggests meanings not available to its hero. His *aporia* is our entertainment. The play of closure and indeterminacy in the story of Hermaphroditus points to a rhetorical shift in mode. The closure of the etiological fable suggests an explanatory mode of narration: we learn why the waters of Salmacis got to be the way they are. In contrast, Ovid's story, taken with all of its ironies and indeterminacies, presumes a kind of conspiratorial relationship between poet and reader to enjoy the conundrum constructed for the protagonist.

THE OVIDIAN SUBTEXT
IN MIDDEST BOOK I

The displacement of the Hermaphrodite from the center of Book I to the conclusion of Book III ratifies the larger structural and thematic shift from the first to the last book of the 1590 *Faerie Queene*. In Book I the allusion to Ovid's Hermaphrodite occurs in the determinate center of a providential structure. Book III makes allusion to that figure in a conclusion that questions the very possibility of closure.[11] The Redcrosse Knight's liaison with Duessa and his encounter with Orgoglio represent a turning point, a fortunate fall, the first Pyrrhic defeat in a series of Pyrrhic victories over projections of his own faithlessness and joylessness. The pun error-*errare* that underlies the narrative of Book I as the hero's epic wanderings proceed from his initial mistake in doubting Una's truth becomes subsumed by the pattern of sin and redemption, which climaxes in the apocalyptic fight between Saint George and the dragon.[12] The hermaphroditic embrace of Scudamore and Amoret, which concludes the 1590 *Faerie Queene*, reminds the heroine, "halfe enuying their blesse" that her own quest is unfulfilled and her own love is unrealized.

At the center of Book I, Spenser revises Ovid's myth of the Hermaphrodite in order to emphasize the moral component of the Redcrosse Knight's experience over the merely physical and to define the hero's identity as his moral self.[13] The indeterminacies Ovid presents for our amusement are transformed into the moral hierarchy Spenser presents for our edification. Spenser separates the Ovidian paradox—that what Hermaphroditus experiences as the loss of manhood can also be regarded as male sexual performance—into moral and physical components. The cause of the enfeebling property of the fountain from which Redcrosse drinks is distinguished from its effect on the knight. Ovid's "causa latet, vis est notissima fontis" (4.287) [The cause is hidden; but the enfeebling power of the fountain is well known] becomes:

> The cause was this: one day when *Phœbe* fayre
>   With all her band was following the chace,
>   This Nymph, quite tyr'd with heat of scorching ayre
>   Sat downe to rest in middest of the race:
>   The goddesse wroth gan fowly her disgrace,
>   And bad the waters, which from her did flow,
>   Be such as she her selfe was then in place.
>   Thenceforth her waters waxed dull and slow,
> And all that drunke thereof, did faint and feeble grow.
>   (1.7.5)[14]

Ovid's erotic myth of the Hermaphrodite purports to reveal the hidden cause. In Spenser's redaction, the cause of the fountain's special properties is presented as an open matter, but the apparently straightforward explanation conceals hidden contradictions in the mythographic commentary that accrued to the Hermaphrodite myth in the centuries between Ovid and Spenser. Mythographic commentators on the Hermaphrodite tended to focus exclusively on either the moral or the erotic dimension of Ovid's story. Spenser secretly shifts from one tradition of interpretation to the other as he establishes a hierarchical relationship between the moral and the sensual. The cause that Spenser initially provides derives from a mythographic tradition that interprets the nymph Salmacis as an emblem of moral laziness.[15] No reference to the erotic aspect of the myth occurs until Redcrosse actually drinks from the stream; his reaction recalls, in part, the other mythographic tradition, which holds that the fountain of Salmacis is aphrodisiac and promotes impotence through sexual overindulgence.[16] The Redcrosse Knight is surprised by sexuality, but his sin is the moral loss he brings from the House of Pride.

In Ovid's myth of the Hermaphrodite, the false closure of the promise of an etiological explanation at the opening and the explanatory curse at the conclusion suppress the punning sexual content of the protagonist's experience. In Spenser's revision, repressed desire returns with a vengeance, as Orgoglio. Throughout his errancy the Redcrosse Knight has been naively confident in himself and in the evidence of his senses and inattentive to his surroundings in their relationship to himself: he understands neither how his feelings cloud his perception nor how external nature gives back projections of his own human nature. In return for his heedlessness, he is assaulted by a sense experience. Orgoglio figures forth both an earthquake, sign of divine anger, and an ambulatory erection, image of the hero's own sensuality.[17] Redcrosse survives his Pyrrhic defeat by Orgoglio because his fall is grounded typologically in Christ's redemption of fallen man. Prince Arthur rescues the Redcrosse Knight by violently demystifying Orgoglio:

> That huge great body, which the Gyaunt bore,
> Was vanisht quite, and of that monstrous mas
> Was nothing left, but like an emptie bladder was.
> (1.8.24.7–9)

The monstrous allegorical figure disappears, leaving nothing behind but a simile. But Redcrosse remains, wasting away, "the chearelesse man" (1.8.43.7) in both appearance and feeling (*OED* s.v. "cheer" 1–4). Orgoglio's defeat is an Ovidian joke that plays unstable language against insecure sexuality: as a purely rhetorical figure, Orgoglio has no more independent physical existence than an erection *post coitum*. But the Redcrosse Knight's manhood is not exhausted by the disappearance of Orgoglio. As a man, he is the pattern for physiological tropes as well as the image of something greater than his mere physical being. Orgoglio's destruction educates the Redcrosse Knight morally because it figures the emptiness of pride. Redcrosse experiences the loss that his physical and spiritual sins bring about and is redeemed through that experience of loss.

The physical is clearly subordinated to the moral in the Redcrosse Knight's encounter with Duessa. Although the allegorical significance of the episode is conveyed by quite specific details of Renaissance sexual physiology, those details contribute to a picture of spiritual transgression. As Thomas P. Roche, Jr., has pointed out, the Redcrosse Knight's sin is that of whoring after strange gods.[18] The seductress Duessa, arrayed in her scarlet robe and papal triple-mitered crown evokes the Whore of Babylon and the Roman Catholic church.[19] She is a figure of institutional temptation to which Redcrosse falls prey because of his pride. Nevertheless, the relationship of the erotic narrative to its allegorical meaning is not entirely stable. Both Ovid's myth and Spenser's revision treat the problematic aspect of appropriating the female in the construction of discourse. The

Ovidian source reflects critically on the use of the female as a semiotic function that defines the protagonist's manhood.[20] In Book I,
Duessa's function in the allegory is signaled by abundant iconographic detail. At the conclusion of the episode, however, we see the
female figure exceeding allegorical control. As Una interprets it for
us, the stripping of Duessa presents the true face of falsehood in all
of its ugliness. Nevertheless, the graphic detail of the description insists on the female gender of the figure and presents a specifically
female body as an object of disgust:

> Then when they had despoild her tire and call,
> Such as she was, their eyes might her behold,
> That her misshaped parts did them appall,
> A loathly, wrinckled hag, ill fauoured, old,
> Whose secret filth good manners biddeth not be told.
>
> Her craftie head was altogether bald,
>   And as in hate of honorable eld,
>   Was ouergrowne with scurfe and filthy scald;
>   Her teeth out of her rotten gummes were feld,
>   And her sowre breath abhominably smeld;
>   Her dried dugs, like bladders lacking wind,
>   Hong downe, and filthy matter from them weld;
>   Her wrizled skin as rough, as maple rind,
> So scabby was, that would haue loathd all womankind.
>
> Her neather parts, the shame of all her kind,
>   My chaster Muse for shame doth blush to write;
>   But at her rompe she growing had behind
>   A foxes taile, with dong all fowly dight;
>   And eke her feete most monstrous were in sight;
>   For one of them was like an Eagles claw,
>   With griping talaunts armd to greedy fight,
>   The other like a Beares vneuen paw:
> More vgly shape yet neuer liuing creature saw.
>   (1.8.46.5–48)

Readers inclined to take this passage as an unambiguous expression of Edmund Spenser's gynophobia should probably turn to the
description of Lust in Book IV as a counterexample. The question
remains, however, what are we to make of this? My own sense is
that an enthusiasm for the carnivalesque body and a kind of Grand
Guignol delight in grossness animate the descriptions of both the
naked Duessa and the hirsute Lust as much as does disgust.[21] Be that

as it may, the function, in context, of the grotesque physical description of "the face of falsehood" is to mark the appropriation of the female body for allegorical purposes. Although the erotic aspect of the episode is subordinated to the moral, revealed in the stripping of Duessa is the resistance of the female body to the imposition of abstract, gender-neutral meaning. The identification of Duessa's "neather parts" as "the shame of all her kind," underscored by Spenser's blushing Muse, blatantly calls attention to the awkwardness of making female physiology express a general moral. The female pronoun "her" is ambiguous. It is impossible to determine whether "all her kind" refers to all evil witches or to all womankind or, indeed, all humankind.[22] The potential gynophobia of the reference highlights the extent to which moral allegory may be destabilized when it derives its tropes from female anatomy.

THE BATTLE FOR INTERPRETATION
IN THE HOUSE OF BUSIRANE

The original conclusion to Book III of *The Faerie Queene*, from Britomart's trial in the House of Busirane through the image of the hermaphroditically embracing Amoret and Scudamore, focuses on this issue of appropriating the female in the construction of discourse in a particularly self-conscious way. The text engages its readers in female-gendered constructs by presenting both Britomart and Amoret as reader surrogates. In the House of Busirane, Britomart plays the role of militantly active reader while Amoret is the passive object of Busirane's fiction making. This is a more constraining and coercive variation on the way the reader is engaged in the Gardens of Adonis by the ambivalent image of the boar imprisoned in the *mons Veneris*. That image, figuring both threat and security, invites an active response from the reader in registering both parts of the paradox. The image of the boar, which figures loss as castration, presents the consequences of conceiving nature metaphorically in gendered terms. The House of Busirane offers no position safe from the ascription of gender and, indeed, from the ascription of female gender. Insofar as femininity is conceived as a metaphor, it can be assigned to any object. Male or female, we are all potentially Marinell being impaled by the fate from which he flees, or Amoret being penned by a manipulative poet.

The House of Busirane reflects critically on conventional, male-authored erotic discourses by exposing the manipulation of gendered constructs. Amoret is the site of battle between Busirane and Britomart over the nature of love. But Amoret is presented as a woman as well as a field of contesting interpretations, and as a woman she offers her own resistance to Busirane's poetic construction of her. As comrades in the struggle against the enchanter, the two female figures enable the text to focus critically on Busirane's art through a kind of triangulation. Both Britomart and Amoret are embattled because Busirane covertly seeks to retain the power of interpretation exclusively for himself. The art both Britomart and Amoret resist, each in her own fashion, is presented as covertly manipulating the reader so as to write the act of interpretation out of the picture:

> For round about, the wals yclothed were
>> With goodly arras of great maiesty,
>> Wouen with gold and silke so close and nere,
>> That the rich metall lurked priuily,
>> As faining to be hid from enuious eye;
>> Yet here, and there, and euery where vnwares
>> It shewd it selfe, and shone vnwillingly;
>> Like a discolourd Snake, whose hidden snares
> Through the greene gras his long bright burnisht backe declares.
>
> And in those Tapets weren fashioned
>> Many faire pourtraicts, and many a faire feate,
>> And all of loue, and all of lusty-hed,
>> As seemed by their semblaunt did entreat;
>> And eke all *Cupids* warres they did repeate,
>> And cruell battels, which he whilome fought
>> Gainst all the Gods, to make his empire great;
>> Besides the huge massacres, which he wrought
> On mighty kings and kesars, into thraldome brought.
>
>> (3.11.28–29)

The ecphrastic description half conceals active designs on the reader, much as the fabric of the tapestry half conceals serpentine threads of gold. Rhymed puns on "entreat" and "repeate" suggest that what might seem straightforward mimesis can be rhetorical manipulation. "Entreat" can signify "treat of given subject matter" but also "beseech" (*OED* s.v. 2–3; 7, 9–10). Similarly "repeate" can mean reproduce mimetically but, in context, can also signify refight Cupid's wars. The series of classical rapes presented in the tapestries gives a highly tendentious picture of sexual love. Moreover, the designation of "Cupids warres" has already imposed an interpretation on love and, indeed, the figure of Cupid himself covertly reifies an interpretation of desire as cupidity.

The interpretation of love as "Cupids warres" is imposed on the audience in an act of warlike aggression. This doubling underscores the homology between sexual love and semiosis that functions throughout Book III. Both are transactions across a gap of consciousness. The embattled reader has a champion, however, in Britomart. Throughout Book III, her adventures have had a strong hermeneutic component, as, indeed, have the adventures of the Redcrosse Knight and Sir Guyon. Nevertheless, Britomart's climactic trial at the House of Busirane is much more explicitly a matter of reading than is either Redcrosse's fight with the dragon at the conclusion of Book I or Guyon's destruction of the Bower of Bliss at the close of Book II. Her struggle with Busirane is cast as an inescapable battle for interpretation. Britomart's movement through the door marked with the inscription "Be bold" explicitly links the act of reading with the active pursuit of her mission to rescue Amoret:

> Tho as she backward cast her busie eye,
>   To search each secret of that goodly sted,
>   Ouer the dore thus written she did spye
>   *Be bold*: she oft and oft it ouer-red,
>   Yet could not find what sence it figured:
>   But what so were therein or writ or ment,
>   She was no whit thereby discouraged
>   From prosecuting of her first intent,
> But forward with bold steps into the next roome went.
>   (3.11.50)

Although the words of the inscription are plain enough, what is meant is mysterious, both because no context is provided in which to place the gnomic imperative and because the source of the inscription—the locus of authorial intention—is unknown. Britomart is unable to decipher the message over the door, but, undaunted by the absence of external validation for what she does, she obeys the command by being bold and passing boldly into the next room. In so doing, Britomart gives the inscription a meaning it did not necessarily have before her particular act of boldness and enacts a model of literary interpretation as invention—simultaneously the creation and discovery of meaning in a collaboration of reader and text.[23]

Britomart's encounter with Busirane presents a reasonably clear-cut model of the relationship of reader to poet. We see the initial metaphor of Cupid's war staged as the struggle between Busirane as a poet figure and Britomart as an exegete, with Amoret in the middle. The model of reading developed in Book III initially posits subjective engagement in the object of perception, as Britomart must think of what might pertain to herself in order to see the magic vision in Merlin's looking glass. The introduction of Amoret's subjective resistance to the magic visions conjured up by Busirane complicates this model. Amoret's dual role as a character in Spenser's *Faerie Queene* and as an unwilling participant in Busirane's Masque of Cupid provides a fictive model of the link between a conscious subject and an object of representation.[24] The episode represents a living person reduced to the status of a fictive object while from a slightly different perspective, the content of the fictive masque apparently comes to life and resists its author's intentions. Spenser's initial model of subjective participation in the object of reading has become an unstable exchange between subject and object as Amoret wavers from one position to the other.[25] Throughout the House of Busirane, we see the interaction of reader and text as a vigorous and highly charged exchange.

The fact that Amoret, the resisting subject matter, and Britomart, the resisting reader, are both women brings into focus gender identification in transactions between the poet and reader and between artificer and work of artifice. The Masque of Cupid examines the appropriation of the female in erotic fiction-making as a special case of poetic referentiality. The Petrarchan dialectic of absence and presence—the physical absence of the beloved permits her presence in the poet-lover's text, just as the presence of the beloved in the poem inscribes her absence—is revised in the pageant as negotiations of resistance and compliance.[26] The motif of resistance and compliance gives a psychological dimension to the binary of physical absence and presence and lends a certain psychological verisimilitude to textual negotiations. In the Petrarchan discourse here subjected to critique, female desire is construed as a function of male desire. The woman's desire varies inversely with that of the male poet. Her unwillingness allows him to continue discoursing on his desire, unchecked by satisfaction. In this scheme, the lady's resistance is fictive resistance, determined by the exigencies of the male-authored discourse. The Petrarchan poet gives the impression of reaching out beyond the bounds of the text, exquisitely rendering the painful desire that is constituted by lack, by the tragic limitations of the individual psyche in an indifferent universe, while at the same time maintaining control over the entire system of discourse.

Amoret upsets this conventional Petrarchan scheme by offering both female resistance and female compliance in one figure. She thereby introduces genuine uncertainty into Petrarchan discourse. If satisfied desire is accepted as a possibility, then unsatisfied desire is something the poet risks, not something that is his tragic destiny. Scudamore's speech to Britomart describing his lady's predicament reveals how incompletely Amoret fits into conventional accounts of romantic love:

> My Lady and my loue is cruelly pend
>   In dolefull darkenesse from the vew of day,
>   Whilest deadly torments do her chast brest rend,
>   And the sharpe steele doth riue her hart in tway,
>   All for she *Scudamore* will not denay.
>   Yet thou vile man, vile *Scudamore* art sound,
>   Ne canst her ayde, ne canst her foe dismay;
>   Vnworthy wretch to tread vpon the ground,
> For whom so faire a Lady feeles so sore a wound.
>
>   (3.11.11)

Scudamore chivalrously blames himself for the injustice done his virtuous and innocent lady, but his language betrays greater complexity than is explicitly acknowledged. Scudamore's castigation of himself "for whom so faire a lady feeles so sore a wound" is a complicated judgment. By punning on the preposition "for," Spenser indicates the ambiguity of the relationship between Amoret's suffering and Scudamore's responsibility. She feels a wound for his sake—because she will not betray him—and she feels a wound because of him—because of his failure to protect her. Both these meanings accord with Scudamore's explicit self-condemnation. There is, however, a third sense that subverts Scudamore's tacit assumption of responsibility, namely that Amoret feels a wound of desire for him. As a conventional lover, Scudamore appropriates all of the active role for himself. In so doing, he connives at Amoret's enforced passivity and, because he has assumed an impossible role, he prevents himself from pursuing it successfully. Like the Petrarchan poet whose attitudes he replicates, Scudamore confines the scope of his action to lyric outburst. Scudamore's explanation for Amoret's predicament, "All for she *Scudamore* will not denay," reveals through the double sense of the words how Amoret exceeds Scudamore's conventional expectations of her and transgresses the conventional role of female beloved. In the context of Scudamore's account, denay has the sense of "to say 'no' to the claims of" (*OED* s.v. "deny" 2). That is to say, Busirane continues to torment Amoret because she will not deny her commitment to Scudamore. However, another meaning of "denay" as "to withold anything desired" (*OED* s.v. "deny" 3.5) suggests that Amoret is tormented by Busirane because she will not deny anything to her lover Scudamore. Scudamore's words reveal both a traditional view of Amoret as a passive object of desire and an unconventional picture of her as a desiring subject.

Critics frequently interpret Amoret's problem as a fear of marriage or of unbridled sexuality, but it makes more sense to see her as the lady who says yes and thereby incurs the animosity of the Petrarchan poet Busirane.[27] Moreover, giving Busirane's torture of Amoret a primarily psychological interpretation risks oversimplifying the critical examination of psychology as a structure of knowledge at work in the episode.[28] Critics tend to read the Masque of Cupid as a representation of Amoret's fear of marriage or as a representation of male erotic psychology, the sight of which terrifies Amoret.[29] Missing in those readings is an appreciation of the extent to which the terms of the masque itself, rather than the particular message it is intended to convey, are subjected to critique. The description of the phantasmagoric close of the masque raises the issue of female fear in order to put it in question:

> There were full many moe like maladies,
>   Whose names and natures I note reden well;
> So many moe, as there be phantasies
> In wauering wemens wit, that none can tell,
> Or paines in loue, or punishments in hell;
>   (3.12.26.1–5)

The near pun on the preposition "in" raises a genuine question about the location of the masque. Is the pageant the product of Amoret's sexual fears and fantasies: does it represent the pain that naturally accompanies love? Or is the masque torture inflicted from without, like the punishments in hell? Is the masque occurring in Amoret's mind, in Britomart's mind, in Busirane's castle, or simply on the page of Spenser's text? Busirane abuses poetry by passing off his own cruelty as both an objective statement about love and as a representation of Amoret's subjective fears. Both men in Amoret's life join in misrepresenting the state of Amoret's psyche. The Petrarchan lover Scudamore describes Amoret in such a way as to suppress her active desire for him. The Petrarchan poet Busirane sets forth an allegorical pageant that presents psychology as a function of his writing. The figures representing mental states are deployed by the poet Busirane in an effort to control meaning.

The pageant consists of traditional figures of erotic personification allegory that might have stepped out of the *Roman de la rose*.[30] After Ease disappears, twelve paired figures march out: Fancy and Desire, Doubt and Daunger, Feare and Hope, Dissemblaunce and Suspect, Griefe and Fury, Displeasure and Pleasaunce. The pageant gives the impression of expressing a coherent meaning, but that is an illusion promoted by its apparent formal coherence. Looking closely at the individual figures, how each expresses its meaning and how each relates to its companion figure, we see a picture of extreme incoherence, systematic discontinuity masquerading as continuous allegory. For example, Doubt exemplifies doubt; Hope does not exemplify hope but provokes it in others. Fancy is linked to its companion Desire through moralized genealogy: Fancy begets Desire. Suspect is defined in relationship to his partner Dissemblaunce: she laughs at him and he lowers at her. But, although Dissemblaunce dissembles, she does not fool Suspect; she just teases him. The iconography of those figures seems rich and complex, but the real poetic point of the masque lies in how the language comes to life the moment Amoret enters. The appearance of a flesh-and-blood woman among the walking allegories gives a genuine shock:

> After all these there marcht a most faire Dame,
>   Led of two grysie villeins, th'one *Despight*,
>   The other cleped *Cruelty* by name:
>   She dolefull Lady, like a dreary Spright,
>   Cald by strong charmes out of eternall night,
>   Had deathes owne image figurd in her face,
>   Full of sad signes, fearefull to liuing sight;
>   Yet in that horror shewd a seemely grace,
> And with her feeble feet did moue a comely pace.

Her brest all naked, as net iuory,
   Without adorne of gold or siluer bright,
   Wherewith the Craftesman wonts it beautify,
   Of her dew honour was despoyled quight,
   And a wide wound therein (O ruefull sight)
   Entrenched deepe with knife accursed keene,
   Yet freshly bleeding forth her fainting spright,
   (The worke of cruell hand) was to be seene,
That dyde in sanguine red her skin all snowy cleene.

At that wide orifice her trembling hart
   Was drawne forth, and in siluer basin layd,
   Quite through transfixed with a deadly dart,
   And in her bloud yet steeming fresh embayd:
   And those two villeins, which her steps vpstayd,
   When her weake feete could scarcely her sustaine,
   And fading vitall powers gan to fade,
   Her forward still with torture did constraine,
And euermore encreased her consuming paine.
                  (3.12.19–21)

Busirane's attempt to impose on Amoret the conventions of courtly love is a forcible troping. He forces her to embody a metaphor, a profane version of the sacred heart, in order to alienate Amoret's chaste affection for Scudamore. Busirane assaults her integrity with those Petrarchan conventions that identify a woman with a heart and mind of her own as Cruel and Despitious.[31]

Busirane's violation of Amoret employs a strategy of literalizing the language of desire and feeling and appropriating her body as a means of achieving exclusive control over psychological states. By imprisoning Amoret in the Masque of Cupid, Busirane has "pend" her in both senses of the word (3.11.1). He seeks to sequester her from any social context in order to assert his own absolute control over states such as fear and desire, which customarily lie in the realm of the interpersonal and, at the very least, are states accessible to multiple consciousnesses. Busirane seeks both to ground his fiction in the mutilated body of Amoret and to transform her body into the spoil of Cupid, the free-floating sign of his power.[32] As Busirane's artworks become increasingly three-dimensional and lifelike—from the tapestries and the idol, to the relief figures and the broken swords and spears, "warlike spoiles . . . of mighty Conquerours and Captaines strong" (3.11.52.2–3), to the Masque of Cupid—they become not more perfect imitations of reality but more perfect spoils.[33]

The final battle of Book III pits Britomart, the champion of chastity, against Busirane, the perpetrator of abuse. At issue in Britomart's rescue of Amoret from the power of Cupid is how meaning is to be determined.[34] By imprisoning Amoret in the Masque of Cupid, Busirane attempts to assert the power of the poet to be supreme arbiter of meaning.[35] By thwarting his attempt, Britomart reaffirms the view of allegory as a shared enterprise figured by the hermaphroditic embrace of the lovers at the conclusion of the 1590 *Faerie Queene*.

Busirane seemingly violates Amoret's physical integrity as he attempts to usurp the steadfast love that is her chastity. But as Britomart discovers, Amoret's wound is an illusion. The version of love named Cupid denies sexual difference in making both men and women Cupid's spoil. Like Hermaphroditus, Amoret suffers spoliation because desire is misnamed. Both are disfigured by a system of signs that repudiates bodily integrity. The Hermaphrodite emasculates himself by misreading his metamorphosed body. In distinguishing male from not-male, he denies physical sexuality and consigns desire to the female other. Amoret is assaulted by the art of Busirane, who attempts to redefine her chastity in order to violate it. Amoret's torment, her heart drawn forth from the orifice riven in her breast, transfixed with a deadly dart, evokes both the literalized alienation of her affections and the graphic penetration of her body. By misrepresenting Amoret's chastity in reductively physical terms, Busirane seeks to deny her desire. In this case, however, desire is not mistakenly assigned to the female in an inadvertent self-castration but deliberately suppressed by Busirane in an attempt to violate both Amoret and audience. The art of Busirane reifies desire by naming it "Cupid" in order to assert the absolute authority of the artificer.

Busirane's duplicity will not withstand a second look, however. When the masque appears the next night, Britomart follows the figures back into the room from which they came and sees Amoret chained to a pillar and Busirane "figuring straunge characters of his art" (3.12.31.2). The masque has been demystified, but not because its characters turn out to be nothing but a pack of tropes. The transformation of the masque into marks on the page is just another of Busirane's tricks. Rather, it is the continued presence of Amoret, her wounded heart still in her breast, that reveals the limitations of

Busirane's authorial control. Busirane can only pen Amoret. He can only confine her; he cannot move her emotionally. "A thousand charmes her formerly did proue; / Yet thousand charmes could not her stedfast heart remoue" (3.12.31.8–9). Busirane's charms are merely incantations; they have no power to move the heart. "The cruell steele which thrild [Amoret's] dying hart" (3.12.38.1) thrills her heart in the sense of "to pierce" (*OED* s.v. "thrill" 1), but her heart is thrilled with desire (*OED* s.v. "thrill" 4–5) only when she is reunited with Scudamore. The pun on "thrill" emphasizes female consciousness as something that eludes Busirane's Petrarchan poetics. Similarly, the narrator's exclamation, "Ah, who can loue the worker of her smart?" (3.12.31.7) suggests Busirane's limitations by pointing to a complex female sensibility and to a linguistic polyvalence both of which are beyond the scope of Busirane's theater of cruelty. The narrator's question seems to point rhetorically to Busirane. The rhetorical answer is, No one. Amoret cannot love Busirane for his abuse of her. But another, real answer to the question is, Britomart.[36] She loves Artegall, the worker of her smart. Resistance to Busirane comes from both Amoret and Britomart as both participate in erotic discourses that elude the control of Busirane.

THE OVIDIAN SUBTEXT
AND THE 1590 CONCLUSION

Book III moves from depicting a poet figure and representing the limitations of his powers of artifice to evoking the limitations of poetry through strategies of aesthetic distancing, as the narrative moves from the defeat of Busirane to the reunion of Amoret and Scudamore. If in the House of Busirane both Britomart and Amoret are figures of the embattled reader, at the conclusion of the 1590 *Faerie Queene* Britomart becomes the reader's surrogate as an onlooker whereas Amoret is sequestered, not in a pageant of erotic cruelty, but in a private space not fully amenable to representation:

> Had ye them seene, ye would haue surely thought,
>   That they had beene that faire *Hermaphrodite*,
>   Which that rich *Romane* of white marble wrought,
>   And in his costly Bath causd to bee site:
>   So seemd those two, as growne together quite,
>   That *Britomart* halfe enuying their blesse,

> Was much empassiond in her gentle sprite,
> And to her selfe oft wisht like happinesse,
> In vaine she wisht, that fate n'ould let her yet possesse.
>
> (1590.3.46)

The image is not a direct reference to a Hermaphrodite, nor to a statue of a Hermaphrodite, nor even a simple metaphor likening the embracing Amoret and Scudamore to a Hermaphrodite. Spenser refers to a specific statue that is not present in the scene he is describing: the reader, were he or she observing the scene directly and not reading about it, would have mistaken the fictional characters for the statue.[37] Britomart's response to the scene is likewise a complex combination of engagement and detachment. Her half-envy is both a desire for the bliss she observes and an awareness that her own love is unsatisfied. She is moved both to wish the like for herself and to pursue her yet unrealized quest.

Britomart's wish for the happiness she sees but does not herself enjoy evokes the theme of imitation in a context of uncertainty and insecurity. Brought together at the original conclusion of Book III are the concerns, present throughout the book, of the epistemology of risk and the efficacy of imitation. The 1590 conclusion imitates Ovid in such a way as to retain the threat implicit in Ovid's myth of the Hermaphrodite while pointing to the possibility of positive revision. The *tout ensemble* of the Hermaphrodite statue set in the Roman bath recalls the most sinister aspects of Ovid's myth. If the statue represents the metamorphosed Hermaphroditus, the bath itself must evoke the infamous fountain of Salmacis, whose waters caused men to become effeminate. The danger presented by this tableau is the danger of repeating the Hermaphrodite's act and fulfilling his curse by misusing art. Just as the rich Roman reduces art to pool decoration, so the reader risks abusing art by avoiding the role of interpreter and by unreflectively treating art as imitation experience rather than as a model for imitation. Underlying the Ovidian-Petrarchan discourse of desire, which Book III subjects to critique as the creation and projection of one consciousness, is the narcissistic self-abuse ironically forced on Marinell by his mother and receiving graphic expression with the image in Busirane's pageant of Cupid pricking himself "that he might tast the sweet consuming woe" (3.11.45.4). The reader is challenged to moralize art, to engage the text in a process of sense-making, rather than to reify art as an instrument of gratification, to undertake humanist, not hedonist imitation.

In this process of humanist, morally productive imitation, the reader has Britomart as a role model. Crucial to her wish for "like happinesse" when faced with the embracing couple is the implied possibility of repetition with a difference.[38] Her response is not simple identification or appropriation. In this respect, she differs from characters such as Cymoent, who sees in her son the "deare image of [her] selfe" (3.4.36.1), the witch's son, for whom the False Florimell is "enough to hold a foole in vaine delight" (3.8.10.7), Paridell, for whom the story of Troy is a blueprint for the seduction of Hellenore, or Malecasta, who furnishes Castle Joyeous with erotic tapestries as well as beds to facilitate the orgiastic goings-on.

The hermaphroditic couple presents a complex object for Sidnean imitation. The project of Sidney's poet, who seeks "to bestow a Cyrus upon the world to make many Cyruses" (24), recalls uncomfortably Ovid's Hermaphroditus, who seeks to give the world many Hermaphrodites by cursing the fountain of Salmacis. The concluding image is an invitation to resist the potentially debilitating and deforming conventions of erotic discourse. Ovid's Hermaphrodite unwittingly emasculates himself when he misreads his own body and distinguishes male from female in such a way as to identify desire with the female. The stanzas originally concluding Book III offer a creative revision of constricting attitudes toward love. The picture of chaste love presented for our edification does not evoke the traditional notion of two becoming one. Rather, the two lovers become a new entity: a couple.[39] Amoret and Scudamore are not the Hermaphrodite precisely because their embrace does not depend on the effacement of sexual difference and the disfigurement of bodily form. Rather, Spenser practices a kind of alternative discourse as he subjects conventional images of the body and of gender to reconfiguration:

> Lightly he clipt her twixt his armes twaine,
>   And streightly did embrace her body bright,
>   Her body, late the prison of sad paine,
>   Now the sweet lodge of loue and deare delight:
>   But she faire Lady ouercommen quight
>   Of huge affection, did in pleasure melt,
>   And in sweete rauishment pourd out her spright:
>   No word they spake, nor earthly thing they felt,
> But like two senceles stocks in long embracement dwelt.
>   (*1590*.3.12.45)

Amoret's body is first a prison, then a lodge, then both lovers dwell in a mutually defined embrace. Her body is metamorphosed, not to the monstrous form of the Hermaphrodite, but to an instrument of mutual pleasure. Considered solely as a dividing barrier, the body is a prison, painfully imprisoning experience.[40] The prison is transformed to a lodge as the body is considered an instrument of sense experience. The lovers' union is a mutually defined relationship—not a monster—which accounts for sexual difference and sexual desire.

Replacing the Hermaphrodite's denial of sexual difference is an androgynous reversal of roles. In an inversion of traditional Petrarchan imagery, Scudamore is compared to a deer "that greedily embayes / In the cool soile, after long thirstinesse" (1590.3.12.44.7–8). Amoret "in sweete rauishment pourd out her spright," a transformed allusion to the Redcrosse Knight "pourd out in loosenesse on the grassy grownd" (1.7.7.2) with Duessa. This ravishment is not the violation attempted by Busirane, but physical and emotional transport, which Spenser renders with great circumspection. Although we are invited to see through traditional formulations of gender to understand how conventional categories may be manipulated and revised, we are also confronted with the limitation of our understanding. The ideal of chaste love figured by the embracing couple is framed as an ideal and therefore not something fully available to us in our sublunary existence. The simile "like two senceless stocks" suggests both that the lovers have gone beyond earthly things and that the onlooker is not privy to their experience. Seen from without, the embracing couple appears like two senseless stocks—whether through transcendence of earthly things or through mere senselessness is a matter we as observers are left to ponder. Saved from the spoils of Cupid, the lovers "each other of loues bitter fruit despoile" (1590.3.12.47.2), while readers, like Britomart, are left with the quest of making sense unfinished.

4

Book IV

Retrospection and the Undoing of Book III

As Spenser moves from Book III to Book IV of *The Faerie Queene*, he shifts focus from discourse to textuality. He moves from considering the function and effect of linguistic constructs and directing attention to the act of reading, to examining how a discursive construct conveys meaning. This shift in focus reflects, in part, the fact that when Book IV appeared in 1596, the first installment of *The Faerie Queene* had already been committed to print. The 1596 edition of *The Faerie Queene* thus incorporates in itself a previously published text. The continuation of the original *Faerie Queene* in the 1596 edition focuses attention on the status of the poem as a text and how, as a text, it absorbs and refracts processes of reading and writing.[1] The existence of *The Faerie Queene* as text takes on particular emphasis through the cancellation of the original 1590 conclusion—that is, by the substitution of one set of printed stanzas for another—and by the reflection in the proem to Book IV on reception of the earlier installment of *The Faerie Queene*.

Book III showcases the pursuit of love. It focuses on the chase as a discursive structure that determines how Eros is understood. Book III treats sexual relations as paradigmatic of other relationships: self and other, reader and object of reading, artificer and objects of artifice. Book III posits a homology between Britomart's quest in pursuit of love and the reader's quest in reading the poem. The major focus is on reading as paradigmatic, morally charged, heroic activity. The icon of the blinded dragon lying at Cupid's feet with a shaft piercing each eye and the narrator's ironic comment "(Ah man beware, how thou those darts behold)" (3.11.48.5) dramatize the agonistic character of reading. Punning on "behold," the passage threatens to reward an injudicious consideration of traditional erotic iconography with graphic violence to the reader. The reader beholds the darts amiss and risks being blinded. Although the subtextual, metaphoric evocation of reading is strong, reading is figured as a purely visual activity. Indeed the violent image of the arrow shafts makes the visual component graphically palpable. Here as elsewhere in Book III, the issue of signification is presented primarily and fundamentally as a question of reading. In Book IV, the text as such is much more the focus. While in Book III Britomart's second look at the Masque of Cupid makes the figures disappear, transformed and diminished by a militant reader to marks on the page, at the opening of Book IV, we see that texts have unsuspected staying power since Busirane's pageant refuses to go away. Not only does Book IV direct attention to the processes by which texts convey meaning, but it emphasizes the institutional power of the received ideas codified textually.[2]

THE HERMAPHRODITE CANCELED
AND AMORET RECONSTRAINED

As the 1596 *Faerie Queene* moves from Book III to Book IV it revises both the stanzas originally concluding Book III and the themes affirmed by the 1590 conclusion.[3] Not only has the triumphant reunion of Amoret and Scudamore, with which the 1590 *Faerie Queene* concluded, been rewritten, so that, in the 1596 version, Scudamore has left to get help by the time Britomart emerges with Amoret from the Castle of Busirane, but Britomart's liberation of Amoret seems oddly nullified as well.[4] Amoret remains subject to all of the attitudes represented by Busirane and his pageant of Petrarchan allegories of male domination. She sees herself as Busirane sought to present her: as an object, the legitimate spoil of her apparently male rescuer. Moreover, Britomart, Amoret's erstwhile champion, now seems to be taking over from Busirane in abusing Amoret with her own imitation of male sexual aggression:

> Thereto her feare was made so much the greater
>   Through fine abusion of that Briton mayd:
>   Who for to hide her fained sex the better,
>   And maske her wounded mind, both did and sayd
>   Full many things so doubtfull to be wayd,
>   That well she wist not what by them to gesse,
>   For other whiles to her she purpos made
>   Of loue, and otherwhiles of lustfulnesse,
> That much she feard his mind would grow to some excesse.
>   (4.1.7)

Busirane's Masque of Cupid attempted to blur the boundaries between male ideology and female psychology in order to violate
Amoret. The comedy of mistaken identity and gender masking that
opens Book IV puts sexual ideology in a new perspective as *The Faerie
Queene* moves from an exploration of private virtues in the first three
books to an exploration of public virtues in the second. The comic
scene evoked at the opening of Book IV shows us what it is like for
those attitudes figured allegorically in Busirane's castle—for example that sexuality is a battle and woman is the spoil—to be unexamined cultural assumptions. We view a dramatic rather than an explicitly allegorical representation of social constructs. If in Book III,
Amoret was imprisoned among Petrarchan allegories, she now finds
herself in a socially untenable situation. As the narrator observes:

> When her from deadly thraldome he redeemed,
> For which no seruice she too much esteemed,
> Yet dread of shame, and doubt of fowle dishonor
> Made her not yeeld so much as due she deemed.
> (4.1.8.4–7)

It is ironic that Amoret's passive resistance here maintains Britomart's bluff since in Book III Amoret suffered Busirane's enmity, "All
for she Scudamore will not denay" (3.11.11.5). The chastely loving
wife provokes the hostility of Busirane, whose Petrarchan art re-
quires a lady who just says no. In Book IV, we see Amoret assuming
as a social constraint what in Book III she resisted as an allegorical
agon. The fundamentally inner-directed conflict over how Amoret's
chastity is to be read has been transformed into a question of how she
fits into a social matrix.[5]

Even before the opening episode, the introductory stanzas reveal
how much Busirane is a part of the social milieu of Book IV:

> For that same vile Enchauntour *Busyran*,
>   The very selfe same day that she was wedded,
>   Amidst the bridale feast, whilest euery man
>   Surcharg'd with wine, were heedlesse and ill hedded,
>   All bent to mirth before the bride was bedded,
>   Brought in that maske of loue which late was showen:
>   And there the Ladie ill of friends bestedded,
>   By way of sport, as oft in maskes is knowen,
> Conueyed quite away to liuing wight vnknowen.
> (4.1.3)

Unless one is either very tolerant or very jaded, it registers, I think, as a shock that what was presented in Book III as a horror show provided part of the entertainment at the wedding of Scudamore and Amoret. In Book III, Britomart's second look at the pageant reveals the emptiness of Busirane's Petrarchan fictions. The second "second look," directed by Book IV at the Masque of Cupid, reveals their power and a reality of socially authorized rape more horrifying than the lurid fantasies Britomart overcomes in Book III. James Nohrnberg observes that epithalamia focusing on male sexual violence were a common feature of Elizabethan weddings (*Analogy* 475). That, I think, is Spenser's point. As Oscar Levant once observed of Hollywood, "When you strip away the phony tinsel, what you have left is the real tinsel." The move from a private experience of the Masque of Cupid to its function as a part of a public celebration gives us a critical perspective on Elizabethan social conventions.

The opening of Book IV calls attention to the contextualizing of the Masque of Cupid. In Book III, Busirane is said to have "pend" Amoret: imprisoned her with language. In Book IV, we see Amoret embedded in social conventions, as are we as readers. Book IV reflects critically on the force of conventions to which a society subscribes as it develops a critique of reading conceived as a solitary, context-free activity. Accordingly, Book IV directs a second look at the quest structure of Book III, which posits the homology between individual heroine and individual questing reader.

RETROSPECTION AS A WAY OF LOOKING

In a number of ways, the continuation of *The Faerie Queene* into Book IV involves retrospection. In Book IV, flashback is a major narrative strategy. The story of Cambel and Triamond, eponymous heroes of the book, is told in flashback, for example. Temporal slippages, particularly with Scudamore's narrative of winning Amoret, call attention to the flashback as a discursive construct. Not only does Amoret apparently disappear from the local present of the story, but pointers in the narrative sequence make the chronology of the story seem inconsistent. In stanzas 20–22 of canto ix, it seems that Arthur and Amoret come upon Britomart and Scudamore observing four knights fighting. There is a flashback to the origin of the quarrel among the four, which goes on to tell of how Britomart and Scudamore are brought into the fight. The flashback apparently ends with stanza 32, which begins, "Whom when the Briton Prince a farre beheld. . . . " Narrative clues indicate both that we are back to Arthur's initial sight of the quarrel and that the quarrel has progressed beyond that initial sight, subverting our expectation that time stands still in the larger story while the narrator addresses a flashback to the reader.

A second look directed at some of the ideas of Book III focuses on problems previously held in abeyance. Book IV reconsiders specular substitutions unproblematically assumed between Britomart and reader, whose projects in Book III can be considered mirror-image quests, as well as the specular exchange of male and female, who are presented as relatively interchangeable. In canto ii of Book III, upon seeing the image of Artegall in a mirror, Britomart expeditiously fashions herself after that image into a knight of chastity. At the conclusion of the 1590 *Faerie Queene*, each of the two lovers united in an embrace is described in terms associated with the other sex. Like the Petrarchan beloved, Scudamore is the deer "that greedily embayes / In the coole soile, after long thirstinesse" (1590.3.12.44.7–8). Amoret, in an androgynous reversal of the Redcrosse Knight "pourd out in loosenesse on the grassy grownd" (1.7.7.2), "in sweete rauishment pourd out her spright" (1590.3.12.45.7).

The cancellation of the original conclusion of *The Faerie Queene* as the poem is continued in 1596 emphasizes how revision can mean change as well as looking again. Indeed, the manipulation of certain classical myths underlying Books III and IV reveals ironic connections between looking again and effecting change. The Hermaphrodite figured the union of the two lovers at the conclusion of the 1590 *Faerie Queene*. When Scudamore compares winning Amoret to Orpheus' recovering "his Leman from the Stygian Princes boure" (4.10.58.4), he explicitly names the myth that has informed the lovers' search for reunion throughout Book IV. Book IV places the 1590 conclusion in a context of retrospection that undoes the sexual union figured by the Hermaphrodite, as Orpheus' gaze undid Eurydice.[6] Concomitantly, Book IV examines retrospection as an intellectual construct, as a way of looking, in short, as theory.[7]

LOSING AND FINDING
VS. LOSING AND WINNING

The examination of retrospection in Book IV focuses on the complexities of loss. Spenser opens up an exploration of loss with a play on words. In the revised conclusion to Book III, we are told that when Britomart returns to where she left Scudamore and Glauce, "Neither of them she found where she them lore" (3.12.44.4). In the sixteenth century, "lore" was the past participle of "to lose" (*OED* s.v. "leese" vb. 1, 6), but, as the *OED* suggests, Spenser uses it as the simple past of the participle "lorn," left or abandoned. Most obviously, Britomart has not found the pair where she left them, but also, in a sense, she has not found them where she lost them because, as the story continues, finding is not the only counterpart to losing: winning is a counterpart as well. The nature of loss is not, therefore, an inescapable given but is theoretically determined. It all depends on how one looks at loss: whether it is seen in relation to finding or to winning. In Book III, the emphasis is on finding and the orientation is prospective. The narrative takes the form of a quest romance to posit an epistemology of learned ignorance in which the truth is always more fully, but never completely, known, as an alternative to Platonic recollection, which postulates origins as the source of authority. Book III traces a shift in focus from origins and certainty to creative growth and risk. Britomart is not conscious of her love for Artegall until it has already taken hold of her. Her anxiety that her love might be illusory, that the image with which she has fallen in love might not correspond to a real person, is eased by Glauce's promise to "find that loued knight" (3.2.46.9). Both heroine and reader are progressively fashioned as part of that ongoing quest.

In Book IV, winning replaces finding as the counterbalance to loss. Throughout Book IV, knights engage in jousts to win a lady, or an artificial lady, or a lady's girdle, with the joust marked as an institutional response to male desire. Scudamore's description of winning Amoret occurs at the point at which, by narrative logic, Amoret and Scudamore should find each other. The nature of the opposition of loss to winning differs from that of loss to finding. Winning and losing are a binary pair as reversible as mirror images in a perpetual zero-sum game of specular exchange. In short, everybody wins some and loses some. Finding pairs in a different way with loss. It does not depend on a binary opposition to losing. No one has to have lost Artegall for Britomart to find him. And while it might be theoretically possible to find again what one has lost, in Book IV what has been lost cannot be found because the theoretical orientation has shifted from an economy of finding and losing to an economy of winning and losing, and this way of looking at things presents itself as all there is. This shift from a view of loss as the counterpart of finding to an economy of winning and losing accompanies a shift from the emphasis on risk in Book III to the critical examination of strategies of logical entailment in Book IV. Book III posits the risk of error and illusion as the precondition of creative growth and knowledge. Book IV examines structures that circumscribe knowledge and purpose to guarantee certainty. It shows how the effort to eliminate uncertainty can be an unwitting strategy of foreclosure, much as Orpheus' backward look to make certain of Eurydice resulted in their separation.

Two narratively inscribed failures of Scudamore and Amoret to be reunited explicate in detail how the binary structure of winning and losing undoes the hermaphroditic union of the lovers. In canto 1, the two lovers miss each other as Amoret's companion Britomart and Scudamore successively engage in jousts with the same group of characters: Amoret rides off before Scudamore rides up. In cantos 9 and 10, Scudamore's flashback account of winning Amoret substitutes for Spenser's narration of their reunion. Canto 1 begins a critique of friendship conceived as sameness, which both perpetuates discord and excludes the sexual relation. The after-you-Alphonse number played by the knights Paridell and Blandamour, as the pair trade the right to attack Britomart and win Amoret back and forth like a hot potato, may well parody the classic story of male friendship, that of Titus and Gesippus.[8] The pattern is comically repeated when Blandamour, having been knocked flat by Britomart, volunteers Paridell to take on Scudamore. These are two of many jousts in Book IV that have the dual purpose of proving martial prowess and either winning a lady or proving the superior beauty of one's own. The joust represents a circumscribed discourse based on the binary opposition of essentially like participants; both are equipped to play the same game, and if one wins, the other loses. In these contests, the logical coherence of the male transaction contrasts markedly with the speciousness of its extension to women. Whoever wins a fight can be designated the better fighter by definition. There is a much more tenuous connection between the military success of a knight and that knight's social and sexual relations, as Britomart ironically demonstrates at the beginning of canto 1 by claiming arbitrarily to be both Amoret's knight and her young opponent's lady so all can spend a Platonic evening together. The sexual ideology attaching to chivalry

seems seriously askew in actual practice in Book IV. We see the traditional view of chivalry as the romantic relations of brave knights
and fair ladies giving place to what Eve Sedgwick has called the homosocial transactions among men and to a general sense of things
running out of control. The knights at Satyrane's tournament award
the prize of Florimell's girdle to the False Florimell although only the
chaste Amoret is able to wear it—it falls off any who is not a virgin—
and then the knights try in vain to award False Florimell to the winner and first two runners-up of the tournament. Third runner-up
Satyrane decides that giving False Florimell her free choice of the remaining suitors is preferable to renewing the combat, which seems
at least as much motivated by mutual jealousy as desire for the artificial lady. Similarly, Blandamour is hostile to Scudamore "both for
his worth, that all men did adore, / And eke because his loue he
wonne by right" (4.1.39.5–6). Since not only is his love Amoret not
present at the fight between Blandamour and Scudamore, but
Blandamour has just tried unsuccessfully to give his friend Paridell
the right to win her from Britomart, one sees here as well as in the
burlesque tournament of Satyrane male jealousy of another man taking precedence over any transaction between the sexes. Significantly,
Scudamore's reaction to the allegorical troublemaker Ate's lie that
Britomart "ha[d his] *Amoret* at will" (4.1.49.1) echoes the canceled
1590 conclusion. Again Scudamore is likened to a deer and again he
is silent, but in Book IV the deer is struck with a dart and Amoret does
not share his silence. "No word they spake, nor earthly thing they
felt" (*1590*.3.12.45.8) becomes "ne word he had to speake for great
dismay" (4.1.50.2).

Scudamore's narrative of winning Amoret explicates how the binarism of winning and losing excludes the heterosexual relation. As
he explains his motives in seeking the lady:

> What time the fame of this renowmed prise
>   Flew first abroad, and all mens eares possest,
>   I hauing armes then taken, gan auise
>   To winne me honour by some noble gest,
>   And purchase me some place amongst the best.
>   I boldly thought (so young mens thoughts are bold)
>   That this same braue emprize for me did rest,
>   And that both shield and she whom I behold,
> Might be my lucky lot; sith all by lot we hold.
>
> (4.10.4)

The pun "prise/emprize" sheds light on Amoret's role in Scud-amore's adventure.[9] Made into a prize she enables his enterprise. She is part of the enterprise—as prize is literally part of the word em-prize—as the nominal goal. Nevertheless, Scudamore initially names honor and a place among the best as his goals and—significantly, I think—only names Amoret by periphrasis as "she whom I behold." If this is, as A. C. Hamilton suggests in his annotations to *The Faerie Queene*, an indication of Amoret's presence, it is a singularly feeble one, since "behold" might mean "relate or belong to" or "consider" as well as "look at" (*OED* s.v. "behold" 3, 6–7). Amoret's presence is marginal at best because the woman's role in the economy of win-ning and losing is at a categorical remove from the man's. It is not that when the man wins, the woman loses but that when he wins, he wins her. She is not part of the transaction in the same capacity as the man. Her constancy camouflages the reversibility of the structure of winning and losing—the fact that there can always be another re-match—in order to give a specious sense of closure and fixity to an open-ended process.[10]

By regarding both the shield of Love and Amoret as his prizes, Scudamore makes himself into Cupid's man instead of being half the androgynous Scudamoret.[11] While the shield and the lady are dou-bled as prizes, the metaphoric connection between the two—both, as it were, on the receiving end—is suppressed. Having defeated the knights guarding the shield, Scudamore rereads the inscription by the shield, *Blessed the man that well can vse his blis: / Whose euer be the shield, faire Amoret be his* (4.10.8.8–9). By doubling the shield and Amoret, Scudamore fails to use either well; by merely repeating the inscription, Scudamore fails to understand the challenge of its opta-tive mode—faire Amoret *be* his. As a reader, he contrasts with Brito-mart before the enigmatic inscription, Be bold:

> *Be bold*: she oft and oft it ouer-red,
> Yet could not find what sence it figured:
> But what so were therein or writ or ment,
> She was no whit thereby discouraged
> From prosecuting of her first intent,
> But forward with bold steps into the next roome went.
> $$(3.11.50.4–9)$$

Britomart "reads" the injunction to be bold by being bold; she goes forward and finds meaning not known a priori but confirmed post hoc, as she succeeds in being bold. The term bold is likewise applied to Scudamore in canto 10 of Book IV. He says, "I boldly thought (so young mens thoughts are bold)" (4.10.4.6) and "Whom boldly I encountred . . . " (4.10.10.1). But his boldness is of a different sort.[12] Britomart's boldness, like her reading, is inventive and improvisatory, open to uncertainty and risk. By way of contrast, consider Scudamore's exegetical performance with the shield:

> Then preacing to the pillour I repeated
> The read thereof for guerdon of my paine,
> And taking downe the shield, with me did it retaine.
>   (4.10.10.7–9)

His repetition accompanies an impulse toward possession and control.

LOOKING BACK TO MAKE SURE:
THE RETROSPECTIVE STANCE
AND THE TOTALIZING GAZE

The difference between Britomart and Scudamore as readers underlines the shift in attitudes to origins and retrospection from Book III to Book IV and suggests why Amoret will never be Scudamore's.[13] While the prospective orientation of Book III simply de-emphasizes origins, in Book IV retrospection is a principle of confirmation. The informal, post-hoc confirmation of invention in Book III is raised to a higher level of abstraction in Book IV as a built-in guarantee: retrospection becomes part of a strategy of totalization. This impulse to build in a guarantee underlies the categorical problem inherent in Scudamore's enterprise of winning his lady, namely the collapsing of discrete logical categories into each other to suppress the fact that one frames the other. In seeking to win Amoret, Scudamore pursues what is nominally a sexual relationship, but the woman stands outside the transaction of winning and losing, remaining aloof and intact as the prize for the victorious male.

For such a totalizing strategy to work, what is seen must be taken for all there is. Spenser traces this reduction specifically as it operates on sexuality as Scudamore describes the Temple of Venus in a revision both of Britomart's gaze at the Hermaphrodite and the Gardens of Adonis in Book III:

No tree, that is of count, in greenewood growes,
   From lowest Iuniper to Ceder tall,
   No flowre in field, that daintie odour throwes,
   And deckes his branch with blossomes ouer all,
   But there was planted, or grew naturall:
   Nor sense of man so coy and curious nice,
   But there mote find to please it selfe withall;
   Nor hart could wish for any queint deuice,
But there it present was, and did fraile sense entice.

  .   .   .   .

Which when as I, that neuer tasted blis,
   Nor happie howre, beheld with gazefull eye,
   I thought there was none other heauen then this;
   And gan their endlesse happinesse enuye,
   That being free from feare and gealosye,
   Might frankely there their loues desire possesse;
                   (4.10.22, 28.1–6)

The repeated locution "no . . . but" bases its claims of universality on taking what Scudamore sees and denominates as a totality. In tracing the reduction from the Gardens of Adonis to the Temple of Venus, Spenser seems to be drawing on certain sixteenth-century mathematical ideas, specifically the distinction between denumerability and non-denumerability. A set of numbers is denumerable if there is a one-to-one correspondence between its members and the set of positive integers; it is non-denumerable if no such correspondence can be established. Thus, the set of rational numbers, although infinite, are denumerable, whereas the real numbers (rational plus irrational) are not.[14] Scudamore's description of the Temple of Venus posits a one-to-one relationship between what Scudamore sees and what is. Spenser reserves the category of non-denumerability to characterize the uncircumscribed plenitude described in the marriage of Thames and Medway at the conclusion of Book IV.

The variant "none other then" hints at the denial of otherness implicit in the totalizing process. Although Scudamore alludes to presumably mixed-sex pairs of lovers, it is "another sort" of lovers, male friends who usurp his attention. Scudamore, pitying his bliss-free past, envies their endless happiness, in contrast to Britomart who, in an alternative reality or at least an earlier edition, half-envies Scudamore and Amoret their bliss and wishes herself similar happiness in the future. There is perhaps an etymological play on the word "envy," a shift from the French "envie," desire, to the Latin "invidia," a looking askance. Britomart, "empassioned in her gentle sprite," is moved to hope. Scudamore is looking at things the wrong way. The happiness he sees seems endless because he is looking back. He is standing on the endpoint and does not know it.

REDUCING SEXUALITY
AND CONTROLLING PLENITUDE

The plenitude on which Scudamore's way of looking works its reduction is associated directly with sexuality. One indication of this occurs with the extended allusion to *De rerum natura* in stanzas 44 through 47 of canto x. Lucretius begins his poem by invoking Venus as the universal principle of generation. The prayer addressed by the lovers to the idol of Venus paraphrases Lucretius' invocation to Venus beseeching the goddess to temper the violence of Mars in an erotic enactment of cosmic *discordia concors*:

> Aeneadum genetrix, hominum divomque voluptas,
> alma Venus, caeli subter labentia signa
> quae mare navigerum, quae terras frugiferentis
> concelebras, per te quoniam genus omne animantum
> concipitur visitque exortum lumina solis:
> te, dea, te fugiunt venti, te nubila caeli
> adventumque tuum, tibi suavis daedala tellus
> summittit flores, tibi rident aequora ponti
> placatumque nitet diffuso lumine caelum.
>
> . . . .
>
> Effice ut interea fera moenera militiai
> per maria ac terras omnis sopita quiescant;
> nam tu sola potes tranquilla pace iuvare
> mortalis, quoniam belli fera moenera Mavors
> armipotens regit, in gremium qui saepe tuum se
> reiicit aeterno devictus vulnere amoris,
> atque ita suspiciens tereti cervice reposta
> pascit amore avidos inhians in te, dea, visus,
> eque tuo pendet resupini spiritus ore.
>
> (1.1–9, 29–37)

[Mother of Aeneas and his race, darling of men and gods, nurturing Venus, who beneath the smooth-moving heavenly signs

fill with yourself the sea full-laden with ships, the earth that
bears the crops, since through you every kind of living thing
is conceived and rising up looks on the light of the sun: from
you, O goddess, from you the winds flee away, the clouds
of heaven from you and your coming; for you the wonder-
working earth puts forth sweet flowers, for you the wide
stretches of ocean laugh, and heaven grown peaceful glows
with outpoured light. . . . Cause meanwhile the savage works
of war to sleep and be still over every sea and land. For you
alone can delight mortals with quiet peace, since Mars mighty
in battle rules the savage works of war, who often casts himself
upon your lap wholly vanquished by the ever-living wound of
love, and thus looking upward, with shapely neck thrown
back, feeds his eager eyes with love, gaping upon you, goddess, and, as he lies back, his breath hangs upon your lips.]

In contrast, Spenser's worshipers pray:

> Great God of men and women, queene of th'ayre,
> Mother of laughter, and welspring of blisse,
> O graunt that of my loue at last I may not misse.
> (4.10.47.7–9)

Venus genetrix has been demoted to the status of a dating service,
and the desire that is the motive power of the universe has been reduced to getting what one wants.[15] Sexual desire, conceived by Lucretius as a cosmic force, is here circumscribed when sexuality is
separated from a cosmic matrix and presented as a one-to-one relationship between lover and object of desire. The description of the
idol as it harks back both to the Gardens of Adonis and to the Hermaphrodite engages Spenser's previous text in the reduction of sexuality. The claim that the idol "in shape and beautie did excell / All
other Idoles" (4.10.40.1–2) echoes the earlier statement that the Gardens of Adonis "All other pleasant places doth excell" (3.6.29.7).
Scudamore's hearsay conjecture that under the veil, that statue
"hath both kinds in one, / Both male and female, both vnder one
name" (4.10.41.6–7) recalls the Hermaphrodite of Book III, but with
some differences. The hermaphroditic union of Scudamore and
Amoret is described with a complexity that resists being reduced to
the univalence of two becoming one, a univalence that easily

becomes male hegemony. For all of Scudamore's approval, the veiled statue, concealed from the people by her priests, placed "vpon an altar of some costly masse" (4.10.39.2) appears Papist—veiled, perhaps, like a Roman Catholic ciborium.[16]

The reduction of sexuality from a cosmic force to a circumscribed desire is accomplished through the degradation of specifically female sexuality. The *mons Veneris*, which in Book III represents the unfolding of cosmic generation in successive states, as allegory, as geography, as physiology, is reduced in Book IV to the lap of Womanhood, which is what Amoret is sitting on when Scudamore finds her. Another revision of Book III links the degradation of female sexuality to narratological retrospection. Glauce's encouragement of Britomart in her pursuit of Artegall, "things oft impossible . . . seeme, ere begonne" (3.2.36.9), is echoed by Scudamore's reflection on his pursuit of Amoret:

> For sacrilege me seem'd the Church to rob,
> And folly seem'd to leaue the thing vndonne,
> Which with so strong attempt I had begonne.
> (4.10.53.3–5)

An obscene reduction and reification of Amoret as "the thing vndonne" indicates the difference between Britomart's quest of an as-yet-unknown lover and Scudamore's conquest of a woman reductively defined a priori.

ORPHEUS AND THE LOSS OF AMORET
TO THE QUEST FOR CERTAINTY

Scudamore's usurpation of the narrative voice from the opening of canto x signals the exclusion of Amoret. Scudamore's assertion,

> For since the day that first with deadly wound
> My heart was launcht, and learned to haue loued,
> I neuer ioyed howre, but still with care was moued.
> (4.10.1.7–9)

echoes the opening of Book IV, "for from the time that *Scudamour* her bought / In perilous fight, she neuer ioyed day" (4.1.2.1–2) but Scudamore has substituted self-pity for the pity Spenser's narrator expresses for Amoret. In effect, the autobiographical "I," which is both present narrator and historical subject of narration, leaves no room for Amoret.[17] The complex structure of Scudamore's narrative functions as a strategy for assuring control as it reveals the solipsism of such efforts. The closure of autobiographical narrative is presented as a substitute for ambiguity of signification. The conflation of rape and rescue in the narrative reworking of the Orpheus myth replaces the semiological complexity of love's wound. In Book III, the bittersweet and complex experience of love is expressed by the paradoxical valuation given to the motif of wounding. When Scudamore accuses himself, "vnworthy wretch to tread vpon the ground, / For whom so faire a Lady feeles so sore a wound" (3.11.11.8–9), his words point with unconscious irony both to Amoret's suffering at the hands of Busirane and to the wound of love that leads her to resist the enchanter. Book IV, in reworking its Virgilian and Ovidian subtexts, conflates the cause of Eurydice's wound—her attempted rape by the bee-keeper Aristaeus as given in Virgil's Fourth Georgic—with the attempted remedy, as Scudamore journeys to the Temple of Venus, not to restore Amoret, but to carry her off. Although Scudamore's autobiographical account of the combined rape and rescue of Amoret is the last we read about the unhappy lovers, it is retrojected to a position of origin. This totalizing gesture suppresses the emotional complexity signified by love's wound as it projects the complexity and uncertainty of signification onto a closed loop of narrative.[18]

The effacement of desire is linked to the silencing of Amoret through the revision of classical subtexts. Scudamore's response to the rebukes of Womanhood,

> Nay but it fitteth best,
> For *Cupids* man with *Venus* mayd to hold,
> For ill your goddesse seruices are drest
> By virgins, and her sacrifices let to rest.
> (4.10.54.6–9)

echoes Musaeus' Leander, who lectures Hero on the contradictions of being Venus' nun (*Hero and Leander*, 141–165). But while Hero's speechlessness betokens her silent arousal at Leander's speech, Womanhood's silence results from terror at the sight of "*Cupid* with his killing bow / And cruell shafts" (4.10.55.3–4) on Scudamore's shield. In direct contrast to Hero, Amoret is both voluble and unwilling:

> She often prayd, and often me besought,
>   Sometime with tender teares to let her goe,
>   Sometime with witching smyles: but yet for nought,
>   That euer she to me could say or doe,
>   Could she her wished freedome fro me wooe;
>   (4.10.57.1–5)

Not only does Scudamore ignore Amoret's words, but he suppresses her voice by giving her protests in indirect discourse. In so doing, Scudamore imitates Ovid who, in his version of the Orpheus legend, reduces the long protest Virgil gives Eurydice to "quid enim nisi se quereretur amatam?" (*Met.* 10.61) [for of what could she complain save that she was beloved?]. Just as Ovid's Eurydice is reduced to silence in the economy of male desire, so Amoret is reduced to a figment of Scudamore's autobiography as she disappears from Spenser's story. Ironically, although the narrator imitates Ovid in silencing the woman's voice, Scudamore the character does not imitate Orpheus in looking on the face of his beloved. Rather, he tells us:

> And euermore vpon the Goddesse face
>   Mine eye was fixt, for feare of her offence,
>   Whom when I saw with amiable grace
>   To laugh at me, and fauour my pretence,
>   I was emboldned with more confidence,
>   (4.10.56.1–5)

Has Scudamore seen through the veil for an unmediated vision of truth, or, having turned from Amoret, does he gaze on the face of his own desire? Scudamore's autobiographical account of the origin of his love forecloses any other representation of that love because the origin, conceived as the object of desire, reflects specularly the endpoint from which Scudamore looks back. Instead of losing himself in an embrace, as at the conclusion of the 1590 *Faerie Queene*, Scudamore finds perfect closure at last, but closure represented in the text, not closure of the text.[19] Scudamore has been led by historically authorized ways of looking to pursue an enterprise with built-in guarantees, but in the larger context of Books III and IV, we can see him embracing the sort of narcissism against which Britomart has struggled. If Book III posits risk as the precondition of creative growth and understanding, Book IV explores the impulse to foreclose risk and examines what might be sacrificed in the attempt to guarantee certainty.

5

The Legend of Cambel and Triamond

The Joust as a Model of Order

Concomitant to the suppression of the Hermaphrodite stanzas at the conclusion of the 1590 *Faerie Queene* is the casting of Book IV—at least insofar as it is, indeed, the legend of Cambel and Triamond—as the continuation of Chaucer's "Squire's Tale." The famous invocation of "Dan *Chaucer*, well of English vndefyled" (4.2.32.8) replaces the Ovidian pool of Salmacis recalled by the "costly Bath" at which the "rich *Romane*" cited in Spenser's canceled stanzas places the statue of the Hermaphrodite, as the fiction of a lost Chaucerian text conceals the actual cancellation of Spenser's stanzas.[1] Spenser's equivocal grounding of his text in spurious literary history calls attention to the play of institutional structure and discursive construct explored throughout the episode of Cambel and Triamond. The combat of the two eponymous heroes is one of a great many jousts represented in Book IV. The joust appears in Book IV as a paradigmatic institution, and the battle between Cambel and Triamond is presented as an etiological fable that demonstrates the development of the joust as a rudimentary system of order. At the same time, the episode provides an allegorical representation of narrative staged as a clash between disparate aspects of the text. The joust as a paradigm of institutional order thus becomes an instrument for an orderly consideration of conflicting aspects of narrative. If there is a moral to the allegory of textual conflict, it is that all structure is provisional, that one cannot press a given order too hard without revealing internal strains and contradictions. Spenser's stance toward the revelation of internal contradiction in narrative structure is far from nihilist, however. Rather, he suggests as a corollary to the breakdown of narrative stability an urbane trust in the reader to appreciate the disorder.[2]

HOLDING THE MIRROR UP TO THE TEXT

By casting the examination of textual process as the rewrite of a prior text, Spenser extends the Book IV exploration of retrospection to recursion, the application of the text's own procedures to itself in order to produce more information. Fundamentally, the process of recursion derives epistemic effects from a structural procedure. Nevertheless, it is significantly different from the strategy of retrospection, which seeks to achieve fixity by imposing closure. While an important project of Book IV is to reveal the pitfalls of depending on structurally built-in guarantees of epistemological certainty, the recursive features of Book IV are designed to produce, not absolute certainty, but a greater degree of knowledge. This recursion is a forward-looking procedure that results in a growth of knowledge.[3] As Daniel Dennet points out, "One 'goes meta-' when one represents one's representations, reflects on one's reflections, reacts to one's reactions. The power to iterate one's powers in this way, to apply whatever tricks one has to one's existing tricks, is a well-recognized breakthrough in many domains: a cascade of processes leading from stupid to sophisticated activity" (29).

This recursion, in which the text's own procedures are taken apart and presented as part of the story, appears as source following as it calls attention to the process, normally taken for granted, of ascribing and imposing structure. Spenser's pose of nostalgia for the irrecoverable masterworks of bygone literature is shown to be the imitation of a thoroughly conventional topos. Spenser's lament,

> But wicked Time that all good thoughts doth waste,
>   And workes of noblest wits to nought out weare,
>   That famous moniment hath quite defaste,
>   And robd the world of threasure endlesse deare,
>   The which mote haue enriched all vs heare.
>   O cursed Eld the cankerworme of writs,
>   How may these rimes, so rude as doth appeare,
>   Hope to endure, sith workes of heauenly wits
> Are quite deuourd, and brought to nought by little bits?
>
> (4.2.33)

echoes Chaucer's complaint in *Anelida and Arcite* (10–21). Spenser alludes to Chaucer, who cites Statius and a mysterious Corinne. While this seems like an infinite regress, the ineluctable drift of language from an unknowable source, it really is no such thing.[4] What purports to be irreparable epistemic loss is a convention eminently transferable from one text to another and Spenser's pose of following Chaucerian "auctoritee" gives way to a freewheeling narrative invention that calls attention to itself by its *copia*.[5]

In addition, Spenser's pose as Chaucer's redactor appears to conflate the positions of writer and reader into one textual configuration:

> Then pardon, O most sacred happie spirit,
>   That I thy labours lost may thus reuiue,
>   And steale from thee the meede of thy due merit,
>   That none durst euer whilest thou wast aliue,
>   And being dead in vaine yet many striue:
>   Ne dare I like, but through infusion sweete
>   Of thine owne spirit, which doth in me surviue,
>   I follow here the footing of thy feete,
> That with thy meaning so I may the rather meete.
>
> (4.2.34)

The pun about following "the footing of thy feete" and the mysterious claim to meet with Chaucer's meaning casts interpretation and signification—reading and writing—in spatial terms in order to give the epistemic aspect of signification, the movement over time from one consciousness to another, the appearance of fixity. Spenser signals this process of spatial translation as the Squire of Dames intervenes in the ongoing and seemingly interminable quarrel between Blandamour and Paridell and, as Jonathan Goldberg insightfully observes, turns Spenser's text into another Squire's Tale (44–46). Spenser remarks of the intervention:

> There they I weene would fight vntill this day,
>   Had not a Squire, euen he the Squire of Dames,
>   By great aduenture trauelled that way;
>
> (4.2.20.1–3)

The locatives "there" and "this" trace a complex web of transactions between writer and reader. "This day" points to the time of writing and each time of reading. "There" points to a fictional place temporally destabilized by the tense of "would fight." "Would have fought until this day" would fix the fight, so to speak, with respect to "this day," but the imperfect tense of "would fight" inhabits the fictional time and space of "There" and not the times of writing and reading referred to by "this day." The complexities evoked of writing and reading over time, where words on a page take on existence through time through successive voicings, give way to the temporally fixed structure of the flashback. As introduction to the story of Cambel and Canacee, the textualized voice of Spenser's narrator quotes Chaucer's Knight, "Whylome as antique stories tellen vs" (4.2.32.1), and concludes "that since their days such louers were not found elsewhere" (4.3.52.9). Although the story of Cambel and Triamond seems to have an almost lapidary stability as an encapsulated text transfused directly from Chaucer to Spenser, that solidity tends to melt on closer inspection. The concluding line, "That since their days such louers were not found elsewhere," can indicate not only that the lovers are exemplary but that their existence is confined to the page of Spenser's text.[6] On closer examination, the monumental solidity of the episode appears to be the product of discursive games.

FIGURING THE TEXT AS BATTLE

Ostensibly, the encapsulated story of the fight between Cambel and Triamond (and his brothers) over Canacee and its amicable conclusion in the marriage of each combatant to the sister of his opponent is an allegory of friendship that shows harmony proceeding from discord and erotic desire subdued by bonds of likeness.[7] But what purports to be a narrative with a moral-allegorical meaning is also an allegorical representation of narrative, in which the relationship between aspects of narrative structure is staged as a fight between two knights over a lady. In many ways, the textual joust Spenser stages prefigures strategies of deconstruction described by Paul de Man: genealogical structure is set against teleological structure and each term is shown to be infected by the other.[8] At stake in Spenser's text, however, is not the revelation of the conditions of its own impossibility. Rather, the text allegorizes its own processes as combat over a woman while showing how that combat occults desire by the way it structures the woman's position. This circumscribed episode characterizes the entire book of Friendship insofar as it reveals the failure of totalizing strategies to guarantee perfect order and links those strategies to the suppression of female desire. The episode stages a complex set of encounters between genealogy and teleology or, to use the pair of terms invoked repeatedly in Book IV, beginnings and ends.[9] On the one hand, Cambel is the protagonist of an etiological fable shown to be already controlled by the teleology of its foreconceit.[10] On the other, the -mond brothers, Pri-, Di-, and Tri-, figure the foreconceit of friendship as likeness, but the intellectual integrity with which they unfold the idea of Agape is shown to be compromised by genealogy in its material form of motherhood.[11]

The joust between Cambel and Pri-, Di-, Triamond is one of a great many such in Book IV, but this particular episode has the character of an etiological fable that shows an institution arising in response to social conditions. Cambel challenges representatives of his sister's many suitors as a way of forestalling further violence:

> So much the more as she refusd to loue,
>   So much the more she loued was and sought,
>   That oftentimes vnquiet strife did moue
>   Amongst her louers, and great quarrels wrought,
>   That oft for her in bloudie armes they fought.
>   Which whenas *Cambell*, that was stout and wise,
>   Perceiu'd would breede great mischiefe, he bethought
>   How to preuent the perill that mote rise,
> And turne both him and her to honour in this wise.
>
> One day, when all that troupe of warlike wooers
>   Assembled were, to weet whose she should bee,
>   All mightie men and dreadfull derring dooers,
>   (The harder it to make them well agree)
>   Amongst them all this end he did decree;
>   That of them all, which loue to her did make,
>   They by consent should chose the stoutest three,
>   That with himselfe should combat for her sake,
> And of them all the victour should his sister take.
>
>   (4.2.37–38)

The joust is presented as a system designed to channel and control violent male desire. Nevertheless, the ambiguity of Cambel's role points to the uncertainty about whether structures of desire—here, male competition over a diffident female—control or create that desire. As combatant for the hand of Canacee, Cambel, if victorious, becomes his sister's designated sexual partner. Spenser's text seems to give no clear signals for reading this disconcerting situation. One might interpret Cambel's challenge as evidence of prior incestuous jealousy or see him as being maneuvered into a compromising position and wonder about the psychological or erotic consequences and implications of that position, but the text leaves it an embarrassingly open question.[12] By extension, the indeterminacy of Cambel's position raises questions about the etiological fable in which he plays a part. Ostensibly, an etiological fable is an exercise in genealogical explanation. That is, a conventional strategy for explaining some aspect of the status quo is to project backward a historical narrative of origins. This historical narrative provides both the ontological grounding for the circumstances under examination and the framework for a meditation on it. But Cambel draws our attention to the chicken-and-egg indeterminacy of such narratives. As implicit, competing claims of logical and historical priority undercut each other, the reader is reminded that we do not necessarily know how things got to be the way they are or whether they are that way for any good, logical reason.[13]

In the other corner, so to speak, are three brothers and a theory. Priamond, Diamond, and Triamond represent the Aristotelian notion of friendship as a relationship of likeness while also figuring forth a Neoplatonic unfolding of Agape as charitable love:[14]

> Amongst those knights there were three brethren bold,
>   Three bolder brethren neuer were yborne,
>   Borne of one mother in one happie mold,
>   Borne at one burden in one happie morne,
>   Thrise happie mother, and thrise happie morne,
>   That bore three such, three such not to be fond;
>   Her name was *Agape* whose children werne
>   All three as one, the first height *Priamond*,
> The second *Dyamond*, the youngest *Triamond*.

> Stout *Priamond*, but not so strong to strike,
>   Strong *Diamond*, but not so stout a knight,
>   But *Triamond* was stout and strong alike:
>   On horsebacke vsed *Triamond* to fight,
>   And *Priamond* on foote had more delight,
>   But horse and foot knew *Diamond* to wield:
>   With curtaxe vsed *Diamond* to smite,
>   And *Triamond* to handle speare and shield,
> But speare and curtaxe both vsd *Priamond* in the field.

> These three did loue each other dearely well,
>   And with so firme affection were allyde,
>   As if but one soule in them all did dwell,
>   Which did her powre into three parts diuyde;
>   Like three faire branches budding farre and wide,

> That from one roote deriu'd their vitall sap:
> And like that roote that doth her life diuide,
> Their mother was, and had full blessed hap,
> These three so noble babes to bring forth at one clap.
>
> (4.2.41–43)

Although the brothers are introduced as a logically complete representation of the foreconceit of the episode (and, indeed, of Book IV), the subsequent account of their origins seriously qualifies that picture of theoretical coherence. In the case of the three brothers, genealogy is conspicuously and intractably a matter of biology. We learn that three brothers are the products of a rape, inflicted by an anonymous "noble youthly knight" on the unpropitiously named Agape, and that they have inherited their adventurous nature from their father. Etiology appears not as a narrative strategy and an intellectual construct, but as blind, biological causality. Moreover, the Eros theoretically controlled by Cambel's tournament and linguistically excluded from the allegory of Agape's progeny returns in a deceptively matter-of-fact description of the nymph's rape:

> There on a day a noble youthly knight
>   Seeking aduentures in the saluage wood,
>   Did by great fortune get of her the sight,
>   As she sate carelesse by a cristall flood,
>   Combing her golden lockes, as seemd her good:
>   And vnawares vpon her laying hold,
>   That stroue in vaine him long to haue withstood,
>   Oppressed her, and there (as it is told)
> Got these three louely babes, that prov'd three champions bold.
>
> (4.2.45)

In her so-called carelessness and maternal concern for the consequent offspring, Agape resembles Marinell's mother, Cymoent. Spenser's point is not, I think, that raping solitary nymphs is unexceptionable behavior for knights errant. Nor does he particularly focus in these two instances on the nymph's own agency in being at risk, alone in the woods, as he does, for example, in the episode of Amoret carried off by Lust. Rather, both episodes of casually, unemphatically described rape, in which the reader is induced to share the nymph's "carelessness," lead to a scene of the mother's attempt to read the future of her progeny. The unmarked irruption of Eros in each instance reveals the reductiveness and limitation of a given scheme of reading. Cymoent mistakes her own narcissistic construction of Proteus' prophecy for an accurate account of her son's future. If Cymoent's response to Proteus' prophecy shows the reader occulted, Agape's visit to the three Fates literalizes textual negotiations: the textual becomes the textile as the lives of her three sons figure as lengths of thread. The resonant images of weaving and spinning and the power of the myth that calls our life a "span" remain dramatically in Agape's single-minded focus on the length of the threads. Having journeyed to the Fates to know "th'end of all [her sons'] dayes" (4.2.47.1), Agape returns contented having obtained the promise that her sons' lives might be "annexet" one to the other, like length of string in a magic show. In the case of Agape, Eros and fertility are that which elude schematic representations of order.

CANACEE, WOMAN AT POINT ZERO

As an involuntary object of desire, Agape represents a shadowy double of Canacee. However, while Agape points us to a biological reality outside the text, Canacee occupies a sort of textual ground zero. She generates and authorizes a transaction among men from which she is excluded, one that resembles what Eve Sedgwick has labeled a homosocial relation.[15] Relations based on an economy of the sameness supplant those based on sexual difference as the social structure epitomized in the joust reveals a curious set of family ties. All of the combatants are brothers, mostly of one another. In no case is sexual desire a primary motivation. Priamond, Diamond, and Triamond are conspicuously not rivals. Indeed, the joust, which illustrates their commutative and collective equality with Cambel is a parable of friendship.

Canacee occupies a strange position in the encounter between her brother and the three sons of Agape. She is a placeholder who authorizes the combat by her presence. Although she stands outside the main action, her position is identified with both subject and object:

> And on the other side in fresh aray,
> Fayre *Canacee* vpon a stately stage
> Was set, to see the fortune of that fray,
> And to be seene, as his most worthie wage,
> That could her purchase with his liues aduentur'd gage.
> (4.3.4.5–9)

Canacee's situation rings changes on issues of specularity and the gendered vision introduced in Book III when Britomart's engagement with the image of her beloved in the magic mirror is contrasted to the glass tower from which Phao could see but not be seen (3.2.19–20). Significantly, the analogous episode in Book III shares with the story of Canacee an allusion to Chaucer's "Squire's Tale." The magic mirror in which Britomart first sees Artegall and the magic ring that Canacee gives to her brother recall magic gifts given by the stranger knight to Cambyuskan in Chaucer's story. But while Britomart's interest in her matrimonial future transforms Merlin's mirror from an instrument of vision to the source of desire, Canacee's ring is transformed through its literary appropriation from Chaucer in such a way as to rewrite and suppress desire. Spenser revises the magic Chaucer ascribes to the ring, substituting the power to stanch all wounds for the power to understand the speech of animals, which Spenser's heroine enjoys by virtue of her learning. When Canacee gives the ring to her brother, she enables him to appropriate female identity in symbolic form while annulling what has been hitherto identified symbolically in *The Faerie Queene* as the wound of desire. For Chaucerian compassion, literally com-passion—feeling together—as Canacee and the female peregrine falcon sympathetically share their feelings of romantic love and loss, Spenser substitutes a kind of male mimetic desire, in which the reciprocal measuring up of one knight with the other takes precedence over sexual love.[16]

What is at stake here is not solely an exploration of the sexual politics within a literary convention. Rather, Spenser focuses on a conventional—even schematic—literary motif as a way of examining issues of textuality, specifically the textual construction of the subject. The Book III project of constructing the reader by presenting Britomart's quest as a lesson in interpretation is reexamined from the point of view of textual process. The opening cantos of Book IV present a series of fights between men over a woman in order to trace a process of change in the construction of the subject. The series itself puts linearity in question. Just as the progress of Paridell and Blandamour to Satyrane's tournament is interrupted by the interpolated story of Cambel and Triamond, so the systematic reduction and abstraction of the female, from (the absent) Florimell to the Snowy Florimell to Florimell's girdle as a counterpart of the male subject play against the more analytic presentation of subjectivity with Canacee.[17]

CAMBINA BREAKS THE STANDOFF

Cambina's appearance as terminatrix of the battle of Cambel and Triamond places the textual hegemony invoked by Canacee's position
as both subject and object and by the narrator's pose as both reader
and writer against the self-awareness invited in the reader by progressively ludicrous plot developments, as the allegory of friendship
begins to resemble a shaggy dog story.[18] In this, Spenser is quite Ariostan as he invites the reader to share his joke and to see the author's
hand in the baroque twists of plot.[19] Cambina seems a figure of stability and closure in every way imaginable. Her name suggests exchange or combination and her accoutrements—from her lion-
drawn chariot of Cybele to the caduceus in her hand—figure forth
order iconographically.[20] She turns the triangle of sexual rivalry into
a gender-balanced foursome: Cambina doubles Canacee, end doubles beginning, a woman is cure as well as cause of the strife, and all
live happily "that since their days such louers were not found
elswhere" (4.3.52.9). Nevertheless, Cambina's intervention emphasizes irregularities in this exemplary story of friendship and allows
those irregularities to ripen to the point of slapstick. There is, after all,
something potentially incongruous about allegorizing friendship as
a knock-down, drag-out fight, and the lengths to which Cambina
must go to stop the fight—after hitting the combatants with the caduceus does no more than distract them briefly, she slips them nepenthe as a thirst-quencher—underscore the incongruity.[21] The
longer the fight continues, the clearer it becomes that the very likeness that supplies the foreconceit for this allegory of friendship is
what perpetuates the bloodshed. The standoff is produced not only
by the equal prowess of the fighters but also by the special attributes
each enjoys as an exemplary figure. Although the interchangeable
souls shared by the three brothers and the magic ring that stanches
all wounds seem to figure concord, their combined effect is to pro-
long the violence of the fight while neutralizing the consequences of
that violence. The result makes the violence farcical.[22]

As both the allegorical personification and narrative agent of ci-
vility, Cambina emphasizes the textual pitfalls of trying to get everything under control. Although seemingly a picture of self-sufficiency,
Cambina is inscribed in a more heterogeneous set of relations than
might first appear. The elaborate iconography with which that figure

is invested presupposes a tradition of conventional representations and of an audience prepared to recognize those conventions. But an audience is invoked not only by what is conventional about the figure of Cambina, but also by what, in the way that figure is deployed, mocks conventional expectations:

> Thereto she learned was in Magicke leare,
>   And all the artes, that subtill wits discouer,
>   Hauing therein bene trained many a yeare,
>   And well instructed by the Fay her mother,
>   That in the same she farre exceld all other.
>   Who vnderstanding by her mightie art,
>   Of th'euill plight, in which her dearest brother
>   Now stood, came forth in hast to take his part,
> And pacifie the strife, which causd so deadly smart.
>
> And as she passed through th'vnruly preace
>   Of people, thronging thicke her to behold,
>   Her angrie teame breaking their bonds of peace,
>   Great heapes of them, like sheepe in narrow fold,
>   For hast did ouer-runne, in dust enrould,
>   That thorough rude confusion of the rout,
>   Some fearing shriekt, some being harmed hould,
>   Some laught for sport, some did for wonder shout,
> And some that would seeme wise, their wonder turnd to dout.
>   (4.3.40–41)

Contemporary readers might dismiss the detail that Cambina begins her pacification by running down a mob of panic-stricken bystanders as a symptom of late Elizabethan antipopulism, rather than as a deliberately crafted narrative glitch, but the sudden appearance of a hitherto unmentioned sister of Priamond, Diamond, and Triamond is more clearly odd. Cambina's appearance is neatly justified by a teleological kind of narrative logic: she is in the text to allow the couples to match up evenly. But teleological closure is achieved at the expense of genealogical probability, as the reader is left to wonder where Agape got the extra baby.

The way Cambina deploys her readily identifiable icons of harmony shows a similar combination of overdetermination and incongruity. She turns the caduceus into an instrument of harmony by using it to hit Cambel and Triamond: narrative agency in beating the combatants into temporary submission ironically contrasts with the iconographic significance of the rod as an emblem of harmony. With the nepenthe, agency forecloses representation: to what extent can one say that Cambel and Triamond have found true friendship when both are drugged? Friendship conceived as the allegorical referent of the nepenthe plays against friendship conceived as the product of the potion.

The fight between Cambel and Triamond sets in counterpoise cultural and textual phenomena. On the one hand, the episode treats the growth and purpose of social institutions and public virtues. On the other, it examines the relationship between allegorical foreconceit and fable. Intellectual and textual relations are presented as mutually reflecting in a fun house of specularity. As homologies of matter and manner proliferate, so does a sense of there being too much of a muchness. The retrospective stance has become a recursive stance in which textual procedures are turned back on the text itself. Although recursion is a strategy for generating more knowledge, deriving epistemic effects from structural procedures, what is produced here is more like epistemic vertigo. If a major procedure of *The Faerie Queene* is to reflect critically on its own discourse, the allegory of Cambel and Triamond suggests that no discourse will stand up under intense scrutiny. Under indictment, in Book IV, however, is not discourse, but strategies of totalization. Spenser shows us, insofar as we as readers are receptive to the ironic amusement of vertiginous regress, that the search for built-in guarantees of certainty is self-defeating.

6

Satyrane's Tournament
and the Combat
of Britomart and Artegall
Extrapolating from Sex and Violence

The specifically erotic component of the joust is the focus of Satyrane's tournament and the private rematch between Britomart and Artegall. These episodes question the use of the relationship between men and women as a paradigm for other relationships, as well as the strategy of deriving signifying structures from the sexual relation. Held up to critique is a tendency to present sexuality in reductive terms in order to generate a structure from the misrepresentation. The many battles of Satyrane's tournament seem pointlessly repetitive and its outcome, as none of the champions can be persuaded to accept the False Florimell as prize, seems inconclusive. The tournament directs attention to the reduction of sexuality to the hymen as a kind of fetish, and to the substitution of an endless alternation of absence and presence for asymmetrically changing, productive relations. Conversely, the sexual politics of the tournament reflect critically on the broader strategy of extrapolating from a tautological structure to something beyond the limited range of tautology. Satyrane's tournament details the transmogrification of sexual relations into discursive structures. The private battle between Britomart and Artegall refigures the relationship between the erotic and the discursive in less critical, more sympathetic terms. We see how gendered bodies can disrupt discursive structures, but also why the stability afforded even by restrictive conventions might be desired.

FRAGMENTING
AND FETISHIZING WOMEN

In the convoluted narrative of Book IV, all roads seem to lead to Satyrane's tournament. Not only does the Squire of Dames take over

99

BELMONT UNIVERSITY LIBRARY

the narrative[1] and redirect its progress to the tournament, but the contest is a large-scale version of the jousts that seem, in endless variation, to be most of what takes place in Book IV. The Squire persuades Blandamour and Paridell to defer fighting over the False Florimell in order to defend the right to her against all the other participants in Satyrane's tournament: narrative deferral corresponds to the Squire's blatant strategy of putting off trouble until later. The ludicrous fight of the two false knights over the even falser lady calls comic attention to the nature of sequentiality itself. Blandamour wins the False Florimell from Sir Ferraugh in a comic replay of the knights' consecutive encounters with Britomart and Scudamore. First Blandamour urges Paridell to fight Britomart for Amoret. Paridell, having been overthrown by Britomart in the previous book, cedes to Blandamour the privilege of being unhorsed by Britomart in return for Blandamour's lady. Then Scudamore appears, Blandamour insists that Paridell take a turn, and Paridell is defeated. When Ferraugh appears with False Florimell and Blandamour urges his friend to fight for the lady, Paridell responds, "Last turne was mine, well proued to my paine, / This now be yours, God send you better gaine" (4.2.6.4–5). This time, Sir Ferraugh loses and Blandamour gets False Florimell.

If this explanation seems confusing, Spenser's text is even more confusing, particularly since the poet's use of syntactically unspecified pronouns makes it very difficult to tell Blandamour from Paridell. This ambiguity is clearly part of the point: the false friends are indistinguishable in their mock selflessness. But the false friends are also hardly distinguishable from true friends such as Cambel and Triamond insofar as for both false and true friends, likeness perpetuates strife. False Florimell focuses attention on this dimension of perpetuity by the way she keeps turning up with first one, then another knight as the perennial prize. Paridell picks the fight with Blandamour by demanding that his friend share his prize:

> Too boastfull *Blandamour*, too long I beare
>   The open wrongs, thou doest me day by day;
>   Well know'st thou, when we friendship first did sweare,
>   The couenant was, that every spoyle or pray
>   Should equally be shard betwixt vs tway:
>   Where is my part then of this Ladie bright,
>   Whom to thy selfe thou takest quite away?
>   Render therefore therein to me my right,
> Or answere for thy wrong, as shall fall out in fight.
>
>   (4.2.13)

Paridell's ludicrous claims to a part of the False Florimell suggest that the pattern of the joust, by means of which friendship is realized throughout Book IV, is a process of fragmentation. Although Paridell's claim threatens to provoke endless conflict, we can see that, ironically, the dispute is much less intractable than the combatants seem to understand. Not only is the False Florimell shareable sequentially, but she is an automaton reducible to her constituent parts.

But Snowy Florimell's peculiar status as a literal construct only underscores the more familiar reduction of the female to a part implied when Florimell's girdle becomes the prize in Satyrane's tournament. The girdle functions as a fetish in almost textbook Freudian terms of absence and presence: it represents female genitalia and signals the presence of the hymen as it substitutes for the absent woman.[2] In addition, Florimell's girdle evokes all of the Elizabethan wordplay on naught and nothing.[3] The point here is not just the reduction and objectification of the female. Rather, the complex, linguistically realized fragmentation of the female body becomes a way to explore textual construction of subjectivity. Spenser subjects his culture's fetishization of female virginity to scrutiny and quite irreverent critique, but he uses that critique to approach intellectual habits that underlie making such a fetish of virginity. Consideration of the economic and social dimensions of prizing female virginity—having to do, for example, with ensuring the legitimacy of heirs—seems largely to be deferred to Book VI, in which, quite unlike Book IV, babies figure prominently.[4]

Spenser's exploration of the figure of naught accords with a renewed interest in sixteenth-century European culture in the zero as a term in mathematics, economics, and the visual arts. In his study, *The Semiotics of Zero*, Brian Rotman notes a fundamental contradiction between the use of zero as a sign of absence and the use of zero as one integer among many:

> If we interpret counting cardinally, then the proto-numbers appear as signs that iconically mark out fixed pluralities via a tallying procedure which assigns the typical protonumber 11 . . . 1 to a *corresponding* plurality of counted objects; a process that makes zero the cardinal number—nought—of the empty plurality. . . . If counting is interpreted ordinally, the proto-numbers 1, 11, 111, etc., appear as records which mark out by iconic repetition the sequence of stages occupied by a counting subject. Zero then represents the starting point of the process.
>
> (13)

In similar fashion the girdle, initially the sign of Florimell's absence, becomes the counter that generates Satyrane's tournament. The description of Satyrane displaying the girdle to all contenders makes explicit both the fetishizing of the object and the complexity of relations that the object engages:

> Then first of all forth came Sir *Satyrane*,
>> Bearing that precious relicke in an arke
>> Of gold, that bad eyes might it not prophane:
>> Which drawing softly forth out of the darke,
>> He open shewd, that all men mot it marke.
>> A gorgeous girdle, curiously embost
>> With pearle and precious stone, worth may a marke;
>> Yet did the workmanship farre passe the cost:
> It was the same, which lately *Florimel* had lost.
>
> (4.4.15)

The blatant repetition of "marke" meaning "to observe" and "a unit of currency" (*OED* s.v. "mark" vb. 3; sub. 2.1) suggests an obscene meaning of mark as well, as female genitalia.[5] The pun associates male observation both with exchange value and female sexuality. The economy of male perception as deployed in Satyrane's tournament both fragments the woman and puts her in circulation.[6]

FLORIMELL'S GIRDLE:
CONTROLLING DESIRE
AND TROPING THE EROTIC

What is at stake in this fragmentation and objectification of woman is the infelicitous attempt to impose structure on a process. The male-female transactions represented by the pun on "marke" subject sexual desire to an elaborate system of ordering in an attempt to assert fixity and control over the intractable to-and-fro-ness of desire. Moreover, the linguistic play on Florimell's girdle calls attention to the close congruence of rhetorical and sexual matters, in Book IV of *The Faerie Queene*, as well as in late Elizabethan culture.[7]

In its erotic connotations, Florimell's girdle enacts a shift from metonymy to metaphor: the girdle represents female genitalia metonymically by contiguity and metaphorically by shape. Moreover, since the girdle falls off the unchaste, it makes manifest the state of the female body it encloses, however temporarily, in such a way as to abstract the signification of absence or presence of the hymen from active heterosexual relations. Making a fetish of the hymen affords but a negative sort of carnal knowledge—the knowledge of lost virginity—and excludes post-hymeneal, married chastity from the universe of discourse. Spenser calls attention to these contradictions in the ideology of virginity by means of comic play on the motif of losing the girdle. Most explicitly, the humor is expressed in the Squire of Dames' comment *"Vngirt vnblest"* (4.5.18.7), as the girdle falls off all but one of the ladies at the tournament.[8] But the joke goes much further than that. That history given for Florimell's girdle, the cestus, is another of those slightly odd Spenserian stories that raise more questions than they answer. In this case, the interpolated narrative ostensibly traces the provenance of the girdle to classical mythology in order to account for its magical properties: Vulcan made the belt to give "vertue of chast loue" (4.5.3.1) to his wife Venus. Nevertheless, the details of the story cast the relationship of the belt to the virtue of chastity in an odd light. The stanzas introducing the story specifically raise the question of whether the cestus contains virtue as an inherent property or whether the belt is a medium of exchange in an economy of vanity. The narrator begins the history of Florimell's girdle by observing:

> That many wish to win for glorie vaine,
> And not for vertuous vse, which some doe tell
> That glorious belt did in it selfe containe,
> (4.5.2.6–8)

Implicitly, the question appears: does the cestus represent chastity as it was defined in Book III, or is it a debased "marke" of exchange? As the story unfolds, we see that Vulcan has fashioned a very peculiar chastity belt. Designed "to bind lasciuious desire, / And loose affections streightly to restraine" (4.5.4.7–8), the belt is easily removed when Venus wants to visit her paramour Mars. Florimell is said to have found the belt where Venus discarded it on Mount Acidale: the chastity belt owes its historical dissemination to Venus' adultery with Mars.

The semiological confusions focusing on the cestus present in microcosm larger problems explored through the extended episode of Satyrane's tournament and its aftermath, fundamentally the problem of deriving signifying structures from erotic transactions. Throughout the episode, each part of the complex—the sexual and the semi-ological—presents a complementary critique of the basic strategy of extending a tautology to Something Else. On the one hand, we see that a sexual ideology focused on physical virginity, focused, that is, on the tautologically paired absence or presence of the hymen, is not extendable to married chastity. For that reason, the fact that Florimell's girdle fits Amoret alone is simply ignored and the prize is awarded to the False Florimell. As the embodiment of married love, Amoret has no place in the contest. The theoretical certainty of binary opposition is shown to have limited practical application as Spenser frames a succinct critique of Elizabethan sexual ideology. Social historians observe that the Elizabethan preoccupation with female chastity reflected the need to ensure the legitimacy of heirs in a system of primogeniture. Insofar as that preoccupation became a cult of virginity, it served its social purposes badly, especially in light of the widely held Elizabethan belief that the initial act of intercourse would not produce offspring.[9]

Representational strategies operating in Satyrane's tournament reveal analogous problems of extending a tautology. In many ways, the contest is set up as a paradigmatic signifying structure: it is a means of designating the best knight and the fairest lady. However, juxtaposing the two parts of the contest reveals both how dissimilar the two really are and how speciously they are connected. The joust provides a relatively clear-cut means of determining martial superiority, although, given the round-robin, tag-team nature of the hostil-ities, some judgment must be exercised in choosing the winner. Hav-ing overthrown the *Salvage* Knight who had previously defeated all the other combatants, Britomart is given the prize for the third and final day as well as the grand championship "for last is deemed best" (4.5.8.8). The relative certainty with which the martial contest deter-mines the most skillful knight only points up how dubious is the con-test to choose his lady. For one thing, the standards of selection do not remain constant: what starts out as a beauty contest turns into the chastity sweepstakes when Florimell's girdle fails to stay around False Florimell, to whom it has been awarded. Moreover, the narra-tor makes clear that Snowy Florimell's beauty is a forgery (4.5.15) and suggests more obliquely a specifically linguistic dimension to that duplicity:

All that her saw with wonder rauisht weare,
And weend no mortall creature she shoud bee,
But some celestiall shape, that flesh did beare:
Yet all were glad there *Florimell* to see;
Yet thought that *Florimell* was not so faire as shee.
                                    (4.5.14.5–9)

In the eyes of her audience, the simulacrum both is and is not Florimell: the proper name cites both presence and absence.

Although it might be tempting for a late twentieth-century critic to see in the False Florimell a paradigmatic representative of the (inescapable? essential?) duplicity of language, that is perhaps to repeat the strategy of unwarranted extrapolation criticized in this episode. In presenting the contradictory status of the figure that both is and is not Florimell, Spenser emphasizes the response of the delighted onlookers. The observers' bias and desires are very clearly relevant. Satyrane's tournament, with all its contradictions, is an important set-piece in Spenser's larger project of examining the impulse to reify epistemic data by projecting them onto a fixed structure. If Book III focuses on problems of making sense of experience, Book IV focuses on problems of representing experience, particularly insofar as narrative structure provides a symmetrical mapping of the one-way asymmetry of experience as it is necessarily lived in time.[10]

As a vehicle for exploring these issues, Spenser sets the basically homosocial economy of the joust, with its indefinitely repeatable choice between fundamentally similar antagonists, against the multiple asymmetries of heterosexual relations.[11] Consequently, Britomart, who embodies chastity as an active, forward-looking virtue, disrupts Satyrane's tournament as she points up its contradictions. Her explicit act of restoring Florimell's girdle to the knights of Maydenhead (4.4.48) accentuates the slippage from asymmetry to symmetry: although the belt figures the hymen, it recycles very easily. Britomart's quest for chaste love emphasizes by contrast the extent to which her comrades are fighting under false colors. Although one side designates itself the Knights of Maydenhead and the other more or less fits under the banner of Friendship, both sides seem engaged in a contest of mutual phallic display. This is particularly emphasized in the description of the first day's fight, in which the knights have at each other "strong and stiffly" with "huge great," "beamlike" spears.[12] The point is not, I think, simply that spears are phallic. Rather, this exaggerated phallic symbolism alerts us to the ensuing critical examination of symbols and other discursive constructs particularly as they engage sexuality and desire.

BRITOMART FINDS ARTEGALL: RETHINKING THE QUEST ROMANCE AND SIDNEAN IMITATION

The erotically charged rematch between Britomart and Artegall appears as an accidental slip from the homosocial into the heterosexual. Following her victory at Satyrane's tournament, Britomart is sought by both Scudamore and Artegall, each of whom desires revenge on what he assumes to be a male rival. Scudamore, in active pursuit of Britomart, encounters Artegall, who lies in wait for her.[13] When Artegall apologizes for mistakenly charging at Scudamore, the latter replies:

> Small harme it were
> For any knight, vpon a ventrous knight
> Without displeasance for to proue his spere.
> (4.6.4.1–3)

Scudamore acknowledges the value of unprovoked jousting between consenting, presumably male, adults. Seen in the context of the homosocial camaraderie of Artegall and Scudamore, as well as their imagined homosocial rivalry with Britomart, the fight between Britomart and Artegall appears anomalous and disruptive. The pair reconfigure the joust as they alter its erotic significance. Although the combat between Britomart and Artegall is highly charged sexually, it explicitly resists the binary structure represented by the absence or presence of the hymen. What emerges is the contrast between paradigmatic and syntagmatic aspects of structure. By focusing on the cestus, Satyrane's tournament represents sexuality in a quintessentially paradigmatic way: in order to have a syntagmatic dimension, to accommodate repetition, the hymen must be fetishized. As a narrative sequel to the great set-piece of Satyrane's tournament, the fight between Britomart and Artegall refocuses attention on the syntagmatic aspect of Spenserian fiction. The violent single combat focuses attention on the quality of asymmetry, as narrative purports to engage one-directional change through time.

Britomart's departure from Satyrane's tournament recalls the opening of Book III. As in the earlier episode, Britomart refrains from joining male knights in pursuit of Florimell (or the person they think is Florimell). But, if in Book III Britomart ignored the distress of another woman in her own single-minded quest, in Book IV Britomart appears as Amoret's guardian, as the two women ride off together, companions in care. On the one hand, Britomart's new role as protectress is in keeping with the more public and political nature of virtue in Book IV. On the other, her performance in the role of protectress is somewhat problematical, since she loses her charge between fights with Artegall. Given the emphasis in Book IV on the permutations and ramifications of loss, Britomart's explanation for Amoret's absence seems ludicrously offhand.

> Till on a day as through a desert wyld
>   We trauelled, both wearie of the way
>   We did alight, and sate in shadow myld;
>   Where fearelesse I to sleepe me downe did lay.
>   But when as I did out of sleepe abray,
>   I found her not, where I her left whyleare,
>   But thought she wandred was, or gone astray.
>   I cal'd her loud, I sought her farre and neare;
> But no where could her find, nor tydings of her heare.
>   (4.6.36)

The plot twist demonstrates the intrusion of narrative contingency into orderly structures of signification. The central episodes of Book IV, as Britomart approaches the object of her quest and finally encounters Artegall, bring into focus the reconsideration of quest romance as a narrative structure that occurs throughout the book. One object of critique is the homology of identity and narrative fundamental to quest romance. As with the Redcrosse Knight and Sir Guyon, Britomart's quest corresponds in a general way to her growing perfection in the virtue of which she is avatar. As Judith Anderson has observed, Britomart "is less simply a metaphor and more simply herself than are the heroes of earlier books" (*SE* 114). Britomart seems to have a life story and that story seems to be a correlative of the anatomy of love presented to us in Book III, even though Britomart herself is absent for the central four cantos. The text gestures toward connections between her *Bildung* as knight of Chastity and the allegory of love in Book III without particularly subjecting those connections to critical scrutiny.

Similarly, Book III tends to deploy gender as a discursive device, as a way of treating general issues of otherness, wholeness, or human sexuality. At the opening of Book III when Britomart declines the general pursuit of Florimell, Spenser makes a joke about deriving general principles from the specifically feminine: Britomart "would not so lightly follow beauties chace" (3.1.19.2) because women do not interest her sexually. Although in Book III Spenser certainly treats female experience, and with considerable sympathy (for a man writing in 1590), in Book III he offers relatively little critical reflection on the problems of a male poet extrapolating from female experience for the edification of a largely male readership.[14] Much that might give trouble in that regard is overlooked in the forward, prospectively oriented movement of Book III. Just as Britomart improvises her identity as Martial Maid, so Spenser puts together the allegory of Book III as a kind of *bricolage*, which he then subjects to retrospection in Book IV. In a witty reversal of Britomart's Book III pursuit of love, both she and Amoret are pursued by their lovers. As with her resistance to "beauties chace," Britomart's concealed gender is an issue. However, while in Book III Britomart's femininity accounts for the single-minded pursuit of her quest, in Book IV the revelation to Scudamore and Artegall that Britomart is a woman refigures retrospectively the object of their jealous pursuit. Britomart's femininity is judged as it fits into a homosocial order as gender is subjected to structures of containment and control.

Part of what is at stake in Spenser's revision of the quest romance is reconsidering the nature of imitation. Book III espouses the Sidnean sort of imitation set forth in the letter to Ralegh. Spenser alludes to Sidney's assertion in his *Defence of Poetry* (24) that poetry works "not only to make a Cyrus . . . but to bestow a Cyrus upon the world to make many Cyruses, if they will learn aright why and how that maker made him"; Spenser champions the "Poets historicall" and prefers Xenophon to Plato:

> for that the one in the exquisite depth of his iudgement, formed a Commune welth such as it should be, but the other in the person of Cyrus and the Persians fashioned a gouernement such as might best be: So much more profitable and gratious is doctrine by ensample, then by rule.[15]

Accordingly, at the conclusion of Book III in 1590, Britomart's wish of "like happinesse" for herself as she observes the hermaphroditic embrace of Scudamore and Amoret, contrasts favorably with the famous Roman's fetishizing of the hermaphrodite statue as he sets it in his bath. Throughout Book III, Spenser contrasts the right use with the abuse of art. Right use involves fashioning oneself after the work of art in virtuous and gentle discipline; abuse comprehends both the misuse of art as a substitute for rather than a model of experience and the capacity of art to abuse and deform the observer. The quest romance of Book III is a moral-tropological model of literary interaction.[16] Representations of self-fashioning extend beyond the frame of the text as models to be imitated.

One gauge of the shift from Book III to Book IV is the career of False Florimell, a grotesque figure of literary artifice. Initially fashioned as a substitute for the real Florimell, she can be passed unaffected from one knight to another because she is an unalloyed figment of the imagination: she has little ontological baggage to weigh her down. As "enough to hold a foole in vaine delight" (3.8.10.7), False Florimell represents the antithesis of the creative and productive sexuality endorsed in Book III. In Book IV, False Florimell is a placeholder in a structure of male homosocial rivalry, much like any number of other female figures including Canacee and Amoret. Book III contrasts Sidnean imitation, which reaches beyond the confines of the text to a community of morally responsive readers, with the sort of literary abuse that short-circuits those transactions. Book IV presents structures of what René Girard has called imitative or triangular desire between rivals in which the drive to imitate the other suitor's desire takes precedence over their drive to win the putative object of desire. The mutual comparison among the male knights in Book IV seems both to generate and to exhaust desire. The woman at the center of male rivalry is so much a structural convenience that the psychological dimension collapses.[17]

Additional perspective on this system of male competition is provided by Scudamore's sojourn in the House of Care. In Scudamore's anguish, we see the return of the emotions largely excluded by the pattern of male jousting. The various feelings that accompany personal relations, of desire, jealousy, hostility, anxiety, and the like, projected outward onto the conventionalized, stylized form of the joust, are allegorized as the archetypal sleepless night spent by Scudamore. John Steadman points out the relationship between the Latin *cura* and *aemulatio*. Scudamore's care, his physical and mental suffering, shows us how male imitative desire really feels. Although

Scudamore is misinformed about Britomart as Amoret's lover, the system of desire in which he participates guarantees that the male lover will suffer the unending care of perpetual male rivalry. Similarly, the six grooms whose hammering keeps Scudamore up all night provide a demonic parody of Pythagorean harmony. Their sameness translates into perpetual discord (665).

The repeat encounter of Britomart and Artegall in canto vi stages a complex critical examination of Sidnean imitation. In Book III, sexual relations provide a paradigm for more general sorts of relations. The relationship of Britomart to Artegall is a model of the relationship of self to other or of reader to text. Much of Britomart's enterprise, from her first view of Artegall in the magic mirror to her last look at the Pageant of Busirane, has a strong exegetical dimension: she seems continually engaged in learning to read what is around her. In Book IV, a literal battle between the sexes presents the interplay between the narrative and what that narrative signifies.

DESIRE AND CONVENTION:
STABILIZING FREE PLAY

One thing the episode seems to say about sexual relationships is that both men and women are strongly motivated to place sexual desire very quickly into some discursive framework. Artegall is stunned by the sight of Britomart's face and "of his wonder made religion" (4.6.22.3), as both he and Britomart assume the conventional pose of erotic idolatry. In a purely tropological sense, Artegall's worship of Britomart is not, I think, a good thing: it is a negative exemplar rather than a model for imitation. Late Elizabethan culture, particularly in its Puritan element, was suspicious of idols, and Spenser himself cast the religion of love in a negative light with Busirane's torture of Amoret.[18] Artegall's idolatry fits reasonably into this negative context. The conventionalized postures of male worshiper and despiteous lady into which Britomart and Artegall fall threaten to short-circuit the creative potential of their desire. Each threatens to become the object of the other's enjoyment in a particularly narrow way. Whereas the Gardens of Adonis showed sexual desire to be part of a cosmic process, here we see desire confined and degraded in a narrow circuit of exchange between worshiper and object of worship.

This closing off of the lovers' desire in a self-limiting circuit of idolatry is part of a larger examination of closure and foreclosure that takes place in canto vi and in Book IV as a whole. Foreclosure is represented paradigmatically by Amoret and Scudamore. Neither is said to have enjoyed a moment since meeting the other: for reasons discussed previously, their relationship is blighted from the outset.[19] Britomart and Artegall enact the process of foreclosure diachronically. In describing the violence of their combat, the narrator playfully alludes to the potentially unstable gap between beginnings and endings in the process when he worries that they risk making "their loues beginning, their liues end" (4.6.17.9). Although the battle is spectacularly bloody, its closure is seen as a function of a discursive shift rather than a fatal wound. At the conclusion of Book IV, with the climactic marriage of Thames and Medway, closure is presented as a categorical shift from one theoretical register to another. A shift into the discourse of idolatry marks the foreclosure of the unconventional mix of love and war in which Britomart and Artegall briefly participate.

The entire encounter of Britomart and Artegall in canto vi is marked by discursive shifts. Their rematch differs from their previous battle—and from Britomart's summary overthrow of Scudamore prior to the main event—because they resort to swords after the first clash of spears. In naively mimetic, fictional terms, the enchanted spear gives Britomart an absolute tactical advantage she no longer has when both contestants use weapons that have no magical powers. But clearly something happens on the symbolic level as well. The shift from one phallic symbol to another calls into question the hitherto unexamined presuppositions encoded in a given choice of symbol. The erotic connotations of the swordplay, as Britomart and Artegall "trauerst to and fro" (4.6.18.1) trading strokes, calls attention to the limitations of breaking spears as an adequate representation of sexual intercourse. The contrast reveals retrospectively the hierarchical nature of the spear as a sexual symbol: penetration is the exclusive focus of the trope, which takes precedence over any other aspect of the sexual act. If the spear symbolically contracts sexuality to one determinate point, Britomart's act of casting aside the spear of Chastity conspicuously resists symbolic determination. Although the description of the battle is erotically charged, what can it possibly mean in this context to ask whether Britomart is still a virgin? The spear as symbol imposes a determinate binary logic on sexuality—did she or didn't she? Britomart and Artegall's battle after they have discarded spears escapes determinacy.

A little too much relevant data, however, proves fatal to the freedom of their relationship. It comes to an end when Artegall shears off Britomart's helmet and reveals the woman within the armor. Tellingly, the verb glance describes the blow that reveals Britomart to Artegall's sight:

> The wicked stroke vpon her helmet chaunst,
>   And with the force, which in it selfe it bore,
>   Her ventayle shard away, and thence forth glaunst
>   A downe in vaine, ne harm'd her any more.
>   With that her angels face, vnseene afore,
>   Like to the ruddie morne appeard in sight,
>   Deawed with siluer drops, through sweating sore,
>   But somewhat redder, then beseem'd aright,
> Through toylesome heate and labour of her weary fight.
>   (4.6.19)

Spenser's pun on "to glance" as the gliding, oblique movement of a weapon (*OED* s.v. "glance" vb. 1.1) and the rapid movement of an eye (*OED* s.v. "glance" vb. 1.5) puts in play the distinction made by Renaissance art historians between the optic and the haptic. The optic appeals to the controlling focus of the eye. The haptic concerns sinuous outlines and an imagined touch.[20] As Clark Hulse has pointed out, the miniaturist Nicholas Hilliard, in his characteristically English adaptation of Albertian theory, resists the complete subordination of the object of representation to the system of visual perspective for the sensuous appeal of the physical and the fleshly. Hulse contrasts the reciprocal gazes envisioned by Hilliard between male artist and female subject with Albrecht Dürer's vision of female subject passively displayed before the male artist viewing her through a perspective grid (145–148). Similarly, when Britomart is uncased, Spenser shows us something more complicated that the female subjected to the male view. Rather, we see how bodies can intrude on theoretical systems of control. Britomart's flushed and sweating face is comically indecorous and ambiguous. Britomart quickly becomes implicated in a circuit of amorous idolatry but not before demonstrating a physicality not appropriate to a *princesse lointaine.*

Although there is something very attractive about the energy and freedom of Britomart and Artegall's encounter, Spenser shows its instability to be a problem: their relationship very quickly turns into something more conventional. If the homosocial transaction between Cambel and Triamond resists closure, so that Cambina must hit them over the head and then drug them to make them stop fighting, the *jouissance* of Britomart and Artegall is all too susceptible to closure. Once the lovers are aware of each other, they fall into a kind of naive mimesis and can no longer participate in a metaphoric eroticism. In a sense, their fight and its aftermath stage certain limitations of Sidnean mimesis: a poet can give us many Cyruses, but it is more difficult to give us many Hermaphrodites. Personal virtues like valor are more susceptible to moral-tropological reproduction than are cosmic principles like *discordia concors*.

Spenser presents the movement from free play to determinacy as a kind of falling off or constriction. In the context of all that has gone before, there are ample reasons to have misgivings about the particular role into which each lover falls. Nevertheless, Spenser is not simply producing an Olympian critique of cultural-linguistic constructs. Rather, he shows us with sympathetic detail how uncomfortable instability is and why people might choose even harmful conventions of behavior and understanding to resolve instability. In a sense, Spenser himself loses some control of his text by making his characters aware of the erotic dimension of their encounter. They cannot then go on exchanging sword strokes however pleasant the metaphoric connotations. The revelation of gendered bodies imposes fatal determinacy on erotic free play. Both Britomart and Artegall undergo a loss of innocence understood, in terms that Blake would understand, as knowledge and experience. This loss of innocence proves genuinely irreversible, in ironic contrast to Pœana's temporarily lost virginity in Book IV, canto viii. While throughout most of Book IV, virginity figures the boundary between innocence and experience, we are shown how fetishized virginity generates structures of reversal and repetition. With Britomart and Artegall, we see an asymmetric, one-directional process, as, first, their combat is grounded in unique sexual desire rather than in arbitrary homosocial display and then, they gain irreversible knowledge of that grounding. The response of each character to that knowledge is expressed not only as a loss of control over the body but as the experience of the body as indeterminate. Consider how Artegall responds to his first sight of Britomart's flushed face and flowing hair:

> And as his hand he vp againe did reare,
>> Thinking to worke on her his vtmost wracke,
>> His powrelesse arme benumbd with secret feare
>> From his reuengefull purpose shronke abacke,
>> And cruell sword out of his fingers slacke
>> Fell downe to ground, as if the steele had sence,
>> And felt some ruth, or sence his hand did lacke,
>> Or both of them did thinke, obedience
> To doe to so diuine a beauties excellence.
>
> (4.6.21)

Instead of enjoying symbolic potency, poor Artegall finds that both hand and sword share in the frailty of the flesh. Britomart also experiences difficulty keeping control of herself:

> When *Britomart* with sharpe auizefull eye
>> Beheld the louely face of *Artegall*,
>> Tempred with sternesse and stout maiestie,
>> She gan eftsoones it to her mind to call,
>> To be the same which in her fathers hall
>> Long since in that enchaunted glasse she saw.
>> Therewith her wrathfull courage gan appall,
>> And haughtie spirits meekely to adaw,
> That her enhaunced hand she downe gan soft withdraw.
>
> Yet she it forst to haue againe vpheld,
>> As fayning choler, which was turn'd to cold:
>> But euer when his visage she beheld,
>> Her hand fell downe, and would no longer hold
>> The wrathfull weapon gainst his countnance bold:
>> But when in vaine to fight she oft assayd,
>> She arm'd her tongue, and thought at him to scold;
>> Nathlesse her tongue not to her will obayd,
> But brought forth speeches myld, when she would haue mis-sayd.
>
> (4.6.26–27)

Her predicament is touchingly similar to Artegall's: both share an adolescent awkwardness as they are both clearly at the mercy of impulses beyond their control.[21] Nevertheless, the differences are subtle and instructive. Britomart's vain efforts at control shift from sword to tongue as she wavers uncertainly between the roles of angry knight and despiteous lady.

Both Glauce and Scudamore help bring the awkward lovers into some kind of accord. Glauce functions more or less as a female go-between, the traditional function of the old nurse figure.[22] Her knowing wordplay domesticates the anarchic semiotic play of their combat and fix their response as smug man and blushing maid (4.6.32). In a more abstract sense, Scudamore reinscribes Britomart and Artegall in a homosocial economy by his interpretation of events. He expresses open glee that Artegall has become "a Ladies thrall" and is "inly glad" at evidence of Britomart's femininity because he defines it as her inability to cuckold him.

With all of this conventional gender role playing, what has become of Merlin's prophecy in Book III of heroic, companionate marriage?

> Great aid thereto his mighty puissaunce,
>   And dreaded name shall giue in that sad day:
>   Where also proofe of thy prow valiaunce
>   Thou then shalt make, t'increase thy louers pray.
>   Long time ye both in armes shall beare great sway,
>   Till thy wombes burden thee from them do call,
>   And his last fate him from thee take away,
>   (3.3.28.1–7)

Judith Anderson observes that "in the closing cantos of Book V it is hard to believe that Artegall can ever return to Britomart to realize those prophecies in time" (*SE* 115 C). Although, given the abundance of work done on Spenserian allegory since the late 1950s no one is likely to mistake *The Faerie Queene* for a nineteenth-century novel, there is considerable temptation to rely excessively on purely narrative coherence in interpreting the poem.[23] Paul Alpers has long observed that *The Faerie Queene* deploys narrative materials rhetorically (3–35). While the poem deploys dramatically realized episodes and narrative plot lines at the service of intellectual and rhetorical structures, both the intellectual structure and the details of plot merit attention. The story of Britomart and Artegall takes some surprising turns in Book IV, canto iv, disturbing if one expects their "story" to exemplify romantic or dynastic fulfillment. However, the narrative twists make a rhetorical point. After finally meeting, the pair behave in unexpected ways: they enact conventional patterns that accord rather badly with the ideal of comrades-in-arms envisioned by Merlin in Book III. Moreover, they are strangely unequal in their attitudes to leave-taking, as Artegall "bound / Vpon an hard aduenture yet in quest" (4.6.42.2–3) departs. Artegall repeats excuses and promises of a speedy return, and Britomart vacillates, now unhappily reconciled to the separation, now vainly pleading, rather like Virgil's Dido, for Artegall to remain with her. Although Spenser supplies considerable human detail, what is held up to scrutiny is not the nature of a domestic relationship. Above and beyond the dramatic particulars of the lovers' parting, we see the quest romance being refigured, as a pattern of interpolated duty and delayed gratification, rather than satisfaction approached. As we will discover in Book V, Artegall's quest carries a deadline: he must rescue Irena before the day of her execution. In some ways, Artegall's limited separation from Britomart resembles the six years' service the Redcrosse Knight owes the Faerie Queene before he can return to his bride Una. Redcrosse's hiatus has apocalyptic connotations and evokes the term of human history at the completion of which the ideas represented by the marriage of Una and the Redcrosse Knight will be realized. Artegall's mission comprises a decidedly secular, political configuration. The uncomfortable intersection of his yet-unnamed quest with Britomart's pursuit of gratified desire presages a conflict of the intellectual orientations represented by each quest.

7

The Allegory of Lust
Imitation at the Limits

The Lust episode extends Spenser's reexamination of Sidnean mimesis. The episode sets the "role model" model of narrative fiction between extreme limiting cases represented by the material body and the imperial reader. On the one hand, the grotesque figure of Lust presents all that exceeds or eludes the moral focus of Sidnean mimesis. On the other, the defeat of Lust by Elizabeth's avatar Belphoebe reveals how real political power functions to determine meaning. In the proem to Book III, Elizabeth is invited to see herself in mirrors more than one and, as Louis Montrose has pointed out, encomia to the queen create the Elizabethan ideal as well as reflect it. Nonetheless, Elizabeth enters the text in the Lust episode as part of a textual intervention that makes clear that she has a kind of authority that places her outside customary transactions of reader and text.

THE (GENDERED) BODY IN ALLEGORY

From the opening of canto vii, as Amoret wanders away from Britomart's protection to be kidnapped by Lust, tropological allegory—the pattern of moral behavior suitable for Sidnean imitation—plays against sheer corporal materiality. In accounting for Amoret's departure, the narrator presents us with a crux:[1]

> The whiles faire *Amoret*, of nought affeard,
> > Walkt through the wood, for pleasure, or for need;
> > When suddenly behind her backe she heard
> > One rushing forth out of the thickest weed,
> > That ere she backe could turne to taken heed,
> > Had vnawares her snatched vp from ground.
> > Feebly she shriekt, but so feebly indeed,
> > That *Britomart* heard not the shrilling sound,
> There where through weary trauel she lay sleeping sound.
>
> (4.7.4)

The alternative explanations "for pleasure, or for need" suggest and subvert a moral reading of Amoret's action. On the one hand, there are hints that Amoret wanders off in a kind of truancy, that her behavior represents some sort of morally culpable heedlessness and hedonism.[2] On the other, there is little doubt about what need would induce someone to visit the bushes in the middle of the night. Spenser's little bathroom joke makes a serious point, of course. Coextensive with the more traditional implication that Amoret falls victim because of some lapse, even if only a lapse of vigilance on her part is the suggestion that what makes her susceptible to Lust—her own or another's—is the mere fact of carnality, of having (or being) a body with all of its functions.

The episode focuses on the material body as that which, in its materiality, is subject to multiple constructions, as well as resistant to totalization. Spenser underscores the corporeal focus with repeated punning reference to Lust bearing Amoret in his arms (4.7.8.1–2, 6; 4.7.9.2). The grotesque figure carrying off Amoret bodily provides a literal counterpart to Scudamore, who, taking Amoret by the hand, carries her off a bit more genteelly as he bears heraldically on his shield the arms of Cupid with his killing bow. The ideological objectification of woman enacted by Scudamore is parodied in the physical predation of Lust. Whereas the totalizing strategies practiced by Scudamore ultimately eliminate Amoret from the text of Book IV, in the earlier episode she eludes her captor by taking to her heels.

Amoret's imprisonment by Lust recalls her imprisonment by Busirane. The contrast between the two episodes reveal how differently the body figures in the allegory of each book. In Book III, the body is part of a moral hierarchy; in Book IV, it is part of a network of social relations. The shift occurs along an axis whose thematic poles are integrity and virginity and whose rhetorical poles are metaphor and metonymy. The key to the shift lies in how the bodily injury threatening Amoret is described. In Book IV, Æmylia relates to the more recent captive Amoret Lust's predatory habits:

> For on the spoile of women he doth liue,
> Whose bodies chast, when euer in his powre
> He may them catch, vnable to gainestriue,
> He with his shamefull lust doth first deflowre,
> And afterwards themselues doth cruelly deuoure.
> (4.7.12.5–9)

The sinister rhyme "deflowre/deuoure" recalls, significantly, the identical play on words that Thomas More used to liken his situation as subject of Henry VIII to the fate of Sejanus' daughter. As Roper reports in his *Life of Sir Thomas More*, More, importuned by the bishops of Durham, Bath, and Winchester to accompany them to the coronation of Queen Anne as part of a scheme to gain assent to the marriage, replies with an anecdote: the Roman emperor is unable to execute the daughter of Sejanus (not identified by More, who adapts the story from Tacitus) because of a prohibition against executing virgins until a member of the council suggests, "Let her first be deflowered and then after may she be devoured!" More ends by assuring the bishops, "it lieth not in my power but that they may devour me. But God, being my good Lord, I will provide that they shall never deflower me!" (229–230). For More, the pair deflower/devour marks the distinction between More's authority over his own conscience and the king's power over More's body. For Lust, both deflowering and devouring mark progressive stages in the violence he inflicts on female bodies. In More's parable, virginity is a metaphor of moral integrity, which contrasts with physical vulnerability. In Spenser's allegory of Lust, virginity is related metonymically to physical integrity, and, for women, both are equally at risk. More's metaphoric wordplay underscores by contrast the metonymic continuity of deflowering and devouring in the allegory of Lust. In turn, the metonymically linked injuries to which Amoret is subject in this episode contrast pointedly with Busirane's metaphoric attack on her chastity in Book III. Although with his magic arts Busirane has opened a wide wound in Amoret's "bleeding brest" and "riven bowels" (3.12.38.4), and has forced her to carry her transfixed heart in a basin, her love for Scudamore remains unchanged. As the narrator comments, "A thousand charmes he formerly did proue; / Yet thousand charmes could not her stedfast heart remoue" (3.12.31.8–9). When Britomart forces Busirane to reverse his spell, Amoret's wound is closed "as it had not bene bor'd" (3.12.38.5) and her body is restored "as she were neuer hurt" (3.12.38.7). Amoret's beleaguered body is the site of struggle between modes of signification. In Book III, the metaphoric integrity and self-possession that represent Amoret's chastity allow her to resist Busirane, allow her to resist being incorporated into his system of Petrarchan metaphor. However violent the struggle, Busirane ultimately loses and Amoret controls how her body is to be read. In Book

IV, the metonymic slippage from deflowering to devouring underscores the uncertainty of how the body is to be read. There is deliberate ambiguity about whether Amoret is at all responsible for her abduction by Lust and, indeed, it is not clear whether she is the subject or object of the lust so personified.[3] When Belphoebe sees Timias comforting Amoret after their fight with Lust, Belphoebe is certain that Timias has betrayed her with Amoret, but Spenser's text offers less than incontrovertible support of Belphoebe's reading. Rather, it is Belphoebe's readerly authority, as the object of Timias' devotion and as an allegorical embodiment of the reigning monarch, that validates her interpretation and then allows her to supersede her judgment of Timias when she restores him to favor. When the disgraced Timias pleads with Belphoebe, his language registers her arbitrary power:

> Ne any but your selfe, O dearest dred,
>> Hath done this wrong, to wreake on worthlesse wight
>> Your high displesure, through misdeeming bred:
>> That when your pleasure is to deeme aright,
>> Ye may redresse, and me restore to light.
>>> (4.8.17.1–5)

The "misdeeming" that bred her displeasure can be either misunderstanding or misjudgment. Although Timias complains, he resists criticizing his lady's judgment unambiguously. Similarly Timias acknowledges that deeming aright is a function of royal pleasure.[4] In the transactions between Timias and Belphoebe, the social dimension of the body takes precedence over its function as a figure of wholeness, soundness, and integrity.

THE MIRROR OF LUST:
THE LIMITS OF SPECULARITY

The Lust episode critiques the Sidnean project of "mak[ing] many" Cyruses by examining how the body impinges on the sort of moral-tropological imitation Sidney advocates. Amoret's predicament focuses thematic attention on the body as it is subject or resistant to moral interpretation. The figure of Lust, a grotesque compilation of body parts, focuses attention on the relationship of reader and text as readers look to the text as a mirror of their condition. Book III shows the reader allegorical representations of reading. Reading and acting are presented as metaphoric counterparts. Britomart's adventures in Book III and our reading of Book III are presented as parallel quests: both reader and heroine pursue heroic activity and perfect exegetical skills. In Book III, Britomart is a role model for the reader and moral-tropological allegory involves imitating her in a complex way. Book III subjects the act of reading, broadly conceived, to moral evaluation. Misreading can result in deforming what one reads or in being deformed by it. Book III implicitly contrasts right reading as using the text as a mirror that gives us images to imitate in our own lives with the misreading and misuse of the text as an instrument of narcissistic solipsism.

Lust is an important figure in the critique Book IV directs toward the unproblematic specular, mirror-image transactions between reader and text assumed by Book III. Lust is a personification allegory but also a witty figure of prosopopoeia. Prosopopoeia, the rhetorical figure that gives voice to inanimate objects, literally means "to make a face" (*OED* s.v. "prosopopoeia"). In the figure of Lust, Spenser has made a face of male genitalia, a thoroughly ignoble prosopopoeia.[5] As Paul de Man has pointed out in his essay "Autobiography as De-facement," prosopopoeia figures the mutual substitution of reader and text. In grave inscriptions, the quintessential prosopopoeia, *sta viator* (stay traveler), both gives voice to the deceased as it figuratively addresses the traveler and gives a kind of death to the passing traveler who, by reading the inscription, occupies the rhetorical position of the deceased. Spenser's prosopopoeia is de-facement of an irreverent sort. He constructs a male-identified figure of desire and presents it to female view, terrified in the case of Amoret and Æmylia, dispassionately appreciative in the case of Belphoebe:

> Yet ouer him she there long gazing stood,
> And oft admir'd his monstrous shape, and oft
> His mighty limbs, whilest all with filthy bloud
> The place there ouerflowne, seemd like a sodaine flood.
> (4.7.32.6–9)

The multiple perspectives of Amoret, Æmylia, and Belphoebe on Lust destabilize the homosocial economy that has the female as place-holder and object of male desire. Moreover, by calling attention to the gendered quality of the gaze, Spenser raises questions about the specular transaction between reader and text. In Book III, all readers are to follow Britomart's adventures and recognize female otherness as part of the human condition. What is the (probably male) reader to recognize in contemplating the face of Lust? And what imitate? The in-your-face irreverence of the figure is a reminder to us all, I think, that there are practical as well as systemic limits to moral allegory. We can, as it were, hold the mirror up to nature and show vice his or her own feature only by maintaining a discreet aesthetic distance.

TIMIAS AND THE "ROLE MODEL" MODEL

Timias' fight with Lust critiques the moral-tropological model by narrative means. Here, as in other appearances in *The Faerie Queene*, Timias attempts to be a perfect Sidnean and act out his ideals. The results are rather bittersweet comedy as Timias demonstrates the difficulties of putting theory into practice. In Book III, he succeeds in living the ideal of the selfless Petrarchan lover of an unattainable lady with great difficulty and at considerable personal cost. Here, he attempts to be the chivalrous protector of women and wounds Amoret, who has been turned into a literal human shield by her captor. Not only do good intentions miscarry in his rescue of Amoret, but his idealism exposes the inconsistency in what, throughout Book IV, is practiced in the name of chivalry. The knights battle, not to shield ladies, but to prove their prowess and win one lady as a prize. As is made explicit with Amoret in canto x, the lady doubles the shield as the object of phallic aggression. At the end of canto ix, Arthur articulates the distance marked out by his squire Timias between chivalric practice and its ideals when he excoriates a group of knights for fighting over False Florimell:

> To whom the Prince thus goodly well replied;
>   Certes sir Knight, ye seemen much to blame,
>   To rip vp wrong, that battell once hath tried;
>   Wherein the honor both of Armes ye shame,
>   And eke the loue of Ladies foule defame;
>   To whom the world this franchise euer yeelded,
>   That of their loues choise they might freedom clame,
>   And in that right should by all knights be shielded:
> Gainst which me seemes this war ye wrongfully haue wielded.
>   (4.9.37)

Although Arthur directs this condemnation at the false knights Claribell, Blandamour, Paridell, and Druon, it applies with equal force to the true knights as well, virtually none of whom fights to shield the lady's free choice.

Timias' battle calls into question its own evident moral significance as "fighting lust." In this regard, the episode is an extreme instance of many such throughout *The Faerie Queene* in which fighting an allegorical personification fails to coincide completely with solving the problem that figure represents. For example, the Redcrosse Knight finds that slaying the monster Errour does not eliminate the problem of error and is only the first step in his education as a knight errant.[6] In Book II, Guyon faces the task of fighting Furor without succumbing to the vice his opponent represents and becoming furious himself.[7] As William Oram has pointed out, "the battle itself becomes an erotic exchange. Whenever Timias's sword lights on Amoret 'with any little blow . . . Then would [Lust] laugh aloud, and gather great delight' (IV.vii.26). Timias is in a terrible situation: his best efforts seem doomed to bring about just what he doesn't want" ("Elizabethan fact" 43).

Timias' fight with Lust raises the moral, psychological and semiological issues of the above episodes and raises the consideration of those issues to a higher level of complexity. From one perspective, it seems that Timias' difficulty is a function of the terms of armed aggression in which his struggle is couched allegorically. One might imagine taking cold showers (or the Elizabethan equivalent thereof) as a more practical means of fighting lust than waving phallic symbols.[8] From another perspective, however, the choice of symbols might be less fortuitous than first appears. The episode allows the interpretation that the way to fight lust is to satisfy it.[9] The fight between Timias and Lust thus enacts the body's resistance to unambiguous signification. That is to say, bodies get in the way of the moral allegory. The meaning of Timias' virtuous opposition to vice is compromised when Amoret's body is interposed between the combatants.

Like Britomart and Artegall in canto vi, Timias stumbles into a sexual relation. The combat, which theoretically carries a determinate meaning—the winner is the winner by definition—acquires complex and complicating erotic significance. Instead of doubling the shield of Cupid as prize and guarantor of prowess as in the Temple of Venus,

Amoret literally doubles as the shield of Lust. The gender ideology that invokes male service and protection to justify male dominance is destabilized by gendered bodies and parts thereof. Belphoebe, who kills Lust and then stands over him "long gazing," has the power to stabilize meaning. But she also has the power to question Timias and not stay for an answer. "Is this the faith, she said, and said no more, / But turnd her face, and fled away for euermore" (4.7.36.8–9). Everyone not so empowered is left to cope.

8

The Marriage of Thames and Medway and the Union of Florimell and Marinell
Plenitude and Closure

Although Book IV is probably the most diffuse and problematic book of *The Faerie Queene*, one that, as Jonathan Goldberg argues, emphasizes its own resistance to closure, it ends with the marriage of Thames and Medway and the restoration of Florimell to the finally responsive Marinell.[1] To be sure, the union of an etiolated knight with a shamefast lady is conspicuously tentative. As Goldberg points out, the consummation is left "to another place . . . to be perfected" (4.12.35.9).[2] Nevertheless, this is a conspicuous gesture toward closure, however problematic that closure may be. At the conclusion of Book IV, marriage figures as an alternative to the joust as a paradigm of institutional order and as a figure of textual functioning. Throughout Book IV, the joust provides a model of an institution that perpetuates strife in an ill-conceived attempt to assure order. In addition, the combat of Cambel and Triamond stages a textual free-for-all in which genealogical conceptions of order are set against teleological ones. In that battle, what begins as a metonymic figure for institutional order becomes a means of self-reflexive exploration of the ordering principles of the text itself. The marriage of Thames and Medway provides a model for the functioning of the text in which fluidity substitutes for rigid structures of order and control.[3] Natural generation evoked by the plenitude of rivers becomes an analogy for the generation of the text as the narrator undertakes to name all of the guests at the House of Proteus. This paradigmatic act of reference— the act of naming—in turn becomes the occasion for a reflection on the nature of referentiality.[4]

FLORIMELL AND MARINELL:
A NEW PAIR OF LOVERS TO CENTER STAGE

At the opening of canto xi, the Spenserian narrator reassumes control from Scudamore and the story of Florimell and Marinell replaces that of Scudamore and Amoret as the paradigm of desire. The narrator returns on an Ariostan note of mock regret:[5]

> BVt ah for pittie that I haue thus long
>   Left a fayre Ladie languishing in payne:
>   Now well away, that I haue doen such wrong,
>   To let faire *Florimell* in bands remayne,
>   In bands of loue, and in sad thraldomes chayne;
>   From which vnlesse some heauenly powre her free
>   By miracle, not yet appearing playne,
>   She lenger yet is like captiu'd to bee:
> That euen to thinke thereof, it inly pitties mee.
>
> Here neede you to remember, how erewhile
>   Vnlouely *Proteus*, missing to his mind
>   That Virgins loue to win by wit or wile,
>   Her threw into a dongeon deepe and blind,
>   And there in chaynes her cruelly did bind,
>   In hope thereby her to his bent to draw:
>   For when as neither gifts nor graces kind
>   Her constant mind could moue at all he saw,
> He thought her to compell by crueltie and awe.
>   (4.11.1–2)

Spenser calls attention to his authorial control over his characters in a transparent little fiction of narrative remorse. In addition to recalling Ariostan mockery, Spenser's lines recall the Chaucerian formula "pitee renneth soone in gentil herte," in "The Squire's Tale" (F 479).[6] Ariostan distance and control coexist with Chaucerian compassion as Spenser refigures the relationship of author and text. Authorial pity is not simply a narrative convention. Rather, Spenser's expression of pity for Florimell points to the temporality of reading and writing. Although the inscribed regret is an ironic convention, it is perfectly true that an author can read what he has already written; both author and text exist in time. This subtle reference to the flow of time introduces a full-scale exploration of fluidity as an intellectual paradigm. Spenser draws on Neoplatonic notions of reality as a series of unfoldings of an infolded wholeness to posit an alternative to a paradigm of fixed totalities that can be wholly possessed by the intellect.[7]

Accordingly, Spenser posits and subverts images of possession and control. The narrator who is responsible for Florimell's imprisonment becomes an analogue for Busirane, who pens Amoret in Book III. But, whereas in Book III the scene of writing is represented in the text, here authorial penning explicitly transgresses boundaries of writer and reader and writer and written. The opening stanzas invite the collusion of the reader: the reader's putative act of remembering how Florimell's story left off corresponds to the narrator's fictive act of abandoning her. The doubling of narrator and reader, as both collude in the fiction of Florimell's book-length imprisonment, reveals narrative continuity to be a discursive effect. Moreover, Spenser's recursive move from representing writing as imprisonment in the allegory of Busirane to representing his own writing as imprisonment, or rather, positing that a fictional character is left in prison because the author writes about something else, opens an exploration of the figurative nature of the trope writing-as-prison. Florimell's fictional jailer calls attention to the games being played with conventional textual categories. In a reversal of the topos of the binding of Proteus, Proteus binds Florimell in chains "in hope thereby her to his bent to draw" (4.11.2.6). Traditionally the figure of change and process, Proteus has been ironically reified into a villainous prison-keeper. The mythic project of binding Proteus carries the traditional interpretation that knowledge is the reward for somehow containing the forces of fluidity and change.[8] Spenser both binds and unbinds Proteus. Proteus is reified as a figure *in* the text, only to be diffused as a figure *of* the text when the House of Proteus becomes the setting for the marriage of rivers. The insight gained from this binding and unbinding of Proteus, as he transgresses boundaries of "in the text" and "of the text," is the fluid nature of those categories, as Spenser develops his alternative model of Neoplatonic implication-explication.

Spenser explores textual unfoldings specifically by transforming models of desire. The concluding movement of Book IV begins by establishing both Florimell and Marinell as, figuratively, prisoners of love: Florimell imprisoned by Proteus because of her constancy to Marinell, Marinell in his mother's thrall (4.11.7.6) because of the injuries inflicted on him by a woman. The model of love as imprisonment is transformed subtly to one that figures desire as being infolded in some greater totality. This model of desire as implication proves to be extremely productive. Marinell's appearance in the story, coming hard upon the disappearance of Scudamore and Amoret from Spenser's text, has the effect of remotivating the wound of desire. In canto x, Scudamore's self-contained, autobiographical flashback conflates the cause and cure of Eurydice's wound in an account of seeking and carrying off a lady as a prize that justifies the heroic enterprise. At the opening of canto xi, a brief narrative flashback that recalls Marinell's wound as his story is to be continued focuses the contrast to the unhappy story of Amoret and Scudamore by reworking some of its major motifs:

> And all this was for loue of *Marinell,*
> > Who her despysd (ah who would her despyse?)
> > And wemens loue did from his hart expell,
> > And all those ioyes that weake mankind entyse.
> > Nathlesse his pride full dearely he did pryse;
> > For of a womans hand it was ywroke,
> > That of the wound he yet in languor lyes,
> > Ne can be cured of that cruell stroke
> > Which *Britomart* him gaue, when he did her prouoke.
> > > (4.11.5)

The complex pun "nathlesse his pride full dearely he did pryse" recalls the earlier play on "prise/emprize" (4.10.4) in Scudamore's flashback. Marinell both prices and prizes his pride (*OED* s.vv. "pryse, pryce"; "price" 1, 2, 4, 5). He pays the price for his haughty disdain of women and he asserts the value of his pride. Whereas the play on "prise/emprize" figures a relationship of categorical containment and separation, the pun prize/price suggests the more dynamic interplay of positing and feedback. The price of Marinell's pride is both determined and discovered by what he pays: that is, by both what he is willing to pay and what he is required to pay. The economy of Marinell's pride is clearly not a structure of totalization but depends on interaction (sometimes painful) with something Out There. In contrast, the structure of reward for Scudamore's quest suppresses feedback by making the lady a supplement. She marks his success by remaining aloof from his battles, a virginal sign both of victory and unfulfillable desire.

Marinell and Scudamore represent ironic counterparts as the story of each reworks motifs of analogous myths. The myth of Orpheus enacted by Scudamore and that of Narcissus explicitly identified with

Marinell both concern looking as, among other things, an epistemological paradigm. Moreover, Scudamore's autobiographical account of his Orpheus-like quest after Amoret manifests a certain narcissistic mirroring of narrating and narrated "I," of the speaker and his past self. If Scudamore shares Marinell's narcissism, Marinell proleptically parodies the narrative retrojection at the heart of Scudamore's flashback account of the rape and rescue of Amoret when he encounters Britomart in canto vi of Book III.[9] In this episode, Marinell experiences a narrative retrojection all his own. We are told that Florimell leaves Gloriana's court after hearing of Marinell's injury while Britomart encounters Florimell narratively prior to attacking Marinell. Marinell seems to have been knocked into the middle of last week by Britomart; however, what is at issue is not simply the violence of the encounter but the fact that the temporal slippage is demarcated by transactions between Marinell and two women. What seems a purely narrative glitch brings our attention to Marinell's paradoxical relationship to women. Although the narrator exclaims "this was that woman, this that deadly wound" (3.4.28.1) when Britomart overthrows Marinell, we note that Florimell, as well as Britomart, merits the designation as the woman fated to wound him.

While Proteus' prophecy and its fulfillment seem to delineate a closed narrative structure, Marinell's story turns out to be more truly protean a narrative than is Scudamore's encapsulated autobiography. Cymoent's interpretation of Proteus' prophecy affects her son's life, and, as she alters her interpretation in response to feedback, so the shape of his life changes. By warning her son to avoid the love of women, Cymoent infantilizes Marinell and makes him vulnerable to women's power.[10] After Britomart impales Marinell, enacting the emasculation of men who fear women, Cymoent revises her reading and decides that "they that loue do liue" (3.4.37.5). When Marinell returns from Proteus' House dying of love for Florimell, his mother first temporizes over whether the prophecy refers to the love of nymphs or of women, then disregards it altogether and seeks help from other authorities. The changing shape of Marinell's story reveals reading to be part of the narrative process, in direct contrast to Scudamore's autobiography, which asserts control over the process of reading and presents reading as a form of control.

The narratives of both Marinell and Scudamore link the search for assurance with the denial of desire. What is presented thematically in Marinell's story reappears as textual process with Scudamore. Marinell seeks safety by fleeing love. Scudamore seeks closure by eliding female otherness. Amoret and Florimell reverse this relationship of thematics to poetics. Amoret's imprisonment by Busirane is a thematic penning. Florimell is left in prison by the narrator's neglect. If Amoret's imprisonment represents the scene of writing *mise en abyme*, Florimell is *prise de l'abyme* as her state is termed a function of the narrator's writing. Mirror-image reflections of theme and process call into question the categorical distinction between a narrative and its frame. We see, instead, a complex interplay between the stories we tell and how we tell stories.

REFIGURING THE TOTALITY

The substitution of Marinell and Florimell for Scudamore and Amoret and of the fluid interplay of the story and its frame for narrative closure introduces a full-scale exploration of referentiality with the marriage of Thames and Medway. This elaborate set-piece offers invention, with the dual sense of finding and making up, as an alternative to narcissistic closure, as it enacts a process of feedback and flow between what one posits as the object of reference and the act of reference itself. Instead of a one-to-one relationship between independent objects and discrete verbal signs, the river marriage offers a Neoplatonic model of universal flow in which what is in the text and what is Out There are both unfoldings of a larger, infolded, never-fully-knowable whole.[11]

Spenser invokes the inexpressibility topos in an overview of this process:

> But what doe I their names seeke to reherse,
>   Which all the world haue with their issue fild?
>   How can they all in this so narrow verse
>   Contayned be, and in small compasse hild?
>   Let them record them, that are better skild,
>   And know the moniments of passed times:
>   Onely what needeth, shall be here fulfild,
>   T'expresse some part of that great equipage,
> Which from great *Neptune* do deriue their parentage.
>   (4.11.17)

The narrator disclaims pretensions to exhaustive naming while he wittily underscores the problematic nature of the guest list, the rehearsal of which fills most of the canto. The pun on "deriue" epitomizes the fluid process of infolding-unfolding. Most obviously, the term signifies both to flow from (*OED* s.v. "derive" 1.1) and to trace back (*OED* s.v. "derive" 1.10). In addition, there may be playful hints of de-rivering, as Spenser's mythopoeic imagination turns rivers into wedding guests.[12]

The list of names that provides the framework of the episode both imposes and subverts linear order since the object of sequential reference is a system in flux.[13] Spenser provides multiple figures and myths of origin while playing the intellectual move "ad fontes" against fluvial movement to the sea. Neptune is father to both sea gods and founders of nations. These genealogies treat complementary political myths: the passing of authority down from father to son and the tracing of authority back to a mythical founder. After Neptune come Ocean and Tethys, whose offspring "afterward both sea and land possest" (4.11.18.4). As A. C. Hamilton, citing Harry Berger, Jr., remarks, "afterward" refers back to the sea gods and founders and forward to the rivers.[14] Moreover, while Ocean and Tethys precede their offspring in the mythical genealogy and fictional procession, rivers flow from their geographic source toward the sea. The parents of the bridegroom, the Thames' tributaries Thame and Isis, are said to go before the groom. The Thames' tributaries precede the Thames: water flows from them into the larger river and they are positioned "before" or behind the Thames with respect to the Thames' outlet in the sea. But the fiction of the wedding procession suggests that the parents go before, that is, in front of the Thames with respect to the sea, contrary to geography. Each tracing back and forth is but one unfolding, one explication of the whole process. This fluidity informs mythopoeia as well. If multiple etiological myths are possible, from where does mythmaking derive its authority and how does it exert its influence? The force of myth seems to be cumulative as the accretion of stories answers a residue of needs.

The river marriage presents us with multiple ways of looking at this totality that accommodate the fixed to the flowing by subverting the power of visualization. Although Spenser provides an abundance of visual detail, it is often impossible to put the details together to form a coherent picture. Consider the description of the groom's parents:

> So went he playing on the watery plaine.
>   Soone after whom the louely Bridegroome came,
>   The noble Thamis, with all his goodly traine,
>   But him before there went, as best became,
>   His auncient parents, namely th'auncient Thame.
>   But much more aged was his wife then he,
>   The Ouze, whom men doe Isis rightly name;
>   Full weake and crooked creature seemed shee,
> And almost blind through eld, that scarce her way could see.
>
> Therefore on either side she was sustained
>   Of two smal grooms, which by their names were hight
>   The *Churne*, and *Charwell*, two small streames, which pained
>   Them selues her footing to direct aright,
>   Which fayled oft through faint and feeble plight:
>   But *Thame* was stronger, and of better stay;
>   Yet seem'd full aged by his outward sight,
>   With head all hoary, and his beard all gray,
> Deawed with siluer drops, that trickled downe alway.
>
>   (4.11.24–25)

As Calvin Edwards observes, Spenser "makes us see at once the person in the river and the river in the person."[15] Trying, however, to imagine both the winding system of rivers and the aged couple at the same time is rather like watching one of those 1930s cartoons in which dogwood blossoms turn into yapping puppies and then back into flowers. Instead of being able to take in the scene with one imaginative *coup d'oeil*, and take this point of view for granted, the reader must go with the flow and shift from one theoretical orientation— one way of looking—to another.

Spenser points to his own theoretical orientation and suggests how his poetry engages a plenitude that exceeds the capacity of that poetry to contain it in the stanzas concluding canto xi and opening canto xii:

> And yet besides three thousand more there were
>   Of th'Oceans seede, but *Ioues* and *Phœbus* kinde;
>   The which in floods and fountaines doe appere,
> And all mankinde do nourish with their waters clere.
>
> The which, more eath it were for mortall wight,
>   To tell the sands, or count the starres on hye,
>   Or ought more hard, then thinke to reckon right.

But well I wote, that these which I descry,
Were present at this great solemnity:
And there amongst the rest, the mother was
Of luckelesse *Marinell Cymodoce*.
Which, for my Muse her selfe now tyred has,
Vnto an other Canto I will ouerpas.

O What an endlesse worke haue I in hand,
    To count the seas abundant progeny,
    Whose fruitfull seede farre passeth those in land,
    And also those which wonne in th'azure sky?
    For much more eath to tell the starres on hy,
    Albe they endlesse seeme in estimation,
    Then to recount the Seas posterity:
    So fertile be the flouds in generation,
So huge their numbers, and so numberlesse their nation.
                                    (4.11.52.6–53,12.1)

The extended pun on count and recount presents counting as a special case of referentiality and measures Spenser's enterprise against it. The endless work of counting the seas' progeny contrasts with counting the sands or the seemingly endless stars. What Spenser presents as a difference in degree of difficulty may also be understood according to mathematical ideas current in the sixteenth century, as a difference in kind, specifically the difference between denumerability and non-denumerability.[16] While sands and stars can, in principle, be counted, the seas are numberless insofar as they are non-denumerably abundant. Nevertheless, Spenser claims, despite the theoretical impossibility of counting the seas' progeny, that all were present in the House of Proteus, wedding guests in his allegory of universal, flowing plenitude.

By implication, the nature of poetic reference depends on the object of that reference. To assume a necessary one-to-one relationship between text and referent may be seeking to count what is really uncountable. And despite the emphasis on naming the wedding guests at the marriage of Thames and Medway, the fundamental poetic strategy of the episode is not establishing a correspondence between name and referent. Rather, Spenser's imagination plays over the map of the British Isles, as well as catalogues and etymological dictionaries, and fastens on salient details of geography and etymology.[17] Of what he finds and what he fashions the poet creates his allegory of the river marriage.[18]

Spenserian invention brings together what the poet finds and what he makes up and claims validity insofar as the generation of the text and natural generation are both unfoldings of the same plenitude. Spenser finally introduces the term invention at the opening of canto xii, having demonstrated it through most of the previous canto:

> Therefore the antique wisards well inuented,
>   That *Venus* of the fomy sea was bred;
>   For that the seas by her are most augmented.
>   Witnesse th'exceeding fry, which there are fed,
>   And wondrous sholes, which may of none be red.
>   Then blame me not, if I haue err'd in count
>   Of Gods, of Nymphs, of riuers yet vnred:
>   For though their numbers do much more surmount,
> Yet all those same were there, which erst I did recount.
>   (4.12.2)

The joke about "wondrous sholes, which may of none be red" links natural plenitude to poetic creation. On the one hand, marine abundance exceeds the power of human understanding. On the other, no one may read of these fry and "sholes" until Spenser has written about them.

The reference to Venus brings the issue of gender ideology to the foreground. Spenser's Neoplatonic model of unfolding plenitude offers a salutary alternative to sexual binarism. In this account, Venus' invention does not depend on the prior castration of Uranus.[19] Spenser revises another myth of castration, the Cybele myth, as he describes Troynovant-London crowning the Thames to show how invention provides a less damaging alternative. The bridegroom Thames is compared to the goddess Cybele. The coronet he wears, in an allusion both to the turreted towers of sixteenth-century London and to the convention of marking the capital city with a crown on sixteenth-century maps, is likened to Cybele's turreted crown:[20]

> But he their sonne full fresh and iolly was,
>   All decked in a robe of watchet hew,
>   On which the waues, glittering like Christall glas,
>   So cunningly enwouen were, that few
>   Could weenen, whether they were false or trew.
>   And on his head like to a Coronet
>   He wore, that seemed strange to common vew,
>   In which were many towres and castels set,
> That it encompast round as with a golden fret.

> Like as the mother of the Gods, they say,
>   In her great iron charet wonts to ride,
>   When to *Ioues* pallace she doth take her way:
>   Old *Cybele*, arayd with pompous pride,
>   Wearing a Diademe embattild wide
>   With hundred turrets, like a Turribant.
>   With such an one was Thamis beautifide;
>   That was to weet the famous Troynouant,
> In which her kingdomes throne is chiefly resiant.
>   (4.11.27–28)

Critics have noted the shift in pronoun gender in stanza 28, line 9. In his edition, Hamilton suggests that "her" refers to Troynovant or obliquely to the Faerie Queene. He cites Berger's suggestion that Cybele is the antecedent and Church's eighteenth-century emendation of "her" to "his." What has not been noted is the analogous, but pernicious pronoun shift in Catullus' poem about Cybele. There the shift to the feminine pronoun inscribes the self-castration of Cybele's follower Attis:[21]

> Svper alta vectus Attis celeri rate maria
> Phrygium ut nemus citato cupide pedi tetigit
> adiitque opaca silvis redimita loca deae,
> stimulatus ibi furente rabie, vague animi,
> devolvit ili acuto sibi pondera silece.
> itaque ut relicta sensit sibi membra sine viro,
> etiam recente terrae sola sanguine maculans
> niveis citata cepit manibus leve tympanum,
> tympanum tuom, Cybebe, tua, Mater, initia.
> quatiensque terga tauri teneris cava digitis
> canere haec suis adortast tremebunda comitibus.
>   (*Poems of Catullus* 63.1–11)

[Borne in his swift bark over deep seas, Attis, when eagerly with speedy foot he reached the Phyrgian woodland, and entered the goddess's abodes, shadowy, forest-crowned; there, goaded by raging madness, bewildered in mind, he cast down from him with sharp flint-stone the burden of his members. So when she felt her limbs to have lost their manhood, still with fresh blood dabbling the face of the ground, swiftly with snowy hands she seized the light timbrel, your timbrel, Cybele, thy mysteries, Mother, and shaking with soft fingers the hollow oxhide thus began she to sing to her companions tremulously:]

Catullus teasingly keeps the reader waiting for the reference to Attis as "she" by a series of words that seem to but do not refer to her. She has been abandoned, *relicta,* but it is the abandoned *membra* to which the apparent feminine refers. She is alone, *sola,* but *sola* here refers to the ground that has been stained with her blood. It is not until *citata* in line 8 that Attis is marked as feminine. In line 11, Attis is identified by the pronoun *haec,* she, as she begins to sing tremblingly, *tremebunda.*[22] The Catullus poem reveals a gender economy with the female as dangerous supplement.[23] The masculine is taken to be normative and universal and the feminine, while gender-marked and extrinsic, nevertheless marks a lack. In Spenser's version, pronouns are fluid in reference and pronoun shifts are reversible. The crown of Troynovant concurrently maps a myth of civic origins, details of geography and architecture and Spenser's allegorical invention. Multiple unfoldings of a greater plenitude provide an alternative to the castrating economy of absence and presence.[24]

MARINELL AND FLORIMELL UNITED
BY TRIAL AND ERROR

Having crafted an elaborate set-piece to elucidate a Neoplatonic model of fluid plenitude, Spenser shows theoria trickling down into praxis as Marinell and Florimell achieve their own union, of sorts. Marinell presents a comic figure of transition from set piece to story. Excluded from the ceremony for being half-mortal, he wanders around the unoccupied rooms until he overhears Florimell, and the pair enact the transformation of mythic archetypes. Marinell has descended to a nether world as Orpheus has but encounters not Eurydice as object of the gaze but an Echo who, heard and not seen, rescues him from narcissism.[25] The story of Florimell and Marinell takes up the other half of signification.[26] The marriage of Thames and Medway examines the relationship of text to referent. The encounter of Florimell and Marinell focuses on the relationship of voice to audience, as Florimell laments, "But O vaine iudgement, and conditions vaine, / The which the prisoner points vnto the free" (4.12.11.1–2). Although her complaint echoes both the lament of Orpheus for Eurydice and the curse of the nameless youth upon Narcissus, Florimell gets more propitious results than either Ovidian precursor.[27] When Marinell hears the complaint and understands himself to be the cause of her suffering, his heart is "toucht with soft remorse and pitty rare"

(4.12.12.5) and he wishes for the power "to redresse" (4.12.12.8) her. The orphic pattern of retrospection and retrojection tragically enacted by Scudamore and Amoret is replaced by the pattern of remorse and redress that brings Florimell and Marinell together. Scudamore achieves closure by positioning himself on an arbitrary endpoint and looking back to an origin conceived as the specular counterpart of the endpoint. Marinell goes with the flow. The remorse he feels is a looking back that admits its own powerlessness and the redress he desires is a looking forward from the context of the past. Both sorts of looking implicitly measure what is perceived of past occurrences against what might have been done or what might be done in improvement; that is, they measure theoria against praxis.

Encapsulated in Spenser's text is a complex scene of semiosis. Although Florimell complains of the limitations of her lyric utterance, the narrative circumstances in which that utterance is embedded subvert her claim of powerlessness. She laments her inability as prisoner to point to the free while she addresses her lyric complaint directly to Marinell: "But where so loose or happy that thou art, / Know *Marinell* that all this is for thee" (4.12.11.6–7). Spenser plays on multiple meanings of "point" as "to indicate position" or "to direct thought in a certain direction" (*OED* s.v. "point" vb. 1.9) and as the aphetic form of appoint "to prescribe" (*OED* s.v. "appoint" 2.7). Florimell's literal powerlessness—as prisoner she is in no position to give directions to one who is free—indicates a broader problem of pointing as reference. The lovesick woman cannot be satisfied by a discursive construct as fictional audience or as lover. Florimell's predicament seems to replicate that of the poet trapped in the prison-house of language whose lyric utterance can never dependably refer beyond itself nor control its reception. More specifically, Florimell's dissatisfaction with a discursively constructed audience mirrors Spenser's revisionary concern with the construction of the reader as he moves from Book III to Book IV.

Florimell's pose of helplessness turns out not to be justified, however. Ironically, Marinell overhears Florimell's lyric despair and falls in love with her. Like Chaucer's Canacee and unlike the Spenserian characters ostensibly taken from "The Squire's Tale," Marinell's desire is grounded in pity.[28] For him, compassion is, in part, sharing the experience of authorial limitation. Marinell understands himself to be an author who cannot invent a happy ending to the sad story he has a hand in creating. Spenser places a scene of lyric utterance in a narrative frame that subverts its denial of signification. The representation in the text of voicing and audition implicitly raises the question of the text's relationship to its own audience and the problem of contextualizing narrative.

In "Signature Event Context," Jacques Derrida has noted that while context determines signification, it is impossible for a text to determine its own context (1–23).[29] Some four centuries earlier, Spenser shows a narrative frame empowering an act of semiosis while denying the explicit content of the semiosis. What claims can the entire package make on Spenser's readers? What is presented is, I think, an alternative construction of meaning. The uniting of Florimell and Marinell both doubles and frames the marriage of Thames and Medway. The human lovers go with the flow: rather than being subject or object of totalization strategies, they are implicated in infolded structures, larger than the two of them. Their mutual embeddedness, such that each participates in the other's discourse but does not control it, points the pair toward a felicitous conclusion. In some ways, the story of Florimell and Marinell is what the allegorical set-piece "means" when meaning is conceived as narrative. Instead of being given the meaning of narrative, we see meaning as narrative, as an unfolding rather than as an encapsulation of a greater plenitude. In this connection, a joke used by the anthropologist Gregory Bateson to illustrate his theory of human cognition is germane:

> A man wanted to know about mind, not in nature, but in his private large computer. He asked it (no doubt in his best Fortran), "Do you compute that you will ever think like a human being?" The machine then set to work to analyze its own computational habits. Finally, the machine printed its answer on a piece of paper, as such machines do. The man ran to get the answer and found, neatly typed, the words: THAT REMINDS ME OF A STORY
>
> (14)

The recourse to narrative as explanation is, moreover, central to the humanist rhetorical tradition Spenser would have inherited (and, indeed, had the authority of Jesus's parables). As Arthur Kinney points out, the standard procedure of humanist rhetoric was to illustrate each abstract point with an anecdote (24–25). The final cantos of Book IV suggest that insofar as narrative is grounded, it is grounded in a relationship among reader, text and referent. As Kinney describes it, "For the humanists, poetics was *never* a matter of aesthetic enjoyment alone but always an instructive activity that made reading exploratory, an activity in which the reader, responding dialectically to the text, found closure to that text only in his own judgment or interpretation" (45).

WHO NEEDS CLOSURE?

The conclusion does not so much question the possibility of closure as suggest why not having closure might be a good thing after all. In being sought by a woman who had refused a god, Marinell gets the validation the jousting knights seek endlessly, but it is a validation that can only be seen in genuine retrospect. It cannot be planned in advance and retrojected. Spenser calls attention with wordplay to the arbitrary way the story concludes. Marinell happens on Florimell "as he to and fro by chaunce did trace, / There vnto him betid a disauentrous case" (4.12.4.8–9).[30] "Disauentrous" here can signify both disastrous (*OED* s.v. "disadventurous") and nonaccidental (*OED* s.v. "adventurous" 1). The prefix both intensifies and contradicts the root: Marinell's encounter with Florimell is both a traumatic accident and an arbitrary manipulation of the plot. Spenser shows narrative cut loose from any source of validation as he constructs a plot that, in a glorious paradox, vindicates such indeterminacy. What emerges is that precisely because discourse is de-centered, some orientations work better than others. Having been subdued by Cupid to love Florimell, Marinell indulges in what seems to be a comically futile series of contingency plans:

> Now gan he in his grieued minde deuise,
>> How from that dungeon he might her enlarge:
>> Some while he thought, by faire and humble wise
>> To *Proteus* selfe to sue for her discharge:
>> But then he fear'd his mothers former charge
>> Gainst womens loue, long giuen him in vaine.
>> Then gan he thinke, perforce with sword and targe
>> Her forth to fetch, and *Proteus* to constraine:
>> But soone he gan such folly to forthinke againe.
>
> Then did he cast to steale her thence away,
>> And with him beare, where none of her might know.
>> But all in vaine: for why he found no way
>> To enter in, or issue forth below:
>> For all about that rocke the sea did flow.

> And though vnto his will she giuen were,
> Yet without ship or bote her thence to row,
> He wist not how her thence away to bere;
> And daunger well he wist long to continue there.
>
> (4.12.14–15)

While Marinell consciously rejects each of his own plots to liberate
Florimell, we can see a discursive shift operating through Spenser's indirect description of those plots, a shift that repositions Florimell and
Marinell favorably vis-à-vis the erotic structures of Book IV. The reference to enlarging Florimell is a felicitous pun that aligns loss of virginity with pregnancy and liberation instead of with the binary phallic structures of absence and presence defined by virginity throughout
Book IV. The pun marks a liberation from repressive and dysfunctional discursive structures: virginity is temporarily liberated from the
economy of male homosocial desire. Marinell enjoys a complementary
enlargement in the range of the animal imagery with which he is described. Once the sacrificial ox, in Book IV he goes from being Cupid's
mount to a hind who mourns her lost calf (4.12.17). Marinell's enactment of female roles at the conclusion of Book IV represents, not the
castration of the ox, but the unfolding of a larger reality. The comparison to the hind recalls Scudamore in the 1590 conclusion as "a Deare,
that greedily embays / In the coole soile" (1590.3.12.44.7–8). Marinell
has fortuitously achieved the androgynous fluidity sacrificed by
Scudamore in his search for built-in guarantees.

Canto IV draws to a close with a complex play on the idea of closure. If, as Jonathan Goldberg suggests (44), Book IV is initially maneuvered to self-consuming closure by the Squire of Dames' intervention, it is manhandled to a conclusion by Marinell's mother, who
acts as both stage manager and designated exegete. Her performance
contrasts explicitly and ironically with her interpretation of Proteus'
prophecy in Book III, which made her son vulnerable to Britomart's
spear by imposing a specious and self-interested closure on his life
story. In trying to understand Marinell's lovesickness, Cymodoche
first attributes his deterioration to "that same former fatall wound of
his" (4.12.22.5) but then decides "it was not time to scan the prophe-
cie" since "it's late in death of daunger to aduize" (4.12.28.3,6)—perhaps the most insouciant rejection of closure in the entire poem. Cymodoche comically posits degrees of fatality as she focuses on
getting the best for her son. In Book III, Cymoent is a castrating
mother who narcissistically sees her son as the image of herself and

interprets his life story according to her destructive self-interest. At the conclusion of Book IV, Cymodoche has not only undergone a change of name, but she has been transformed into a Ceres figure of renewal, who descends to the underworld to rescue her future daughter-in-law and save her son's life.[31] Cymodoche has metamorphosed from a figure of originary castration who reads her own lack into her progeny to what Patricia Parker calls a literary fat lady (*Literary Fat Ladies* 8–35), who "see[s] her losse before her eyne" (4.12.21.7) and then sets out to find a remedy. Although her son suffers physical deterioration, he does not become disembodied in the manner of Echo. His physical debilitation is as incremental as his prophesied death. Seeing and seen by Florimell, he "reuiued with her sweet inspection" (4.12.34.4), but "his limbs could not his bodie beare" (4.12.35.3). Marinell's relative weakness attests to the continued presence of his etiolated body.[32] He suffers a loss of weight rather than an absolute loss of self.

Cymodoche's rescue of Florimell is her own version of the invention of Venus. As Hamilton observes, Florimell imitates the Venus *anadyomene* as she arise from the sea.[33] Cymodoche uses her considerable powers of self-interested reading to manipulate legal structures to achieve Florimell's release from the sea. In pleading her case before Neptune, she makes use of legal fiction to define Florimell as the property of Neptune, as a "waift," legal property left ownerless, or property "wafted" by the sea.[34] This deliberate objectification of Florimell paradoxically liberates Florimell from Proteus. The term is not a marker of presence or absence but is a hypothetical sign that admits of multiple referents, like the names John Doe and Richard Roe in English common law.[35] The legal fiction of Florimell as flotsam and property of Neptune allows Neptune and Cymodoche to do what they want in a legal manner and take Florimell from Proteus. As a broader allegory, her transfer from Proteus to Neptune implicates and situates Florimell in the larger infolded flow.

The conclusion to Book IV validates what has been implicit throughout Books III and IV: the value of invention, risk, and improvisation over against the temptation to play it safe and seek guarantees. These are concerns central to the early modern period, as well as to the postmodern, and whatever has followed that. The celebration of risk extends from Spenserian theme to Spenserian poetics. Spenser's characters flourish or fail according to their openness to risk. Similarly,

Spenser insists on the riskiness of poetic enterprise itself as a sense-making process. Spenser's reader is denied the security of separating the meaning of Spenser's work from the process through which that meaning is produced and conveyed. The sublunary world offers no refuge from telling stories and interpreting them. And while there exist Archimedean points from which both experience and its narrative inscription can be apprehended as coherent entities, that retrospective vision cannot be assured in advance, and the ultimate "Sabaoths sight" is something for which one must pray.

Spenser exposes fictions of total understanding and total control as just that: fictions, seductive and empowering ones, but fictions nonetheless. In his poetry, we see such late twentieth-century preoccupations as the dialectic of absence and presence or the relationship of the literary sign to its referent and to its audience taken seriously, but framed as questions of mere theory, ultimately dependent on how one chooses to look at earthly things.

Although Spenser reveals total control to be an illusory aim, he nonetheless exercises considerable control over his poem.[36] Critics risk doing a serious disservice to that poem and to their own understanding of a major cultural artifact of early modern Europe if they underestimate the conscious complexity of *The Faerie Queene* and are too ready to dismiss problematic features of it as symptoms of the benightedness of an earlier era (or to celebrate problematic feature of it as relics of the stability of an earlier era).[37] For all Spenser's idealism, *The Faerie Queene* may be seen as a thirty-thousand-line excursus on how people ruin their lives. Little is presented to us that is not framed critically and subjected to the play of a very good Elizabethan mind.

In fashioning a gentleman or noble person, Spenser posits one who is embedded in and beset by a variety of social constructs but who exercises some freedom in that context and bears the consequences, both of resisting social norms and of submitting to them. Spenser's vision is the opposite of what M. H. Abrams has characterized as absolutism without absolutes. Spenser invites us to apprehend both the One and the Many. In the words of Giovanni Pico della Mirandola, "he who cannot attract Pan approaches Proteus in vain" (Wind 191). Because Spenser understands the nature of absolutes, he is able to give contingency its due. This means learning to live with contingency, a task requiring constant attention and invention.

Notes

ABBREVIATIONS

DNB   Dictionary of National Biography
G.l.   Gerusalemme liberata
Met.   Metamorphoses
OED   Oxford English Dictionary
O.f.   Orlando furioso
SE   Spenser Encyclopedia
Var.   Spenser Variorum

INTRODUCTION

1. My reading of *The Faerie Queene* considers that poem as much more critical of conventional Elizabethan sexual ideology than do most feminist analyses of Spenser. One of the best and fullest versions of the feminist reading of Spenser as implicated in the sexual politics of his age may be found in Sheila Cavanagh's lucid and learned book, *Wanton Eyes and Chaste Desires: Female Sexuality in* The Faerie Queene, which I had the privilege of reading in manuscript.

2. A notable exception is James Nohrnberg who, as the modern heir to Renaissance mythographers, has written an encyclopedic work in *The Analogy of* The Faerie Queene.

3. I came upon Susanne Wofford's important study of epic after this manuscript was completed, too late to take account of its argument about the dialectic of allegory and narrative in *The Faerie Queene*. My general sense of this book's position vis-à-vis Wofford's work, without being able to do anything like justice to her dense argument, is that what she considers a division between classes of discursive effects, I should see as reconcilable in a sufficiently intense and sustained reading of the narrative, although that reading would probably not be supportive of any particular ideological orthodoxy.

4. Of Holiness or Of Chastity reproduce the form of an essay title such as *De Senectute* or *Of Friendship*.

5. The classic study of Books III and IV as a unit is *The Kindly Flame* by Thomas P. Roche, Jr.

6. Compare *Amoretti* 67 in which the hunter gets the deer by giving up the chase. This hunt is brought to a fruitful conclusion not by a simple reversal of pursuer and pursued but by a creative merging of characteristics: active and passive, animal and human. To be sure, deer of the four-legged variety do, in fact, double back when pursued.

143

7. For a discussion of the gendered exercise of control through male spectatorship of a female object, see Laura Mulvey. To be sure, in the classical versions of the myth, Orpheus' backward look has a variety of significances. Virgil's Orpheus is overcome by a sudden, inexplicable frenzy to see Eurydice. In Ovid's *Metamorphoses* we are told, "hic, ne deficeret, metuens avidusque videndi / flexit amans oculos, et protinus illa relapsa est" (10.56–57) [he, afraid that she might fail him, eager for sight of her, turned back his longing eyes; and instantly she slipped into the depths]. Orpheus' desire to assure himself of Eurydice's presence brings about her loss. As we shall see, Spenser's meditations on the Orpheus myth in Book IV explore the ironic connections between loss and desire for assuraurance.

8. On this point, see Stephen Toulmin, *The Uses of Argument*.

1. BRITOMART'S QUEST

1. As James I. Wimsatt points out in his *Allegory and Mirror*, the medieval mirror tradition, elaborating, in part, on the Ciceronian dictum that comedy is an "imitation of life, a mirror of custom, and an image of truth," comprised encyclopedic compendia of positive and negative exemplars. In literary contexts, the term mirror most often denoted a courtesy book that presented its readers with a series of ideals to be imitated (29–31; 137–159). As Sister Ritamary Bradley notes, medieval and Renaissance literature in the mirror tradition had "the double function of showing the world what it is and what it should become" ("Backgrounds" 101). See also Grabes.

2. Vulgate and Geneva versions.

3. I have argued elsewhere that Book II provides an ironic transition from Book I to Book III as it explores the problems of adapting an epistemology grounded in revealed truth for the purposes of understanding, rather than transcending the fallen world. See Silberman, "*The Faerie Queene*, Book II and the Limitations of Temperance."

4. In some ways this alternative discourse resembles the resistance from within existing discourses advocated by Julia Kristeva (rather than the *écriture feminine* of Hélène Cixous with the privileged status it accords the body). For a lucid and thoughtful analysis and critique of notions of *écriture feminine*, see Ann Rosalind Jones. What concerns me here is largely a rhetorical strategy of using gender difference as a way of gaining a certain internal distance from the discursive structures we all inhabit. As an example of this strategy, one might consider Donne's Holy Sonnet 10, in which the speaker systematically assumes a feminized posture with respect to God as a way of comprehending mortal experience of the divine. Such strategy clearly risks a problematic appropriating of alien experience. While appreciating Donne's artistry, one might question, as some of my students have done, his conventional appropriation of rape as a metaphor of spiritual ravishment. As we shall see, *The Faerie Queene* III registers both the distinction between sex as a biological category and gender as a cultural one and the unavoidable instability involved in negotiating that difference.

5. For a discussion of Renaissance habits of allegorizing the imagination as conception and pregnancy and the relation of these notions to faculty psychology, see Jay L. Halio.

6. S. K. Heninger argues learnedly and persuasively for considering *The Faerie Queene* as a microcosm that in its complex patterning imitates Pythagorean notions of harmony (*Touches of Sweet Harmony* esp. 372–377). Heninger counters the earlier position held by Paul J. Alpers (107–134) that neither the books of *The Faerie Queene* nor the poem as a whole has what one would call structure. To defend this claim Alpers appeals (112) to the experience of the common reader who is intensely absorbed by local detail and has difficulty remembering earlier details. I would agree that the reader is absorbed by local detail but question how readily that detail disappears from memory.

7. See especially A. S. P. Woodhouse and A. C. Hamilton ("Like Race to Runne").

8. See the headnote to Book III in A. C. Hamilton's edition of *The Faerie Queene* 299; also Maurice Evans 151; Kathleen Williams 81; and Judith Anderson's article on "Britomart" in the *Spenser Encyclopedia* (hereafter *SE*) 114. All my quotations from *The Faerie Queene* come from Hamilton's edition (hereafter often *F.Q.*).

9. The theory of the paradigm shift is developed by Thomas S. Kuhn in *The Structure of Scientific Revolutions*.

10. See the headnote to the proem of Book I in Hamilton's edition of *The Faerie Queene*, 27.

11. D. W. Robertson quotes the following doggerel, attributed to Augustine of Dacia (ca. 1260): "Littera gesta docet, quid credas allegoria, / Moralis quid agas, quo tendas anagogia," and gives a succinct account of fourfold exegesis (292–293). I use the term tropological in the conventional, historical way as the equivalent of moral sense, rather than as "having to do with tropes."

12. See Mark Rose (*Spenser's Art* 143–144). Carol Kaske gives a comprehensive account of the theological allegory figured by the dragon fight.

13. In *Spenser's Art* Mark Rose points out Spenser's witty wordplay.

14. According to Jacques Derrida, the absence of the transcendental signified looses linguistic play (see particularly *Of Grammatology* 44–65). If it seems disorienting to translate Christian eschatology into Derridean terms, one might consider whether one is not retranslating Derridean terminology back into into the terms from which it derives. Arguably, postmodernism results when one removes God from a Judeo-Christian epistemology. Spenser's Christianity is therefore less mystified about the structure of its belief than much contemporary theory.

15. On Renaissance traditions of skepticism, see Richard Popkin and Victoria Kahn. In his *Spenser and the Motives of Metaphor*, A. Leigh DeNeef writes eloquently on the problematic and provisional nature of reading as presented in *The Faerie Queene*.

16. Hamilton annotates Una's father's injunction to the Redcrosse Knight "Soone as the terme of those six yeares shall cease, / Ye then shall hither

backe returne againe, / The marriage to accomplish vowd betwixt you twain" (1.12.19) with the Geneva gloss to Rev. 19:7, "God made Christ the bridgrome of his Church at the beginning, and at the last day it shalbe fully accomplished when we shal be joyned with our head" and notes with regard to "accomplish" the distinction between "wedlock which is contracted or performed . . . and completed, i.e. consummated" (158).

17. I am grateful to my colleague Timothy Peltason for this point.

18. On the tradition of the ladder of lechery, see Fowler; Friedman; Gilbert; and Hutton.

19. For a discussion of *The Faerie Queene*, II as a critique of the attempt to use inappropriate discourses to comprehend earthly desire, see my article "The Limitations of Temperance." For a sustained focus on the element of discursive critique in Book II, see Harry Berger, Jr., "Narrative as Rhetoric." The earliest treatment of *Faerie Queene*, II as a self-conscious critique of its own allegory is by Madelon Sprengnether Gohlke.

20. Ronald Levao identifies this paradox as fundamental to the thought of Nicholas of Cusa. As he summarizes Cusanus' attitude, "The longing for God is the mind's fundamental impulse, the profoundest revelation of its ignorance, and its guarantee that its desires are not vain" (21).

21. A genuine epistemology of randomness would not register the manifestations of that randomness as anything but normative.

22. Consider the crucial pun on "carnal knowledge." One of the primary sources for the idea that love is the counterpart of knowledge is St. Augustine, *De trinitate* 10.11.17–18. On this point, see Colish, passim.

23. The extent to which modern notions of a "self" correspond to sixteenth-century constructs, for example to an entity composed of a spirit, soul, and body or to a mental self composed of reason, will, and appetite affected by a body composed of earth, air, fire, and water is problematic. In the sixteenth century, particularly in the texts of Spenser, the word "selfe" begins to be used to refer to some discrete entity, rather than as an intensifier of the noun or pronoun to which it is attached. I proceed from the working hypothesis that modern notions of a self are in some way indebted to whatever concepts Spenser develops as he fashions virtuous readers and exemplary characters, and I attempt to look at the text closely for evidence of those concepts.

24. Harry Berger, Jr., has a subtle analysis of the interplay of erotic discourses in Book III of *The Faerie Queene* in his "Kidnapped Romance." For a more general treatment of the various discourses of love current in Elizabethan England, see Mary Beth Rose. Reed Way Dasenbrock argues that Spenser criticizes Petrarchism as an injurious interpersonal dynamic.

25.   Le donne antique hanno mirabil cose
fatto ne l'arme e ne le sacre muse;
e di lor opre belle e gloriose
gran lume in tutto il mondo si diffuse.
Arpalice e Camilla son famose,
perché in battaglia erano esperte ed use;

Safo e Corinna, perché furon dotte,
splendono illustri, e mai non veggon notte.

Le donne son venute in eccellenza
di chiascun'arte ove hanno posto cura;
e qualunque all'istorie abbia avvertenza,
ne sente ancor la fama non oscura.
Se 'l mondo n'è gran tempo stato senza,
non però sempre il mal influsso dura;
e forse ascosi han lor debiti onori
l'invidia o il non saper degli scrittori.

Ben mi par di veder ch'al secol nostro
tanta virtù fra belle donne emerga,
che può dare opra a carte ed ad inchiostro,
perché nei futuri anni si disperga,
e perché, odiose lingue, il mal dir vostro
con vostra eterna infamia si sommerga:
e le lor lode appariranno in guisa,
che di gran lunga avanzeran Marfisa.

(O.f. 20.1–3)

[In feats of arms, as in the cultivation of the Muses, the women of old achieved distinction, and their splendid, glorious deeds irradiated the whole earth. Harpalice and Camilla achieved fame for their practised skill in battle; Sappho and Corinna shine, on account of their learning, with a radiance that night will never darken. / Women have proved their excellence in every art in which they have striven; in their chosen fields their renown is clearly apparent to anyone who studies the history books. If the world has long remained unaware of their achievements, this sad state of affairs is only transitory—perhaps Envy concealed the honours due to them, or perhaps the ignorance of historians. / In our own day I can clearly see such virtues evident among fair ladies that ink and paper is needed with which to record it all for posterity; this way, too, the calumnies of evil tongues may be drowned in perpetual shame. The praises of our womenfolk will then be such as to surpass those accorded to Marfisa.] Translations of *O.f.* by Guido Waldman, in Oxford edition.

The classic study of the narrator in the *Orlando furioso* is by Robert Durling.

26. All emphasis in primary and secondary sources is as in the original.

27. Thomas P. Roche, Jr., pointed out this reading to me. In an analogous scene from *Gerusalemme liberata* (hereafter *G.l.*), Tasso's Clorinda, rather than being hurled across the river bound to her father's spear, is carried by her faithful eunuch-nurse, who holds up the infant with one hand while he swims with the other. In Christianizing Virgil, Tasso replaces the biological father with a spiritual father who is a eunuch for the kingdom of God, while emphasizing the associations of the river with baptism and spiritual rebirth.

28. In sixteenth-century usage, "bowels" refer to viscera in general (*Oxford English Dictionary* [hereafter *OED*] s.v. "bowel" 2.2.c). Significantly, in her study of Tudor and Stuart obstetrics and gynecology, Audrey Eccles cites a seventeenth-century work, *The Compleat Midwife's practice* (1698), to the effect that dysmenorrhea is sometimes produced by corruption of the blood (221). Nohrnberg discusses Britomart's coming of age primarily from a psychological perspective (*Analogy* 442–446).

29. Camilla's father feeds his infant daughter with the milk of a wild mare (*Aeneid* 11.570–572), Ariosto has Atlante feed both Ruggiero and Marfisa with the milk of a lioness (*O.f.* 36.62), and Tasso's Clorinda is suckled by a tigress (*G.l.* 12.30–33). Clearly the breakfast of champions. Camilla's early military training is described explicitly in *Aeneid* 11.573–584. Tasso describes Clorinda's habitual activity thus:

> Costei gl'ingegni feminili e gli usi
> tutti sprezzò sin da l'età più acerba:
> a i lavori d'Aracne, a l'ago, a i fusi
> inchinar non degnó la man superba.
> Fuggì gli abiti molli e i lochi chiusi,
> chè ne' campi onestate anco si serba;
> armò d'orgoglio il vólto, i si compiacque
> rigido farlo, e pur rigido piacque.
>   (*G.l.* 2.39)

> [She scorn'd the arts these seely women use,
> Another thought her nobler humor fed;
> Her lofty hand would of itself refuse
> To touch the dainty needle, or nice thread:
> She hated chambers, closets, secret mews,
> And in broad fields preserv'd her maidenhead:
> Proud were her looks, yet sweet, though stern and stout,
> Her dame a dove thus brought an eagle out.]

All translations of *G.l.* are by Edward Fairfax, from the Renaissance version. Tellingly, in her new guise as Martial Maid, Britomart plagiarizes Clorinda's childhood when describing herself to the Redcrosse Knight:

> Faire Sir, I let you weete, that from the howre
> I taken was from nourses tender pap,
> I haue beene trained vp in warlike stowre,
> To tossen speare and shield, and to affrap
> The warlike ryder to his most mishap;
> Sithence I loathed haue my life to lead,
> As Ladies wont, in pleasures wanton lap,
> To finger the fine needle and nyce thread;
> Me leuer were with point of foemans speare be dead.
>   (3.2.6)

30. The term "self-fashioning" has become something of a commonplace since Stephen Greenblatt's important study *Renaissance Self-Fashioning: From More to Shakespeare*. For a subtle and detailed treatment of the complex dynamic of literary self-creation, see Arthur Kinney's chapter on Castiglione in *Continental Humanist Poetics* 87–134. *Reconstructing Individualism*, a collection edited by Thomas Heller, Morton Sosna, and David Wellbery, brings together a number of useful essays about Western ideas of the self. Of particular relevance are those by John Freccero (16–29); Natalie Zemon Davis (53–63), and Carol Gilligan (237–252).

31. Karl Popper identifies an epistemological tradition of learned ignorance, originating with Xenophanes, Democritus, and Socrates (of the *Apol-*

ogy rather than the *Meno*) and revived by Nicholas of Cusa, Erasmus, and Montaigne (15–17). For a discussion of Cusa's doctrine of learned ignorance and its implications for Renaissance notions of conjecture and creativity, see Levao 33–96.

32. For a discussion of the mirror episode, see Kathleen Williams 93–94.

33. As Elizabeth Bieman points out, in Platonic and Neoplatonic writing, the term methexis or participation refers to the relationship between model and likeness and the relationship between the One and the Many. She uses the term participatory mimesis in relation to Spenser's fiction. See *Plato Baptized* passim. For an account of participation written from a position in the Christian Platonist tradition several hundred years subsequent to Spenser, see Owen Barfield's *Saving the Appearances: A Study in Idolatry*. In his essay "The Mirror Stage," Jacques Lacan asserts that the infant at a stage when it lacks full control over its body identifies itself with the image it sees in the mirror, which it conceives both as exterior to itself and as an image of ideal wholeness. As the individual self develops beyond this infant stage, that self attempts to pattern itself after this ideal. What Spenser puts in question in Book III of *The Faerie Queene* is, however, precisely the fictiveness and pertinence of ideal images.

34. As Nohrnberg points out, there is a long tradition, going back through Erasmus to Augustine, of interpreting the Pauline "in aenigmate" as an allusion to allegory (*Analogy* 90n, 97n).

35. See Roche 71; MacCaffrey 298–300; and Edwards.

36. Among commentators who consider Narcissus as an icon of moral failure are Arnolphe d'Orléans (3.5–6); John of Garland, *Integumenta* (2.165); Giovanni del Virgilio (3.6); the author of the *Ovide moralisé* (3.1904–1964); and Giovanni Boccaccio, *Genealogie deorum gentilium libri* (7.59). Commentaries that interpret Narcissus as the victim of a mistake include that attributed to Lactantius Placidus (3.5.44–45); and those of the first two Vatican mythographers (I: 185.11.21–22; II: 180.11.19–20).

37. See note 1.

38. All classical quotations and translations are taken from the Loeb editions unless otherwise noted.

39. This point is mentioned by John Brenkman in a subtle application of contemporary theoretical insights to Ovid's myth.

40. See Nohrnberg, *Analogy* 431–432; 645–646.

41. In his note to *F.Q.* 3.4.17, Hamilton observes that the "sacrifice of the castrated male animal provides a fitting simile for the male figure overcome by a woman" (339).

42. For a discussion of the pun on "dismay," see Schroeder 149.

43. In his note to the passage, Hamilton observes that Spenser's disdain may signify "pride for women or contempt for men; or indignation that he does not have such matter for his song" (336).

44. Patricia Parker has an extensive discussion of the phenomenon of rhetorical dilation as an aspect of the genre of romance in her *Inescapable Romance*.

45. The following discussion is indebted to Berger's "Kidnapped Romance."

46. Consider Chaucer's punning description of the Monk "that lovede venerie" ("General Prologue" 166). In *Amoretti* 67, Spenser emphasizes and revises the conceit of the beloved lady as the pursued deer found in Petrarch and Wyatt, as well as in Horace (*Odes* I.23) and Tasso ("Questa fera gentil" I.93). Note also Spenser's pun on venery in 1.6.22.5.

47. For a discussion of the motif of the chase in Renaissance literature and the reversals characteristic of that motif, see Michael J. B. Allen. One of the best treatments of deer in Spenser, which takes into account the complexities and ambivalence of the traditions the poet draws on, is by Anne Lake Prescott ("The Thirsty Deer"). See Cassell and Kirkham 3–95, as well as Bath, Thiébaux and Nancy Vickers's feminist treatment of the Actaeon myth. Leonard Barkan gives a comprehensive treatment of the literary and mythological traditions through which the myth of Diana and Actaeon is disseminated. Worth considering in this regard is the extent to which Ovid's story of Actaeon in *Metamorphoses* (3.138–252) works its reversals in relationship to the companion story of Callisto (2.401–507). Both Callisto and Actaeon are innocent victims of Diana's wrath. Callisto, raped by Jupiter who has disguised himself as Diana, is banished when the girl's pregnancy is revealed as she bathes; Juno then turns her rival Callisto into a bear. When Actaeon inadvertently sees Diana bathing, Diana turns him into a stag. Not only, then, has Actaeon been transformed into prey but, by analogy with Callisto, has been placed in the position of a rape victim as well. Barkan points out that Titian painted *Diana Surprised by Actaeon* and *Diana and Callisto* as companion pieces for King Philip of Spain (345–349).

48. See Berger's reading of this passage ("Kidnapped Romance" 224).

49. Neoplatonic theory moves readily between a kind of androgyny—each lover becomes the other—and a kind of hermaphroditism—they become one as each becomes both in microcosm. For a useful survey of the relevant love treatises, see A. R. Cirillo.

50. Compare Britomart's words of self-reproach to Glauce about having fallen in love with what might be merely the shadow of a man. (3.2.36, 41).

51. Alpers has cogent observations about Spenser's use of the Fiordespina episode (179–185).

2. THE WOUNDS OF ADONIS

1. As Arthur Kinney points out, "It may astonish us now, but it is surely clear . . . that students of Continental humanists were asked again and again to *construct narrative situations* which, though cast in the *forms* of declamations and disputations, nevertheless established situations that were like stories, situations that were *probable* and *persuasive*" (27–28; original emphasis).

2. On the importance of the phrase "in the middest," see Baybak, Delany, and Hieatt. William Nelson has observed that the description of the Gardens of Adonis echoes Ovid's description of Gargaphie, where Actaeon accidentally encounters Diana (208–209). Compare *F.Q.* 3.6.43–44 and the detail of the cave under the mount with the classical site:

Vallis erat piceis et acuta densa cupressu,
nomine Gargaphie succinctae sacra Dianae,
cuius in extremo est antrum nemorale recessu
arte laboratum nulla: simulaverat artem
ingenio natura suo; nam pumice vivo
et levibus tofis nativum duxerat arcum;
fons sonat a dextra tenui perlucidus unda,
margine gramineo patulos incinctus hiatus.
                                     (*Met.* 3.155–162)

[There was a vale in that region, thick grown with pine and cypress with their sharp needles. 'Twas called Gargaphie, the sacred haunt of high-girt Diana. In its most secret nook there was a well-shaded grotto, wrought by no artist's hand. But Nature by her own cunning had imitated art; for she had shaped a native arch of the living rock and soft tufa. A sparkling spring with its slender stream babbled on one side and widened into a pool girt with grassy banks.]

See also Quilligan, *Milton's Spenser* 191–193.

3. See Merrit Y. Hughes for a discussion of the Virgilian Venus-virago.

4. On the "soft" and "hard" hunts as they apply to *The Faerie Queene*, see Iris Tillman Hall.

5. "Kidnapped Romance" 230. To be sure, Berger and I are emphasizing different parts of the same paradox.

6. In similar fashion, the perverse independence of Ariosto's Angelica, who spurns all suitors until she nurses and falls in love with the wounded Medoro, reveals the solipsism of the suitor's love. Although rivals, they can share in a fantasy of Angelica without encroachment on the rights of their fellow suitors.

7. See Berger, "Kidnapped Romance" 223–224.

8. William Oram observes: "What Spenser does in his portrait [of Timias] is to take Ralegh's *role* as love-struck swain and to isolate it from the complexities of Ralegh's character, showing what might happen if someone lived according to the absolutes of its passionate rhetoric" ("Spenser's Raleghs" 353). For other discussions of the historical dimension of Timias as Ralegh, see Bednarz; Oram ("Elizabethan Fact"); O'Connell; and Koller.

9. In Book IV, Timias encounters Lust personified. See discussion in chapter 7.

10. See Mark Rose, *Spenser's Art* 30–33; 65–68.

11. A contrasting shift occurs in Spenser's source, the *Orlando furioso* (18.165–19). Ariosto traces a shift from the sentimental, homoerotic tableau of Medoro nearly dead beside the body of his slain comrade Cloridano to Medoro's restoration to life and heterosexuality by the ministrations of Angelica. Unlike Belphoebe, Angelica inflicts a wound on herself as she heals Medoro and, also unlike Belphoebe, Ariosto's heroine quickly helps herself to a cure. For another, detailed analysis of Spenser's adaptation of the Angelica and Medoro episode, see Alpers 185–194.

12. Berger made this point in a lecture delivered to an NEH seminar on Spenser at Princeton in July 1989.

13. See chapter 4.

14. *Meno* 82–85C, alluded to in *Phaedo* 73B.

15. We first learn Britomart's name after, in the guise of an unknown, male knight, she has unhorsed Sir Guyon:

> Euen the famous *Britomart* it was,
> Whom straunge aduenture did from *Britaine* fet,
> To seeke her louer (loue farre sought alas,)
> Whose image she had seene in *Venus* looking glas.
>   (3.1.8.6–9)

Spenser plays on "far fet," Puttenham's term for metalepsis (193), or the substitution of one figurative sense for another. The presence in Faerieland of the Briton maid is partly Spenser's rhetorical trope.

16. Consider, for example, Socrates' discussion of how all things are generated from their opposites (*Phaedo* 70D–72D).

17. On theories of spontaneous generation underlying Chrysogone's pregnancy, see Umunc.

18. The passage is as follows:

> Socrates sat up on the bed and drew up his leg and massaged it, saying as he did so, What a queer thing it is, my friends, this sensation which is popularly called pleasure! It is remarkable how closely it is connected with its conventional opposite, pain. They will never come to a man both at once, but if you pursue one of them and catch it, you are nearly always compelled to have the other as well.
>
>   (*Phaedo* 60B)

19. See Berleth for a discussion of the astrological lore underlying this episode.

20. Frank Kermode observes, with sublime understatement, "When we come to the allegory of Venus and Adonis the going is harder" (77). Kermode explicitly rejects the interpretation of Adonis as matter and decides that he is the entire biological cycle. Roche sees Adonis as form and Venus as matter (123).

21. On the shifting nature of Spenser's description of the garden, see also Harry Berger, Jr., "Spenser's Gardens of Adonis: Force and Form in the Renaissance Imagination."

22. In *Worlds Apart*, Owen Barfield distinguishes familiar from inferred nature, a very useful approach to Platonic categories of the sensible and the intelligible.

23. On the philosophical background of the Gardens of Adonis, see Kermode 67–89; Colie 335–349; Tonkin; and Milne. Roche makes some judicious comments about the difficulties of assigning a piece of poetry to any particular philosophy (117–128).

24. On female geography, see Miller 215–281; Woodbridge; and Stallybrass.

25. David Miller notes: "Is the poet modestly disclaiming virginity? Since the fable of Chrysogonee and the Garden itself both sustain a detailed and elaborate physical allegory, the answer would appear to be yes. But since the fable of Chrysogonee and the Garden itself both make intellection analogous

to natural begetting, we may also take the hint that Spenser has visited Nature's lap in a more visionary mode: insofar as the Garden is everywhere, one need only grasp the metaphor to have been there" (263). I should argue that the Gardens of Adonis question just that analogy between intellection and natural begetting.

26. Remarkably little work has been done on the myth of the *vagina dentata* in Western culture. However, Brundage cites a medieval European version of the myth given by Psuedo-Albertus in the *Secreta mulierum* (467).

27. The positive consequence of this resolution of dualism is figured by the progression from the binary of Venus and Adonis, to Cupid and Psyche, to the product of the latter union: Pleasure.

3. THE HERMAPHRODITE

1. The classic study of the hermaphrodite figure in *The Faerie Queene* is Donald Cheney's "Spenser's Hermaphrodite and the 1590 *Faerie Queene*." See also Roche 133–136.

2. See John Charles Nelson 91.

3. This hierarchy of soul over body never becomes a Manichaean dualism that holds souls to be good and bodies evil. Rather, Redcrosse learns that he is more than his body, theologically and allegorically.

4. For a fascinating discussion of the Western tendency to suppress epistemological concerns in deliberations on free will and determinism, see Daniel C. Dennet 123–130.

5. Physicist and philosopher of science David Bohm discusses the problem of mistaking one's ideas and perceptions of the world—that is, one's theories—for what actually exists. See particularly *Wholeness and the Implicate Order* and *Science, Order, and Creativity*.

6. David Miller observes that "what Plato must exclude from his dialectic, insofar as it pretends to a system of truth, is the possibility that ideal forms are derived not from heaven but precisely from the material objects he wants to call their copies" (94). Miller is right that Plato accords absolute privilege to the ideal over the material. Instead of inverting the dialectic as Miller tacitly does, however, and favoring the material as true source, Ovid presents the dialectic as indeterminate. In *Faerie Queene* I, Spenser affirms the priority of spiritual truth and in Book III explores the *apparent* indeterminacy of the material world and the confusion of mortal desire.

7. Ovid also plays "uterque parens" [each of his parents—my translation] against "neutrumque et utrumque videntur" [They seemed neither, and yet both] (*Met.* 4.379). The parents' oneness contrast with their son's sense of noneness, of being neutered. One might consider in this regard Nohrnberg's observations (*Analogy* 606–607) about the hermaphroditism of Spenser's couples: Scudamoret, Britomartegall, Osirisis, Paridellenore, Thamedway, and Claribellamour.

8. As Thomas Laqueur points out, from classical antiquity to the eighteenth century, it was a medical commonplace that female reproductive or-

gans were homologous with the male organs, differing hierarchically in perfection rather than absolutely in kind. For a discussion of Renaissance medical theory of biological hermaphrodites, see Stephen Greenblatt, "Fiction and Friction."

9. The standard work on essentialist and social constructionist theories of gender is by Diana Fuss.

10. Marie Delcourt surveys what little is known about the cult of the Hermaphrodite. She points out that references prior to Ovid ascribe the Hermaphrodite's bisexuality to birth, not metamorphosis (43–78).

11. See Goldberg, *Endlesse Worke* passim.

12. See chapter 1. Patricia Parker gives a subtle treatment of the motif of error-*errare* in *Inescapable Romance* (54–77).

13. A number of mythographic commentators on Ovid's Hermaphrodite read the myth in terms of hierarchies of rational over physical and male over female. Thus, Hermaphroditus' effeminacy represents the subordination of masculine reason to feminine sensuality. See my "Mythographic Transformations of Ovid's Hermaphrodite."

14. Compare Ovid's description of Salmacis:

> nympha colit, sed nec venatibus apta nec arcus
> flectere quae soleat nec quae contendere cursu,
> solaque naiadum celeri non nota Dianae.
> saepe suas illi fama est dixisse sorores
> 'Salmaci, vel iaculum vel pictas sume pharetras
> et tua cum duris venatibus otia misce!'
> nec iaculum sumit nec pictas illa pharetras,
> nec sua cum duris venatibus otia miscet,
> sed modo fonte suo formosos perluit artus,
> saepe Cytoriaco deducit pectine crines
> et, quid se deceat, spectatas consulit undas;
> nunc perlucenti circumdata corpus amictu
> mollibus aut foliis aut mollibus incubat herbis,
> saepe legit flores.
>
> (*Met.* 4.302–315)

[A nymph dwells in the pool, one that loves not hunting, nor is wont to bend the bow or strive with speed of foot. She only of the naiads follows not in swift Diana's train. Often, 'tis said, her sisters would chide her: 'Salmacis, take now either hunting-spear or painted quiver, and vary your ease with the hardships of the hunt.' But she takes no hunting-spear, no painted quiver, nor does she vary her ease with the hardships of the hunt; but at times she bathes her shapely limbs in her own pool; often combs her hair with a boxwood comb, often looks in the mirror-like waters to see what best becomes her.]

15. Specifically, Arnolphe d'Orléans (3.13); *Ovide moralisé* (4.2284–2311); Thomas Peend (B2v).

16. Vitruvius, *De architectura* (2.8.12); Sextus Pompeius Festus, *De verborum significatione* 439; and Giraldi, *De deiis gentium* 181D & E.

17. See S. K. Heninger, "The Orgoglio Episode in *The Faerie Queene*"; Mark Rose, *Spenser's Art* 91–92; and Shroeder 140–159.

18. References to idolatry as whoring after strange gods occur in the following passages: Exod. 34:15–16; Lev. 17:7, 20:5–6; Num. 15:39; Deut. 31:16; Judg. 2:17, 8:27, 8:33; 1 Chron. 5:25; Ps. 73:27, 106:39; Ezek. 6:9, 23:30; Hos. 4:12, 9:1. Of course, the biblical metaphor has a material basis in the Canaanite practice of cult prostitution.

On the connection in Spenser between idolatry and eroticism, see Linda Gregerson.

19. See Hamilton's note to 1.7.16–17 (99). For a witty and erudite treatment of the association of Rome with the Whore of Babylon, and some of its literary ramifications, see Anne Lake Prescott (*Translatio Lupae*).

20. The use of Salmacis as a function of the Hermaphrodite's self-definition is considered wholly unproblematic in medieval and Renaissance commentaries on the Hermaphrodite. See Arnolphe d'Orléans (3.13); the *Ovide moralisé* (4.2284–2311); Thomas Peend; Georgius Sabinus (131); and Charles Estienne (807–808).

21. The term "carnivalesque body" is borrowed from Mikhail Bakhtin. However, considerable scholarship exists on the grotesque in Renaissance culture. See particularly Neil Rhodes.

22. The *OED* lists (gender nonspecific) private parts as a possible meaning of shame (*OED* s.v. "shame" 7).

23. On the collusion of reader and allegorical text, see A. Leigh Deneef 142–156 and Maureen Quilligan, *The Language of Allegory* 224–278. Arthur Kinney observes, "Part of the joy of reading humanist fiction now, as it must have been for its earliest readers, is the infectious way it invites us to participate and the multiple meanings it allows us to discover for ourselves. . . . When the number of such meanings diminishes, when verisimilitude grows so dense that a sense of constricting circumstances takes over the narrative and robs it of its conspiritorial quality, the realistic novel we associate with the eighteenth century emerges" (45).

24. In this regard, Amoret represents a significant variation on a typical pattern in which characters in Spenser's narrative double as personification allegories. Here, Amoret *as a character* is forced to play a role in Busirane's allegory as part of Spenser's story.

25. One might see this shift in perspective as a literary example of the technique of anamorphosis in the visual arts, whereby objects come into focus only when we view a painting from an oblique angle. See Fred Leeman, *Hidden Images*; also see the discussion in Greenblatt, *Renaissance Self-Fashioning* 18–23.

26. See Freccero, "The Fig Tree and the Laurel" for a discussion of the dialectic of absence and presence in Petrarchan lyric.

27. See especially Nohrnberg 474–478; Nelson 224–225; Hough 172–176; and Williams 110.

28. James Broaddus applies Renaissance faculty psychology to Book III. According to Ian Maclean, by the end of the Renaissance, terms of scholastic faculty psychology were "seen as words which designate in an organized

fashion interrelationships which can only be analysed—and perhaps which only exist—in discourse" (87).

29. Critics who locate the pageant inside Amoret's head tend to see Busirane as trying to frighten Amoret with a distorted or reductive vision of sexuality that plays on her fears of marriage. Versions of this interpretation are given by Janet Spens (105); A. C. Hamilton (*The Structure of Allegory in* The Faerie Queene 145–146); William Nelson (230); and Thomas P. Roche, Jr. (473–475). Harry Berger, Jr., shows a much greater appreciation of the role of the imagination in Amoret's plight in "Busirane and the War Between Sexes." For a discussion of the element of fictionmaking in the Masque of Cupid, see MacCaffrey 107–117.

30. See C. S. Lewis, *The Allegory of Love* 343–344; Roche 74.

31. See Roche 75 and Rose (*Heroic Love* 123).

32. Elaine Scarry describes torture as a structure "that allows real human pain to be converted into a regime's fiction of power" (18). In war, she argues, the injured bodies of the participants function to confirm the outcome of winning or losing (20–21).

33. For specific references to spoils and despoiling, see *F.Q.* 3.11.45; 3.11.52; 3.12.20; 3.12.22; and 1590.3.12.47.

34. On the liberation of Amoret from *Amor*, see DeNeef 157–173.

35. C. S. Lewis first identified the Masque of Cupid with courtly love (*Allegory of Love* 340–344). Since then, the nature of Busirane's abuse has been the subject of much critical debate. A useful summary of the main positions is given by Hugh Maclean and Anne Lake Prescott in *Edmund Spenser's Poetry* (741–752).

36. Paul de Man discusses the distinction between rhetorical and real questions in *Allegories of Reading* 3–19.

37. Similarly, in 1.2.11.9 readers are told they would mistake the disguised Archimago for Saint George himself.

38. Jacques Derrida discusses the interdependence of difference and iterability (or repeatability) in "Signature Event Context" reproduced in *Limited Inc.* (1–23). The Renaissance, of course, was well aware of the notion of imitation as creating a true counterfeit. See, especially, the discussions by Thomas M. Greene and Arthur Kinney.

39. For Protestant ideas of companionate marriage, see William Haller; Mary Beth Rose 2–16, 29–42, 93–177.

40. On strategies of defense that turn the body into a prison, see my "*The Faerie Queene*, Book II and the Limitations of Temperance."

4. BOOK IV

1. An analogous sense of a work as a published text appears in the second part of the *Quixote*, as Don Quixote and Sancho Panza must cope with the expectations of people who have read about them in part 1.

2. Nohrnberg gracefully observes of Book IV, "Spenser shows great virtuosity in making storytelling so much of his story" (*SE* 274). I should add that story*telling* is only part of the story of textuality.

3. Nohrnberg succinctly describes the relationship of Book IV to Book III. "Book IV also looks back to Book III, the narratives of which it extends, recycles, updates, culminates, or prolongs, and the happy ending of which it begins by deferring." He goes on to observe that Book IV implies a deflationary critique of the "reformist, expansionistic and desirous" expectations of Book III (*SE* 273).

4. As Maureen Quilligan observes, "the cancellation of the hermaphrodite image would also suggest that the gynandromorphic flexibility that Spenser had asked of his readers in Book III would be canceled as well" (*Milton's Spenser* 203).

5. One might see the Protestant insistence on the primacy of individual experience in reading Holy Scripture underwriting Amoret's resistance to Busirane in Book III.

6. In *Milton's Spenser*, Maureen Quilligan shows how the Orpheus myth reflects ironically on Scudamore. She points out that Orpheus-like, "Spenser himself has just lost Amoret moments before Scudamour begins his narration in one of the more frustrating narrative dissolves in the whole poem" (205). While Quilligan sees Spenser identifying himself with Orpheus' poetic failure, I would argue that Spenser presents Amoret's disappearance as the function of the discourse he is subjecting to critique.

7. Historians and philosophers of science often provide the most lucid discussions of the nature of theory. See particularly Stephen Toulmin (*The Uses of Argument*) and the philosophical writing of the physicist David Bohm. I have found Bohm's work particularly useful in thinking about Spenser partly, I think, because Bohm and Spenser both write from slightly beyond the borders of the epoch of classical physics, which extended from the seventeenth through the nineteenth century. Bohm's critique of classical physics seems to hark back in intriguing ways to ideas developed in *The Faerie Queene*. For example, Bohm argues that a modern misconception of theory as a form of knowledge rather than as a form of insight leads people to mistake the content of their thought for "a description of the world as it is" and to posit a direct correspondence between thought and objective reality. The consequence of this mistake is the fragmentation of the essential wholeness of the world into units circumscribed by thought (*Wholeness* 3–4). This view seems to me highly relevant to aspects of Book IV of *The Faerie Queene*. As we shall see, Bohm's view of reality as an unfolding, fluid wholeness recalls both *The Faerie Queene* and aspects of Neoplatonic thought influencing *The Faerie Queene*.

General studies of Renaissance theories of vision and visual perspective are by Samuel Y. Edgerton and David C. Lindberg. Claudio Guillén emphasizes the fictiveness and conventionality of Renaissance perspective, for all it purported to reproduce things seen. For a catalogue raisonné of the motif of vision in *The Faerie Queene*, see Joseph B. Dallett.

8. In this tale, adapted from the *Decameron* by Sir Thomas Elyot (*The Book Named the Governor*), Gesippus selflessly allows his friend Titus to take his place on Gesippus' wedding night since Titus is more enamored of Gesip-

pus' betrothed than is the intended husband. Years later, Titus confesses to a murder for which Gesippus is wrongfully about to be executed. The real murderer, overcome by the spectacle of friendship, confesses and all live happily ever after.

9. Nohrnberg observes, "Much in the Temple of Venus canto suggests that Scudamour originally sought Amoret as the prize of male aggressiveness" (*SE* 227).

10. It might seem that marriage would short-circuit this problem (absent a Paridell), but I would argue that marriage, as represented by the hermaphroditically embracing couple of the 1590 conclusion is a different order of relationship from what we see in Book IV, which is why the lovers fail to be reunited. Marriage is a relationship of man and woman. What passes for such a relationship in Book IV is really a transaction between men.

11. Nohrnberg points out the hermaphroditic names of Spenser's couples: Scudamoret, Britomartegall, Osirisis, Paridellenore, Thamedway, and Claribellamour (*Analogy* 606–607). Scudamore has been identified with both Sir John Scudamore and his son, Sir James Scudamore ("Scudamore, John" *DNB*). Sir John's wife Mary fell from the queen's favor for marrying in the 1570s but was apparently restored to favor in the 1590s. Sir James' armor is on display at the Metropolitan Museum of Art in New York, where it may be seen, if sought. Although the spelling of the family name varied during the sixteenth century (Skydmore, Skudmore, Scudamour) it was becoming standardized by the 1570s as Scudamore (Galyon 634–635). A comparison of the spelling in Book III (in 1590 and 1596 editions) and Book IV (in 1596) gives some support to this shift from Book III to Book IV. In Book III, the knight's name is spelled both Scudamore (6.53.2, 11.11.5, 11.11.6, 11.19.1, 11.24.4) and Scudamour (11.argument, 11.22.6, 11.26.1, 1590.12.43.2). In Book IV, the spelling Scudamour (the shield of love rather than half the hermaphrodite) is consistent throughout, and in the revised conclusion to Book III (12.44.2), it is spelled Scudamore.

12. A. Kent Hieatt notes the echo of "Be bold," "Be bold," "Be not too bold" and observes that Scudamore's overboldness transgresses the final injunction in the House of Busirane ("Scudamour's Practice").

13. At least Amoret will never be Scudamore's in Book IV. In a (theoretically) unfinished work, we ought to be agnostic about what would have happened to characters. Nonetheless, what we have in 1596 is the cancellation of stanzas figuring the union of Amoret and Scudamore at the conclusion of Book III and the abrupt disappearance of Amoret from Spenser's text in Book IV, canto ix. My argument is that these textual anomalies—which flout narrative logic—are central to Spenser's story.

14. Irrational numbers were a Pythagorean discovery. Before then, mathematicians had assumed that all points on a line corresponded to a rational number—a ratio of two integers—and that any two line segments could be divided evenly by a third smaller line segment, which would make the two segments "commensurable" in Pythagorean terms. As Eves points out, the discovery that the square root of two did not correspond to the ratio of two

integers "seemed to deal a mortal blow to the Pythagorean philosophy that all depends upon the whole numbers" (60; see Eves's discussion 58–61). Greek mathematics was seriously limited by the inability to treat these irrational—literally crazy-seeming—quantities as a number (Kline 173). It was the contribution of Hindu and Arabic mathematics to treat incommensurable magnitudes as a number (Kline 185–186, 191–192). Although Hindu and Arabic work in mathemetics was disseminated in Europe throughout the high Middle Ages, the status of irrationals was a major question in sixteenth-century European mathematics. In his *Arithmetica Integra* (1544), German mathematician Michael Stifel argues that although irrationals behave like numbers, "other considerations compel us to deny that irrational numbers are numbers at all. To wit, when we seek to subject them to numeration [decimal representation] . . . we find that they flee away perpetually, so that not one of them can be apprehended precisely in itself" (Kline 251). As we shall see with the marriage of Thames and Medway, Spenser, like Stifel, is perplexed by the problem of what resists numeration.

Interestingly, the earliest use cited by the *OED* of "irrational" as referring to a number is English mathematician Robert Recorde's *The Pathway to Knowledge* (London, 1551). There are tantalizing hints that Spenser might have read Recorde's book and echoed passages in *The Faerie Queene*. Glauce's assurance to Britomart, "Things oft impossible . . . seeme, ere begonne" (3.2.36.9), might reflect Recorde's prefatory announcement to his reader, "Whereby shallbe plainly perceaued, that many thynges seme impossible to be done, whiche by arte may very well be wrought." In addition, Recorde mentions a marvelous glass fashioned by Roger Bacon that resembles Merlin's mirror in *Faerie Queene* III.

15. Harry Berger, Jr., observes: "The singer's emphasis is on pleasure, laughter, and bliss, and from her point of view generation has its primary significance as a means of relief. The mother of laughter is more important to him than the mother of the species" ("Two Retrospects" 198). Berger reads the temple as a dead end but for different reasons than I do. He sees the Temple of Venus enacting the worship of Venus as Great Mother to promote generation through whatever cultural and psychological forms expedient, sometimes at the expense of human lovers through which she operates. I argue that the Temple of Venus is dysfunctional because of the restrictive way it contains natural forces.

16. As Sean Kane points out, in England after 1540 the term idolatry customarily referred to the Roman Mass, although Kane sees the reference to the idol of Venus in *F.Q.* IV as benign (387–388).

17. For another view, see Judith Anderson ("Whatever happened to Amoret?" 198).

18. Isabel MacCaffrey notes that Scudamore's comparison of his feat of winning Amoret to that of Orpheus winning Eurydice "is designedly ironic in light of his later loss of the lady to another Stygian Prince, Busirane. . . . Doubt as Venus' porter looks back as well as forward, but the Scudamour/Orpheus who wins Amoret has not yet looked back, and the atem-

porality of Spenser's narrative, which places the Busirane crisis before the Temple of Venus, allows the triumph at the Temple to become part of the celebration of love and art in Book IV" (327–328). One might object to characterizing this complex system of flashbacks and narrative retrojection as atemporality. Much of *The Faerie Queene* does take place in an atemporal, allegorical present but the episodes under discussion exhibit hypertemporality, if anything. MacCaffrey's positive reading of the Temple of Venus posits a ghostly restoration of the canceled stanzas describing the lovers' reunion. As she tellingly puts it, "Even without rewriting Spenser's poem for him, or repairing his oversights, we can see a remnant of this pattern" (327). Without belaboring the point, one might remark that condescension to Spenser's imagined oversights prevents closer attention to Spenser's text.

19. For treatments of the issue of closure in *The Faerie Queene*, see Balachandra Rajan 44–84; Goldberg, *Endlesse Worke* passim; Judith Dundas; Susanne Woods offers a particularly good bibliography of studies of unity in *The Faerie Queene*.

5. THE LEGEND OF CAMBEL AND TRIAMOND

1. Jonathan Goldberg argues that the lost conclusion to "The Squire's Tale" doubles the canceled conclusion of Book III, as both function metacritically to deny the possibility of narrative closure. According to Goldberg, "These stories in search of a lost ending arrive in Scudamour's story at a beginning principle, the principle of inevitable loss. Scudamour's tale forcefully insists that the end of narration is always lost and can never be restored. The text always stands in place of the lost text; its doing is undoing" (*Endlesse Worke* 66). As is clear from the previous chapter, I am heavily indebted to Goldberg's reading of Book IV. However, what Goldberg sees as the textual inscription of inevitable loss, I consider to be a self-critical representation of the consequences of a particular theoretical orientation.

2. Arthur Kinney argues persuasively for a humanist "collusive poetics" of the sixteenth century that actively invites the reader's participation (40–45).

3. The classic study of recursive processes is Douglas R. Hofstadter, *Gödel, Escher, Bach: an Eternal Golden Braid*.

4. For an eloquent treatment of Renaissance anxiety about linguistic drift, see Greene 4–27.

5. For discussions of Spenser's response to his precursor Chaucer, see Esolen; Anderson, "A Gentle Knight"; Hieatt, *Chaucer, Spenser, Milton* 75–94; and Miskimin. For a thorough study that focuses specifically on "The Squire's Tale," see Patrick Cheney.

6. According to Goldberg, "the admission that [the lovers] are 'not found elsewhere' is the precondition for dismissal" (44).

7. Nohrnberg observes: "The most notable analogical friendship in Book IV—that of Cambel and Triamond—is consolidated by means of an archetypal marriage of convenience in the Renaissance sense of the term: each marries the other's sister, thus affirming the likeness of things pre-likened by

the sharing of boundaries or adjacency"; he describes the various tetradic re-lationships obtaining among the four characters (*SE* 274).

8. On genealogical and teleological structures, see De Man, *Allegories of Reading* 79–102.

9. Most notable examples are the defense of love as heroic subject matter in the proem to Book IV:

> Which who so list looke backe to former ages,
>   And call to count the things that then were donne,
>   Shall find, that all the workes of those wise sages,
>   And braue exploits which great Heroes wonne,
>   In loue were either ended or begunne:
>   (4.P.3.1–5)

and the narrator's observation of the battle of Britomart and Artegall:

> Certes some hellish furie, or some feend
> This mischiefe framd, for their first loues defeature,
> To bath their hands in bloud of dearest freend,
> Thereby to make their loues beginning, their liues end.
>   (4.6.17.6–9)

but also see 4.1.20.9; 4.5.7.5; and 4.10.3.4.

10. Nohrnberg reminds us that the name given to Pri-Di-Triamond in the title of Book IV is Telamond, apparently from the Greek *telos* (*SE* 275). Note, however, that there was a Telamon who married the sister of the Trojan king Priam. See the third edition of the Norton Spenser (401n).

11. On the unfolding of Agape, see Wind 210. On motherhood in Spenser, see Goldberg, "The Mothers in Book III of *The Faerie Queene*.

12. The incestuous possibilities of the relationship between Cambel and Canacee have been remarked by Patrick Cheney; Nohrnberg 622; and the note to 4.3.11.2 in Hamilton's edition (445).

13. David Lee Miller presents a subtle view of the dialectical relationship of versions of priority developed by Plato and inherited by Spenser. See especially the discussion of "epistemological romance" (92–98).

14. Several critics, most notably Thomas P. Roche, Jr. (15–30, 166) have observed that, in general, the terms concord and discord describe the relationships in *Faerie Queene* IV as well as the term friendship. I am taking this observation further to argue that Spenser shows certain ideas of harmony, especially those that purport to offer built-in guarantees, produce discord. On Concord and Discord in *The Faerie Queene*, see also Kate W. Warren *Var.* IV.282–284. On Spenser's use in this episode of Aristotelian notions of like-ness, see William Fenn DeMoss *Var.* IV.296–297; David R. Pichaske notes the coexistence of Aristotelian and Platonic ideas in the allegory of Pri-Di-Triamond, which he interprets as an account of the genesis of friendship. Barry Weller has useful comments about Renaissance notions of friendship. Charles G. Smith *Var.* IV.327–333 cites Plutarch's *Moralia* as another source of the idea of friendship as likeness.

15. Drawing on René Girard and Luce Irigaray, among others, Eve Sedg-wick identifies a paradigmatic erotic triangle in which emotional relation-

ships between men, overtly sexual or otherwise, are mediated by the nominal female object of their desire.

16. In *Deceit, Desire, and the Novel* and *"To double business bound,"* René Girard argues that human desire is fundamentally imitative and that works that portray desire in that way therefore seem more realistic and appealing. Luce Irigaray posits a dynamic she terms "hom(m)o-sexuality. She argues:

> The use of and traffic in women subtend and uphold the reign of masculine hom(m)o-sexuality, even while they maintain that hom(m)o-sexuality in speculations, mirror games, identifications, and more or less rivalrous appropriations, which defer its real practice. Reigning everywhere, although prohibited in practice, hom(m)o-sexuality is played out through the bodies of women, matter, or sign, and heterosexuality has been up to now just an alibi for the smooth workings of man's relations with himself, or relations among men.
>
> (172)

17. See chapter 6.

18. Over half a century ago, Jefferson B. Fletcher noted how very uncomfortably the details of the episode's narrative square with its apparent significance as a straightforward allegorization of doctrine. As he observes, "We might say a cat with nine lives equals (in fight) one able dog, but I question if that is the kind of equality that would make for cat and dog friendship" (196). Unfortunately, having trusted Spenser's story far enough to register its contradictions, Fletcher decides that "all this hocus-pocus of magic is merely a device to give variety to the inevitably monotonous combats" (196).

19. See Durling 114–123.

20. See the note to 4.2.31 in Hamilton's edition (439).

21. One might consider the episode in canto 27 of the *Orlando furioso* in which the Archangel Michael beats Discord with a cross (27.24–41) as a comparable example of discrepancy between the iconographic significance of an object and the use to which it is put, as well as a possible source of Cambina's appropriation of the caduceus as a cudgel. See also Erasmus' colloquy, "Cyclops, or the Gospel Bearer," in which Erasmus' servant Polyphemus hits someone on the head three times with a metal-bound Gospel in the name of the Trinity.

22. Nohrnberg points out that "Pri-Di-Triamond must fight Cambel in three incarnations because traditionally only a knight who had prevailed thrice in the lists had proven himself worthy of a lady's love" (*SE* 275). Nevertheless, the series of violent but impermanent deaths inflicted on Pri-Di-Triamond makes the episode begin to resemble a Monty Python parody rather than a traditional joust.

6. SATYRANE'S TOURNAMENT

1. See Goldberg, *Endlesse Worke* 45–46.

2. Freud theorized that the fetish is a substitute the male imagines for the woman's penis, since if he accepts the absence of a female penis he is threatened with the possibility of his own castration. Spenser posits the hymen as the locus of male anxiety. See Freud, "Fetishism" 152–157.

3. See Pyles; and Willbern.

4. For a judicious analysis of this view, see Keith Thomas. Thomas concludes that male desire for absolute property rights in women is a more fundamental source of the importance attached to female chastity.

5. See Eric Partridge 146. The *OED* also lists target as a meaning of mark (*OED* s.v. "mark" 2.7).

6. On the woman as object of male perception in *The Faerie Queene*, see Theresa M. Krier passim.

7. The *locus classicus* of the analogy of rhetoric and sexuality is the writing of the twelfth-century author Alain de Lille. On the association of sex and grammar in Alain's work, see Ziolkowski. For studies of Alain's influence on European literature, including *The Faerie Queene*, see Quilligan, "Allegory, Allegoresis," "Words and Sex." Carolyn Dinshaw describes the association of gender with acts of literary signification in the works of Chaucer and the tradition of gendered poetics on which he draws. See also Lee Patterson's chapter on the Wife of Bath. On the gendering of language in Shakespeare and the association of reading and interpretation with sexual mastery, see Carol Cook.

8. Compare the magic cup in *Orlando furioso* (42.98–43.9) that spills its contents on any man whose wife is unfaithful. When offered a drink from the cup, Rinaldo prudently refuses.

9. Rosemary Kegl quotes George Puttenham's *The Arte of English Poesie* (1589; rpt. London, 1869), "the first embracementes never bred barnes, by reason of their overmuch affection and heate but only made passage for children and enforced greater liking" (66–67) in a thoughtful treament of how erotic discourse impinges on other Elizabethan ideological concerns.

10. See Ilya Prigogine for a fascinating treatment of theories of asymmetry.

11. Prince Arthur's expression of official chivalric ideology is conspicuously inapplicable to actual practice throughout Book IV: true and false knights fight among themselves over the lady, who functions as prize, all of them at odds with Arthur's vision of ideally chivalrous relations between loving ladies and their male protectors. Maureen Quilligan points out the dissonance between Arthur's idealistic pronouncement and Scudamore's claim of rights to Amoret (*Milton's Spenser* 206–207).

12. The term "beamlike" is very likely an allusion to the Latin slang use of "trabs" or beam for phallus (Lewis and Short s.v. "trabs" b.8).

13. Consider that one source of the battle of Britomart and Artegall is the combat between Bradamante and Ruggiero in canto 45 of the *Orlando furioso*. Ruggiero, having acquired the emotionally charged friendship of Leone, heir to the eastern emperor, agrees to fight in Leone's armor to win Bradamante for the Greek prince. In borrowing from Ariosto, Spenser tends to transform incipiently homoerotic relationships into heterosexual ones, as in his transformation of the erotic triangle comprising Leone, Ruggiero, and Bradamante into the mistaken rivalries of Artegall and Scudamore with Britomart (in this case moving through a mediating position of the homosocial), as well as in his adaptation of the Fiordespina episode (see chapter 1). One might see an

element of what one might today term homophobia ("concern with the Italian vice" might be more accurate historically) in this. Or one might argue that Spenser transfers the sense of transgressiveness associated with the sodomitical desires of Leone and Cloridano and Fiorodespina's nameless desire for Bradamante in the *Orlando furioso* to heterosexual relations.

14. Both Maureen Quilligan and Harry Berger, Jr., have raised the issue of how the reader's point of view on the Gardens of Adonis is gendered (see chapter 2 note 12). It strikes me that that question is rather like the curious incident of the barking dog in *The Hound of the Baskervilles* (curious because the dog never barked). Although the Gardens of Adonis raise the issue of how gender functions as a metaphoric construct, there seems to be remarkably little overt concern for the gender of the reader. Compare, for example, the analogous description of the Temple of Venus in Book IV, which is given explicitly from Scudamore's point of view.

15. See letter to Ralegh in Hamilton's edition, 737.

16. Rosemond Tuve distinguishes moral allegory as a pattern of behavior from allegory strictly conceived as a pattern of belief and describes the potential interplay between one sort of reading and the other (3–55).

17. Oddly enough, Canacee's desires in the choice of a mate are given less consideration than those of the False Florimell.

18. For a succinct treatment of negative images of idolatry in *Faerie Queene* III, see Nohrnberg *SE* 279. He goes on to argue that Book IV transforms and transvalues the evils of idolatry represented in *F.Q.* III. I am not so sure that idolatry completely sheds its negative connotations in *F.Q.* IV.

Major studies of English Renaissance attitudes toward iconoclasm and idolatry are by Ernest B. Gilman and Kenneth Gross. See also Sean Kane's article "idols, idolatry" in the *Spenser Encyclopedia*.

19. Compare 4.1.2.1–2 with 4.10.1.7–9.

20. Wölfflin draws the classic distinction in Renaissance art between the linear style, which appeals to the tactile sense, as if one could move one's finger along the clearly defined boundaries of objects, and the visual style, which appeals exclusively to the eye (18–72).

21. Julia Walker perceptively remarks that the "secret fear" felt by both Britomart and Artegall is the "fear of losing the male empowerment of knightly armor" (177n).

22. See the pseudo-Virgilian *Ciris*, which Spenser virtually paraphrases in Book III.

23. Donald Cheney has remarked that one might consider *The Faerie Queene* as a hyper Jamesian novel in which everyone is acutely self-conscious. I do not exempt myself from the criticism of relying excessively on narrative. I indulge in the convenience of describing characters and actions as a critical shorthand for broader textual processes.

7. THE ALLEGORY OF LUST

1. Britomart seems in this episode to be imitating Odysseus in his propensity to sleep soundly at inopportune moments.

2. According to Hamilton's note to 4.7.4, the text "suggests that Amoret exposes herself to rape under some inner compulsion" (473). See also Oram, "Elizabethan Fact" 42.

3. For a lucid discussion of this point, see Oram, "Elizabethan Fact" 42–43.

4. For a reading of the ambiguity of this passage that emphasizes the element of reproach in Timias' statement, see Bednarz 64–65. For a discussion of the psychological dimension of the episode, see Donald Cheney, "Spenser's Fortieth Birthday" 22–25; see also Oram, "Spenser's Raleghs" 358.

5. Oram sees female associations in Lust's "wide deep poke, down hanging low" and thus interprets Lust as a bisexual figure ("Elizabethan Fact" 42). I am more inclined to agree with Anne Lake Prescott that what is represented is a *scrotum dentatum*, although the ambiguity seems not inappropriate.

6. On this point, see particularly Williams 6–7; and Donald Cheney, *Spenser's Images of Nature* 25–29.

7. See Silberman, "Limitations of Temperance"; and Berger, "Narrative as Rhetoric."

8. In *The Castel of Helthe*, Sir Thomas Elyot recommends cucumbers and lettuce because of the cold humors they engender (62).

9. In a sense, this is the method St. Paul recommends: if you are burning, marry, although marriage is presumably not what Lust has in mind.

8. THE MARRIAGE OF THAMES AND MEDWAY

1. Volume 4 of the *Spenser Variorum* provides a selection of critical opinion about the supposed lack of unity in Book IV of *The Faerie Queene*. See particularly Warren 282; and Erskine 289.

2. Goldberg observes, "The only way to tell a story is never to have it end" (*Endlesse Worke* 72).

3. For a discussion of the river marriage as a literary convention, see Roche 168–178; Quint 156–166; and Herendeen.

4. For a treatment of Renaissance alternatives to the model of sign-referent that is informed by contemporary literary theory and historically grounded in the primary texts, see Waswo.

5. See Durling 112–124.

6. Variations of this tag also appear in "The Knight's Tale" (A 1761) and "The Merchant's Tale" (E 1986).

7. Edgar Wind describes the logic of unfolding and infolding (christened *explicatio* and *complicatio* by Cusanus) as characteristic of—significantly enough—orphic theology. Each unfolded element of the infolded whole is plainer and less complicated, but each element partakes of the nature of all the others. According to orphic and hermetic lore, the Hermaphrodite represented such an infolded, universal being (191–217). Wind judges that Spenser is heavy-handed in tracing the logic of unfolding through Pri-Di-Triamond, but that, I think is the point. The obvious *explicatio* of the -mond brothers contrasts with the subtle treatment of *explicatio* in the marriage of Thames and Medway, just as reductive orphic retrospection contrasts with the orphic mystery unfolded in the river marriage.

8. For a full and elegant treatment of the motif of Proteus in the Renaissance, see A. Bartlett Giamatti, "Proteus Unbound: Some Versions of the Sea God in the Renaissance"; for a specific discussion of Proteus in *The Faerie Queene*, see Giamatti, *Play of Double Senses* 118–133.

9. The intertextual connections between orphic Scudamore and narcissistic Marinell are more complex than I have been able to indicate. One source of Marinell's descent to Cymoent's undersea bower is a similar descent in Virgil's Fourth Georgic by the bee-keeper Aristaeus to the undersea home of his mother Cyrene and thence to Proteus, who tells him of the wrong he has done Orpheus and Eurydice (333–558).

10. See Goldberg, "The Mothers in Book III."

11. For other readings of the marriage of Thames and Medway, see Goldberg, *Endlesse Worke* 70–72; Braden; and Roche 167–184.

12. On derivation as linguistic drift, see Greene 14–15.

13. As Nohrnberg notes, "Since the persons are rivers, theirs is a courtship that is always proceeding, a wedding that never ends, and a marriage continuously consummated in extinction" (*SE* 275).

14. See Hamilton's note to 4.11.18 (511).

15. Quoted in Hamilton's note to 4.11.27 (513).

16. See chapter 4.

17. For some penetrating observations on how the pageant of rivers functions as a meditation on a map of the British Isles, see Berger, "Two Spenserian Retrospects" 210–211.

18. Herendeen points out that medieval allegorical descriptions of landscape, in particular of rivers, assimilated geographical fact and allegorical idea with no sense of dissonance (88–94). He remarks the seamless overlap of "imaginary" and "real" description of geography (119).

19. See Hesiod, *Theogony* 155–205.

20. See Hamilton's note to 4.11.28 (513).

21. For positive connotations of Cybele as goddess of civilization, see Roche 182. For some of the darker aspects of that figure, see Berger, "Two Spenserian Retrospects" 208. Neither critic mentions the very negative associations of Cybele with castration in the Catullus poem that, given the conspicuous pronoun shift in Spenser's text, seems to be an obvious source. Braden notes the Catullus poem as part of the Cybele tradition (44–45), but not the specific allusion in 4.11.28.

22. I am indebted to Donald Cheney for this reading.

23. The classic discussion of the logic of the supplement, the addition that, while purporting to complete the prior term, reveals its incompleteness is given by Jacques Derrida (*Of Grammatology* 141–164).

24. Note that the lion-drawn chariot of Cambina is a feature traditionally associated with Cybele. For discussions of the iconography of Cybele, see O'Connell 93–94; Roche 181–182; and Hawkins.

25. On this point, see Nohrnberg, *SE* 278.

26. Arthur Kinney has a thorough treatment of the interplay of rhetorical and mimetic dimensions of sixteenth-century poetics. Particularly apt in this

regard is his quotation of Bernard Weinberg's account of Julius Caesar Scaliger's *Poetices libri septem*: "Poetry is conceived of, in Scaliger's system, primarily as language. As language, it must enter into two distinct relationships: (1) with the things which are signified by the words employed and (2) with the audience for whom the signification is intended" (Kinney 41–42).

27. Compare Florimell's plaint:

> Ye Gods of seas, if any Gods at all
>> Haue care of right, or ruth of wretches wrong,
>> By one or other way me woefull thrall,
>> Deliuer hence out of this dungeon strong,
>> In which I daily dying am too long.
>> And if ye deeme me death for louing one,
>> That loues not me, then doe it not prolong,
>> But let me die and end my daies attone,
> And let him liue vnlou'd, or loue him selfe alone.
>
> But if that life ye vnto me decree,
>> Then let mee liue, as louers ought to do,
>> And of my lifes deare loue beloued be:
>> And if he shall through pride your doome vndo,
>> Do you by duresse him compell thereto,
>> And in this prison put him here with me:
>> One prison fittest is to hold vs two:
>> So had I rather to be thrall, then free;
> Such thraldome or such freedome let it surely be.
>> (4.12.9–10)

with Orpheus' plea to the Stygian gods:

> "pro munere poscimus usum;
> quodsi fata negant veniam pro coniuge, certum est
> nolle redire mihi: leto gaudete duorum."
>> (*Met.* 10.37–39)

[I ask the enjoyment of her as a boon; but if the fates deny this privilege for my wife, I am resolved not to return. Rejoice in the death of two.]

and the youth's curse of Narcissus, " 'sic amet ipse licet, sic non potiatur amato!' "(*Met.* 3.405) [So may he himself love, and not gain the thing he loves!]

Nohrnberg has observed that the episode of Marinell and Florimell "reconstructs the myth of Narcissus and Echo" (*Analogy* 432).

28. See discussion in chapter 5.

29. A few years ago the Metropolitan Museum of Art in New York held an exhibit of Renaissance picture frames conceived, for the first time in European art history, as entities separable from the paintings. It seemed the height of urban decadence to be part of a large crowd of people staring raptly at empty picture frames, but the frames were indeed beautiful, and the point was borne home that the issue of framing was of historical significance in the Renaissance.

30. Perhaps this is yet another Spenserian allusion to the "Tale of Sir Thopas." Showing a conspicuous lack of narrative control, Chaucer's pilgrim

announces "I telle it yow, hym hadde almest / Betid a sory care" (VII 758–759 or B² 1948–1949).

31. Contrast Cymodoche's determination to find "how she [Florimell's] libertie might enterprize" (4.12.28) with Scudamore's "braue emprize" (4.10.4.7) to carry off Amoret as his prize.

32. By contrast, the wasting away of the Redcrosse Knight to "the cheareless man" (1.8.43.7) in Orgoglio's dungeon evidences the priority of his spiritual being to his physical self.

33. See Hamilton's note to 4.12.33 (523): he points out that Scudamore seizes Amoret by the same gesture of taking the hand in 4.10.58.4–5.

34. See Hamilton's note to 4.12.31 (522).

35. In "Poetic Diction and Legal Fiction" Owen Barfield considers such legal fictions as a paradigm of poetic language.

36. This is not to deny meanings to a work of literature of which the artist was unconscious. But it seems to me that critics often foreclose their readings when they assume their own superior insight, especially on matters of poetics but sometimes on matters of politics as well. Contemporary ideas have a history, and that history is made up in large measure of earlier texts.

37. Annabel Patterson has an insightful treatment of the tendency of modern critics to appropriate earlier text for dubious political causes.

Bibliography

Abrams, M. H. *Doing Things With Texts: Essays in Criticism and Critical Theory*. New York: W. W. Norton, 1989.

Allen, Don Cameron. *Image and Meaning: Metaphoric Traditions in Renaissance Poetry*. 1960. Baltimore: Johns Hopkins University Press, 1968.

Allen, Michael J. B. "The Chase: A Development of a Renaissance Theme." *Comparative Literature* 20 (1968): 301–312.

Alpers, Paul. *The Poetry of* The Faerie Queene. Princeton: Princeton University Press, 1967.

Anderson, Judith. "Britomart." In *The Spenser Encyclopedia*, ed. A. C. Hamilton, Donald Cheney, W. F. Blisset, David A. Richardson, and William W. Barker, 113–115. Toronto: University of Toronto Press, 1990.

———. " 'A Gentle Knight was Pricking on the plaine': The Chaucerian Connection." *English Literary Renaissance* 13 (1983): 166–174.

———. "Whatever Happened to Amoret? The Poet's Role in Book IV of 'The Faerie Queene.' " *Criticism* 13 (1971): 180–200.

Anderson, W. S. "The Orpheus of Virgil and Ovid: *flebile nescio quid*." In *Orpheus: the Metamorphosis of a Myth*, ed. John Warden. Toronto: University of Toronto Press, 1982.

Ariosto, Ludovico. *Orlando furioso*. Ed. Edoardo Sanguineti. 2 vols. 1974. Milan: Garzanti, 1985.

———. *Orlando Furioso*. Trans. Guido Waldman. Oxford: Oxford University Press, 1983.

Bakhtin, Mikhail. *Rabelais and His World*. Trans. Helene Iswolsky. 1968. Bloomington: Indiana University Press, 1984.

Barfield, Owen. "Poetic Diction and Legal Fiction." In *Essays Presented to Charles Williams*, ed. C. S. Lewis, 106–127. 1947. Grand Rapids, Mich.: Eerdmans, 1966.

———. *Saving the Appearances: A Study in Idolatry*. New York: Harcourt Brace Jovanovich, 1965.

———. *Worlds Apart: A Dialogue of the 1960s*. Middletown, Conn.: Wesleyan University Press, 1963.

Barkan, Leonard. "Diana and Actaeon: The Myth as Synthesis." *English Literary Renaissance* 10 (1980): 317–359.

Bateson, Gregory. *Mind and Nature: A Necessary Unity*. New York: Bantam, 1979.

Bath, Michael. "The Legend of Caesar's Deer." *Medievalia et Humanistica*, n.s. 9 (1979): 53–66.

Baybak, Michael, Paul Delany, and A. Kent Hieatt. "Placement 'In the Middest' in *The Faerie Queene*." *Papers on Language and Literature* 5 (1969): 227–234.

Bednarz, James. "Ralegh in Spenser's Historical Allegory." *Spenser Studies* 4 (1984): 49–70.

Berger, Harry, Jr. "Busirane and the War Between the Sexes: An Interpretation of *The Faerie Queene* III.xi.xii." *English Literary Renaissance* 26 (1959): 171–187.

———. " 'Kidnapped Romance': Discourse in *The Faerie Queene*." In *Unfolded Tales: Essays on Renaissance Romance*, ed. George M. Logan and Gordon Teskey, 208–256. Ithaca: Cornell University Press, 1989.

———. "Narrative as Rhetoric in *The Faerie Queene*." *English Literary Renaissance* 21 (1991): 3–48.

———. "Orpheus, Pan, and the Poetics of Misogyny: Spenser's Critique of Pastoral Love and Art." *ELH* (1983): 27–60.

———. "Spenser's Gardens of Adonis: Force and Form in the Renaissance Imagination." In *Revisionary Play: Studies in Spenserian Dynamics*, 131–153. Berkeley: University of California Press, 1988.

———. "Two Spenserian Retrospects: The Antique Temple of Venus and the Primitive Marriage of Rivers." *Texas Studies in Language and Literature* 10 (1968): 5–25. Rpt. in *Revisionary Play: Studies in the Spenserian Dynamics*, 195–214. Berkeley: University of California Press, 1988.

Berleth, Richard J. "Heavens Favorable and Free: Belphoebe's Nativity in *The Faerie Queene*." *ELH* 40 (1973): 479–500.

Biblia sacra: Iuxta vulgatam versionem. 2 vols. Stuttgart: Württembergische Bibelaustalt, 1975.

Bieman, Elizabeth. *Plato Baptized: Towards the Interpretation of Spenser's Mimetic Fictions*. Toronto: University of Toronto Press, 1988.

Boccaccio, Giovanni. *Genealogie deorum gentilium libri*. Ed. Vincenzo Romano. Bari: Laterza, 1951.

Bode, Georg Heinrich. *Scriptores rerum mythicarum latini tres Romae super reperti*. Celli: Schulze, 1834.

Bohm, David, and F. David Peat. *Science, Order, and Creativity*. Toronto: Bantam, 1987.

Bohm, David. *Wholeness and the Implicate Order*. London: Routledge and Kegan Paul, 1980.

Braden, Gordon. "riverrun: An Epic Catalogue in *The Faerie Queene*." *English Literary Renaissance* 5 (1975): 25–48.

Bradley, Sister Ritamary. "Backgrounds of the Title *Speculum* in Medieval Literature." *Speculum* 29 (1954): 100–115.

———. "The *Wife of Bath's Tale* and the Mirror Tradition." *Journal of English and Germanic Philology* 55 (1956): 624–630.

Brenkman, John. "Narcissus in the Text." *Georgia Review* 30 (1976): 293–327.

Broaddus, James. "Renaissance Psychology and Britomart's Adventures in *Faerie Queene* III." *English Literary Renaissance* 17 (1987): 186–207.

Brundage, James A. *Law, Sex, and Christian Society in Medieval Europe*. Chicago: University of Chicago Press, 1987.

Callimachus Fragments. Musaeus Hero and Leander. Trans. C. A. Trypanis [Callimachus] and Cedric Whitman [Musaeus]. Cambridge, Mass.: Harvard University Press, 1978.

Cassell, Anthony K., and Victoria Kirkham, eds. and trans. *Diana's Hunt: Caccia di Diana: Boccaccio's First Fiction.* Philadelphia: University of Pennsylvania Press, 1991.

Castiglione, Baldassare. *The Book of the Courtier.* Trans. Thomas Hoby. London: Dent, 1974.

Catullus, Gaius Valerius. *Catullus Tibullus and Pervigilium Veneris.* Trans. F. W. Cornish. 1913. Rev. ed. Cambridge, Mass.: Harvard University Press, 1976.

Chaucer, Geoffrey. *The Riverside Chaucer.* Ed. Larry D. Benson. 3d ed. Boston: Houghton Mifflin, 1987.

Cheney, Donald. "Spenser's Fortieth Birthday and Related Fictions." *Spenser Studies* 4 (1984): 3–31.

———. "Spenser's Hermaphrodite and the 1590 *Faerie Queene*." *PMLA* 87 (1972): 192–200.

———. *Spenser's Images of Nature: Wild Man and Shepherd in "The Faerie Queene."* New Haven: Yale University Press, 1966.

Cheney, Patrick. "Spenser's Completion of *The Squire's Tale*: Love, Magic, and Heroic Action in the Legend of Cambell and Triamond." *The Journal of Medieval and Renaissance Studies* 15 (1985): 135–155.

Cirillo, A. R. "The Fair Hermaphrodite: Love Union in the Poetry of Donne and Spenser." *Studies in English Literature* 9 (1969): 81–95.

Colie, Rosalie. *Paradoxica Epidemica: The Renaissance Tradition of Paradox.* Princeton: Princeton University Press, 1966.

Colish, Marcia. *The Mirror of Language: A Study of Medieval Theory of Knowledge.* New Haven: Yale University Press, 1968.

Cook, Carol. " 'The Sign and Semblance of Her Honor': Reading Gender Difference in *Much Ado about Nothing*." *PMLA* 101 (1986): 186–202.

Craig, Martha. "The Secret Wit of Spenser's Language." In *Elizabethan Poetry: Modern Essays in Criticism*, ed. Paul Alpers, 447–472. New York: Oxford University Press, 1967.

Dallet, Joseph B. "Ideas of Sight in *The Faerie Queene*." *ELH* 27 (1960): 87–121.

Dasenbrock, Reed Way. "Escaping the Squires' Double Bind in Books III and IV of *The Faerie Queene*." *Studies in English Literature* 26 (1986): 25–45.

Davis, Natalie Zemon. "Boundaries and the Sense of Self in Sixteenth-Century France." In *Reconstructing Individualism: Autonomy, Individuality, and the Self in Western Thought*, ed. Thomas C. Heller, Morton Sosna, and David E. Wellbery, 53–63. Stanford: Stanford University Press, 1986.

Dean, Leonard F. "Bodin's *Methodus* in England before 1625." *Studies in Philology* 39 (1942): 160–166.

de Boer, Cornelis, ed. «*Ovide moralisé*»: *poème du commencement du quatorzième siècle.* Verhandelingen der koninklijke Akademie van Wetenschappen te Amsterdam. Afdeeling Letterkunde, Nieuwe Reeks, nos. 15, 21. Amsterdam: J. Müller, 1915, 1920.

Delcourt, Marie. *Hermaphrodite: Mythes et rites de la bisexualité dans l'antiquité classique.* Paris: Presses Universitaires de France, 1958.

de Man, Paul. *Allegories of Reading: Figural Language in Rousseau, Nietzsche, Rilke, and Proust.* New Haven: Yale University Press, 1979.

———. "Autobiography as De-Facement." *The Rhetoric of Romanticism.* New York: Columbia University Press, 1984.

DeNeef, A. Leigh. *Spenser and the Motives of Metaphor.* Durham, N.C.: Duke University Press, 1982.

Dennet, Daniel C. *Elbow Room: the Varieties of Free Will Worth Wanting.* Cambridge, Mass.: MIT Press, 1984.

Derrida, Jacques. *Limited Inc.* Trans. Samuel Weber. Evanston, Ill.: Northwestern University Press, 1988.

———. *Of Grammatology.* Trans. Gayatri Chakravortry Spivak. Baltimore: Johns Hopkins University Press, 1974.

Dinshaw, Carolyn. *Chaucer's Sexual Poetics.* Madison: University of Wisconsin Press, 1989.

Diodorus Siculus. *Diodorus of Sicily.* Vol. 2. Trans. C. H. Oldfather. Cambridge, Mass.: Harvard University Press, 1979.

Dundas, Judith. "*The Faerie Queene*: The Incomplete Poem and the Whole Meaning." *Modern Philology* 71 (1974): 257–265.

Durling, Robert. *The Figure of the Poet in Renaissance Epic.* Cambridge, Mass.: Harvard University Press, 1965.

Eccles, Audrey. *Obstetrics and Gynaecology in Tudor and Stuart England.* Kent, Ohio: Kent State University Press, 1982.

Edgerton, Samuel Y. *The Renaissance Rediscovery of Linear Perspective.* New York: Basic Books, 1975.

Edwards, Calvin R. "The Narcissus Myth in Spenser's Poetry." *Studies in Philology* 74 (1977): 63–88.

Elyot, Thomas. *The Book Named the Governor.* Ed. S. E. Lehmberg. London: Dent, 1963.

———. *The Castel of Helthe.* Ed. Samuel A. Tannenbaum. New York: Scholars Facsimiles and Reprints, 1937.

Erasmus, Desiderius. *Ten Colloquies.* Trans. Craig R. Thompson. Indianapolis: Bobbs-Merrill, 1957.

Esolen, Anthony M. "The Disingenuous Poet Laureate: Spenser's Adoption of Chaucer." *Studies in Philology* 87 (1990): 285–311.

Estienne, Charles. *Dictionarium historicum geographicium . . . complectens.* Ursellis, 1601.

Evans, Maurice. *Spenser's Anatomy of Heroism: A Commentary on* The Faerie Queene. Cambridge: Cambridge University Press, 1970.

Eves, Howard. *An Introduction to the History of Mathematics.* 3d ed. New York: Holt, Rinehart and Winston, 1969.

Festus, Sextus Pompeius. *De verborum significatu quae supersunt Pauli Epitome.* Ed. Wallace Lindsay. Leipzig: B. G. Teubner, 1913.

Fletcher, Jefferson B. " 'The Legend of Cambel and Triamond' in the *Faerie Queene.*" *Studies in Philology* 35 (1938): 195–201.

Fowler, Alastair. "Six Knights at Castle Joyeous." *Studies in Philology* 56 (1959): 583–599.

Freccero, John. "Autobiography and Narrative." In *Reconstructing Individualism: Autonomy, Individuality, and the Self in Western Thought*, ed. Thomas C. Heller, Morton Sosna, and David E. Wellbery, 16–29. Stanford: Stanford University Press, 1986.

———. "The Fig Tree and the Laurel: Petrarch's Poetics." *Diacritics* 5 (Spring 1975): 34–40.

Freud, Sigmund. "Fetishism." In *The Standard Edition of the Complete Psychological Works of Sigmund Freud*, trans. James Strachey. Vol. 21, *The Future of an Illusion; Civilization and Its Discontents; and Other Works*, 152–157. London: The Hogarth Press, 1961.

Friedman, Lionel J. " 'Gradus amoris.' " *Romance Philology* 19 (1966): 167–177.

Fuss, Diana. *Essentially Speaking: Feminism, Nature, and Difference*. New York: Routledge, 1989.

Galyon, Linda. "Scudamore family." In *The Spenser Encyclopedia*, ed. A. C. Hamilton, Donald Cheney, W. F. Blisset, David A. Richardson, and William W. Barker, 634–635. Toronto: University of Toronto Press, 1990.

The Geneva Bible: A Facsimile of the 1560 Edition. Madison: University of Wisconsin Press, 1969.

Ghisalberti, Fausto. *Arnolfo d'Orléans: Un cultore di Ovidio nel secolo xii*. Memorie del R. Istituto Lombardo di scienze e lettere: Classe di lettere, scienze morale storiche. 3d s., no. 15, 157–234. Milan: Ulrico Hoepli, 1932.

———, ed. *Giovanni del Virgilio: espositore delle «Metamorfosi»*. Florence: Leo S. Olschki, 1933.

———, ed. *Integumenta Ovidii: Poemetto inedito del secolo xii* [by John of Garland]. Messina: Giuseppe Principiato, 1933.

Giamatti, A. Bartlett. *The Play of Double Senses: Spenser's* Faerie Queene. Englewood Cliffs: Prentice Hall, 1975.

———. "Proteus Unbound: Some Versions of the Sea God in the Renaissance." In *The Disciplines of Criticism: Essays in Literary Theory, Interpretation and History*, ed. Peter Demetz, Thomas Greene, and Lowry Nelson, Jr., 437–475. New Haven: Yale University Press, 1968.

Gilbert, Allan H. "The Ladder of Lechery, *The Faerie Queene*, III, i, 45." *MLN* 56 (1941): 594–597.

Gilligan, Carol. "Remapping the Moral Domain: New Images of the Self in Relationship." In *Reconstructing Individualism: Autonomy, Individuality, and the Self in Western Thought*, ed. Thomas C. Heller, Morton Sosna, and David E. Wellbery, 237–252. Stanford: Stanford University Press, 1986.

Gilman, Ernest B. *Iconoclasm and Poetry in the English Reformation: Down Went Dagon*. Chicago: University of Chicago Press, 1986.

Giraldi, Lilio Gregorio. *De deis gentium*. Leyden, 1696.

Girard, René. *Deceit, Desire, and the Novel: Self and Other in Literary Structure*. Trans. Yvonne Freccero. 1961. Baltimore: Johns Hopkins University Press, 1965.

———. *"To double business bound": Essays on Literature, Mimesis, and Anthropology*. Baltimore: Johns Hopkins University Press, 1978.

Gohlke, Madelon Sprengnether. "Embattled Allegory: Book II of *The Faerie Queene*." *English Literary Renaissance* 8 (1978): 123–140.

Goldberg, Jonathan. *Endlesse Worke: Spenser and the Structures of Discourse.* Baltimore: Johns Hopkins University Press, 1981.

———. "The Mothers in Book III of *The Faerie Queene.*" *TSLL* 17 (1979): 5–26.

Grabes, Herbert. *The Mutable Glass: Mirror-Imagery in Titles and Texts of the Middle Ages and English Renaissance.* Cambridge: Cambridge University Press, 1982.

Greenblatt, Stephen. "Fiction and Friction." In *Reconstructing Individualism: Autonomy, Individuality, and the Self in Western Thought,* ed. Thomas C. Heller, Morton Sosna, and David E. Wellbery, 30–52. Stanford: Stanford University Press, 1986.

———. *Renaissance Self-Fashioning: From More to Shakespeare.* Chicago: University of Chicago Press, 1980.

Greene, Thomas M. *The Light in Troy: Imitation and Discovery in Renaissance Poetry.* New Haven: Yale University Press, 1982.

Gregerson, Linda. "Protestant Erotics: Idolatry and Interpretation in Spenser's *Faerie Queene.*" *ELH* 58 (1991): 1–34

Gross, Kenneth. *Spenserian Poetics: Idolatry, Iconoclasm and Magic.* Ithaca: Cornell University Press, 1985.

Guibbory, Achsah. *The Map of Time: Seventeenth-Century English Literature and Ideas of Pattern in History.* Urbana: University of Illinois Press, 1986.

Guillén, Claudio. "On the Concept and Metaphor of Perspective." In *Comparatists at Work,* ed. Stephen G. Nichols, Jr., and Richard B. Vowles, 29–90. Waltham, Mass.: Blaisdell, 1968.

Guillory, John. *Poetic Authority: Spenser, Milton, and Literary History.* New York: Columbia University Press, 1983.

Halio, Jay L. "The Metaphor of Conception and Elizabethan Theories of the Imagination." *Neophilologus* 50 (1966): 454–461.

Hall, Iris Tillman. "Britomart and *Be Bold, Be Not Too Bold.*" *ELH* 38 (1971): 173–187.

Haller, William. " 'Hail Wedded Love.' " *ELH* 13 (1946): 79–97.

Hamilton, A. C. " 'Like Race to Runne': The Parallel Structure of *The Faerie Queene,* Books I and II." *PMLA* 73 (1958): 327–334.

———, Donald Cheney, W. F. Blisset, David A. Richardson, and William W. Barker, eds. *The Spenser Encyclopedia.* Toronto: University of Toronto Press, 1990.

———. *The Structure of Allegory in* The Faerie Queene. Oxford: Clarendon Press, 1961.

Hawkins, Peter S. "From Mythography to Myth-making: Spenser and the *Magna Mater* Cybele." *The Sixteenth-Century Journal* 12 (1981): 51–64.

Heller, Thomas C., Morton Sosna, and David E. Wellbery, eds. *Reconstructing Individualism: Autonomy, Individuality, and the Self in Western Thought.* Stanford: Stanford University Press, 1986.

Heninger, S. K. "The Orgoglio Episode in *The Faerie Queene.*" *ELH* 26 (1959): 171–187.

———. *Sidney and Spenser: the Poet as Maker.* University Park, Pa.: Penn State University Press, 1989.

————. *Touches of Sweet Harmony: Pythagorean Cosmology and Renaissance Poetics*. San Marino, Calif.: The Huntington Library, 1974.

Herendeen, Wyman H. *From Landscape to Literature: The River and the Myth of Geography*. Pittsburgh: Duquesne University Press, 1986.

Hesiod. *Theogony; Works and Days*. Trans. M. L. West. Oxford: Oxford University Press, 1988.

Hieatt, A. Kent. *Chaucer, Spenser, Milton: Mythopoeic Continuities and Transformations*. Montreal: McGill–Queen's University Press, 1975.

————. "Scudamour's Practice of *Maistrye* upon Amoret." In *Essential Articles for the Study of Edmund Spenser*, ed. A. C. Hamilton, 199–201. Hamden: Archon, 1972.

Himelick, Raymond, trans. *The Enchiridion of Erasmus*. Bloomington: Indiana University Press, 1963.

Hofstadter, Douglas R. *Gödel, Escher, Bach: an Eternal Golden Braid*. 1979. New York: Vintage, 1980.

Horace. *The Odes and Epodes*. Trans. C. E. Bennett. Cambridge, Mass.: Harvard University Press, 1978.

Hough, Graham. *A Preface to* The Faerie Queene. New York: Norton, 1962.

Hughes, Merrit Y. "Virgilian Allegory and *The Faerie Queene*." *PMLA* 44 (1929): 696–705.

Hulse, Clark. *The Rule of Art: Literature and Painting in the Renaissance*. Chicago: University of Chicago Press, 1990.

Hutton, James. "Spenser and the 'Cinq Points en Amours.' " *MLN* 57 (1942): 657–661.

Irigaray, Luce. *This Sex Which Is Not One*. Trans. Catherine Porter with Carolyn Burke. Ithaca: Cornell University Press, 1985.

Jones, Ann Rosalind. "Writing the Body: Toward an Understanding of *L'écriture feminine*." *Feminist Studies* 7 (1981): 246–263.

Kahn, Victoria. *Rhetoric, Prudence, and Skepticism in the Renaissance*. Ithaca: Cornell University Press, 1985.

Kane, Sean. "Idols, idolatry." In *The Spenser Encyclopedia*, ed. A. C. Hamilton, Donald Cheney, W. F. Blisset, David A. Richardson, and William W. Barker, 387–388. Toronto: University of Toronto Press, 1990.

Kaske, Carol. "The Dragon's Spark and Sting and the Structure of Red Cross's Dragon-Fight." In *Essential Articles for the Study of Edmund Spenser*, ed. A. C. Hamilton, 425–446. Hamden: Archon, 1972.

Kegl, Rosemary. " 'Those Terible Aproches': Sexuality, Social Mobility, and Resisting Courtliness of Puttenham's *The Arte of English Poesie*." *English Literary Renaissance* 20 (1990): 179–208.

Kennedy, William J. "Petrarchan Textuality: Commentaries and Gender Revisions." In *Discourses of Authority in Medieval and Renaissance Literature*, ed. Kevin Brownlee and Walter Stephens. Hanover, N.H.: University Press of New England, 1989.

Kermode, Frank. *The Sense of an Ending: Studies in the Theory of Fiction*. London: Oxford University Press, 1966.

Kinney, Arthur F. *Continental Humanist Poetics: Studies in Erasmus, Castiglione, Marguerite de Navarre, Rabelais, and Cervantes.* Amherst: University of Massachusetts Press, 1989.

Kline, Maurice. *Mathematical Thought from Ancient to Modern Times.* New York: Oxford University Press, 1972.

Koller, Katherine. "Spenser and Raleigh." *ELH* 1 (1934): 37–60.

Krier, Theresa M. *Gazing on Secret Sights: Spenser, Classical Imitation, and the Decorums of Vision.* Ithaca: Cornell University Press, 1990.

Kuhn, Thomas S. *The Structure of Scientific Revolutions.* Chicago: University of Chicago Press, 1970.

Lacan, Jacques. *Écrits: A Selection.* Trans. Alan Sheridan. New York: Norton, 1977.

Lactantius Placidus. "Metamorphoses." In *Historiae poeticae: Scriptores antiqui.* Ed. Thomas Gale. Paris: F. Muguet, 1675.

Laqueur, Thomas. "Orgasm, Generation, and the Politics of Reproductive Biology." *Representations* 14 (Spring 1986): 1–41.

Leeman, Fred. *Hidden Images: Games of Perception: Anamorphic Art. Illusion: From the Renaissance to the Present.* Trans. Ellyn Childs Allison and Margaret L. Kaplan. New York: Harry N. Abrams, 1976.

Levao, Ronald. *Renaissance Minds and Their Fictions: Cusanus, Sidney, Shakespeare.* Berkeley: University of California Press, 1985.

Lewis, C. S. *The Allegory of Love: A Study in Medieval Tradition.* 1936. New York: Oxford University Press, 1958.

Lewis, Charlton T., and Charles Short. *A Latin Dictionary.* 1879. Oxford: Clarendon Press, 1969.

Lindberg, David C. *Theories of Vision from Al-Kindi to Kepler.* Chicago: University of Chicago Press, 1976.

Lucretius. *De rerum natura.* Ed. and trans. W. H. D. Rouse. Cambridge, Mass.: Harvard University Press, 1966.

MacCaffrey, Isabel G. *Spenser's Allegory: The Anatomy of Imagination.* Princeton: Princeton University Press, 1976.

Maclean, Ian. *The Renaissance Notion of Woman: A Study in the Fortunes of Scholasticism and Medical Science in European Intellectual Life.* Cambridge: Cambridge University Press, 1980.

Miller, David Lee. *The Poem's Two Bodies: the Poetics of the 1590* Faerie Queene. Princeton: Princeton University Press, 1988.

Milne, Fred L. "The Doctrine of Act and Potency: A Metaphysical Ground for Interpretation of Spenser's Garden of Adonis Passages." *Studies in Philology* 70 (1973): 279–287.

Miskimin, Alice. *The Renaissance Chaucer.* New Haven: Yale University Press, 1975.

Montrose, Louis A. "The Elizabethan Subject and the Spenserian Text." In *Literary Theory / Renaissance Texts,* ed. Patricia Parker and David Quint, 303–340. Baltimore: Johns Hopkins University Press, 1986.

———. "*A Midsummer Night's Dream* and the Shaping Fantasies of Elizabethan Culture: Gender, Power, Form." In *Rewriting the Renaissance: The*

Discourses of Sexual Difference in Early Modern Europe, ed. Margaret W. Ferguson, Maureen Quilligan, and Nancy Vickers, 65–87. Chicago: University of Chicago Press, 1986.

Mulvey, Laura. "Visual Pleasure and Narrative Cinema." In *Visual and Other Pleasures*, 14–26. Bloomington: Indiana University Press, 1989.

Nelson, John Charles. *Renaissance Theory of Love: The Context of Giordano Bruno's* Eroici furori. New York: Columbia University Press, 1958.

Nelson, William. *The Poetry of Edmund Spenser*. New York: Columbia University Press, 1963.

Nohrnberg, James. *The Analogy of* The Faerie Queene. Princeton: Princeton University Press, 1976.

———. "*The Faerie Queene*, Book IV." In *The Spenser Encyclopedia*, ed. A. C. Hamilton, Donald Cheney, W. F. Blisset, David A. Richardson, and William W. Barker, 273–280. Toronto: University of Toronto Press, 1990.

O'Connell. *Mirror and Veil: The Historical Dimension of Spenser's* Faerie Queene. Chapel Hill: University of North Carolina Press, 1977.

Oram, William A. "Elizabethan Fact and Spenserian Fiction." *Spenser Studies* 4 (1984): 33–47.

———. "Spenser's Raleghs." *Studies in Philology* 87 (1990): 341–362.

Ovid. *Metamorphoses*. Trans. Frank Justus Miller. 2 vols. Cambridge, Mass.: Harvard University Press, 1971.

Parker, Patricia. *Inescapable Romance: Studies in the Poetics of a Mode*. Princeton: Princeton University Press, 1979.

———. *Literary Fat Ladies: Rhetoric, Gender, Property*. London: Methuen, 1987.

Partridge, Eric. *Shakespeare's Bawdy: A Literary and Psychological Essay and A Comprehensive Glossary*. New York: Dutton, 1969.

Patterson, Annabel. *Reading Between the Lines*. Madison: University of Wisconsin Press, 1993.

Patterson, Lee. *Chaucer and the Subject of History*. Madison: University of Wisconsin Press, 1991.

Peend, Thomas. *The Pleasant Fable of Hermaphroditus and Salmacis*. London: T. Colwell, 1565.

Pichaske, David R. "*The Faerie Queene* IV.ii and iii: Spenser on the Genesis of Friendship." *Studies in English Literature* 17 (1977): 81–93.

Plato. *The Collected Dialogues*. Ed. Edith Hamilton and Huntington Cairns. Princeton: Princeton University Press, 1963.

Popkin, Richard H. *The History of Skepticism from Erasmus to Spinoza*. Rev. ed. Berkeley: University of California Press, 1979.

Popper, Karl. *Conjectures and Refutations: the Growth of Scientific Knowledge*. 1965. New York: Harper and Row, 1968.

Prescott, Anne Lake. "The Thirsty Deer and the Lord of Life: Some Contexts for *Amoretti* 67–70." *Spenser Studies* 6 (1985): 33–76.

———. "*Translatio Lupae*: Du Bellay's Roman Whore Goes North." *Renaissance Quarterly* 42 (1989): 397–419.

Prigogine, Ilya. *Order Out of Chaos: Man's New Dialogue with Nature*. New York: Bantam, 1984.

Puttenham, George. *The Arte of English Poesie*. Ed. Edward Arber. 1869. English Reprints, 4. New York: AMS Press, 1966.

Pyles, Thomas. "Ophelia's 'Nothing.' " *Modern Language Notes* 64 (1949): 322–323.

Quilligan, Maureen. "Allegory, Allegoresis, and the Deallegorization of Language: The *Roman de la Rose*, the *De Planctu Naturae* and the *Parlement of Foules*." In *Allegory, Myth, and Symbol*, ed. Morton W. Bloomfield. Harvard English Studies 9. Cambridge. Mass.: Harvard University Press, 1981.

———. *The Language of Allegory: Defining the Genre*. Ithaca: Cornell University Press, 1979.

———. *Milton's Spenser: The Politics of Reading*. Ithaca: Cornell University Press, 1983.

———. "Words and Sex: The Language of Allegory in the *De Planctu Naturae*, the *Roman de la Rose*, and Book III of *The Faerie Queene*." *Allegorica* 2 (1977): 195–216.

Quint, David. *Origin and Originality in Renaissance Literature: Versions of the Source*. New Haven: Yale University Press, 1983.

Rajan, Balachandra. *The Form of the Unfinished: English Poetics from Spenser to Pound*. Princeton: Princeton University Press, 1985.

Recorde, Robert. *The Pathway to Knowledge*. London, 1551.

Rhodes, Neil. *Elizabethan Grotesque*. London: Routledge and Kegan Paul, 1980.

Robertson, D. W. *A Preface to Chaucer: Studies in Medieval Perspectives*. Princeton: Princeton University Press, 1963.

Roche, Thomas P., Jr. *The Kindly Flame: A Study of the Third and Fourth Books of Spenser's* Faerie Queene. Princeton: Princeton University Press, 1964.

Rose, Mark. *Heroic Love: Studies in Sidney and Spenser*. Cambridge, Mass.: Harvard University Press, 1968.

———. *Spenser's Art: A Companion to Book One of* The Faerie Queene. Cambridge, Mass.: Harvard University Press, 1975.

Rose, Mary Beth. *The Expense of Spirit: Love and Sexuality in English Renaissance Drama*. Ithaca: Cornell University Press, 1988.

Rotman, Brian. *The Semiotics of Zero*. Houndmills, Basingstoke, Hampshire: Macmillan, 1987.

Sabinus, Georgius. *Metamorphoses*. 1589. Reprint, New York: Garland, 1976.

Scarry, Elaine. *The Body in Pain: The Making and Unmaking of the World*. New York: Oxford University Press, 1985.

Schroeder, John W. "Spenser's Erotic Drama: The Orgoglio Episode." *ELH* 29 (1962): 140–159.

"Scudamore, John." *The Dictionary of National Biography*. Eds. Leslie Stephen and Sidney Lee, 17:1092–1096. London: Oxford University Press, 1973.

Sedgwick, Eve Kosofsky. *Between Men: English Literature and Male Homosocial Desire*. New York: Columbia University Press, 1985.

Sidney, Sir Philip. *A Defence of Poetry*. Ed. Jan A. Van Dorsten. Oxford: Oxford University Press, 1966.

Silberman, Lauren. "Mythographic Transformations of Ovid's Hermaphrodite." *The Sixteenth-Century Journal* 19 (1988): 643–652.

———. "*The Faerie Queene*, Book II and the Limitations of Temperance." *Modern Language Studies* 25 (1988): 9–27.

Spens, Janet. *Spenser's Faerie Queene: An Interpretation*. 1934. Reprint, New York: Russell and Russell, 1964.

Spenser, Edmund. *Edmund Spenser's Poetry*. Ed. Hugh Maclean. 2d ed. New York: Norton, 1968.

———. *Edmund Spenser's Poetry*. Eds. Hugh Maclean and Anne Lake Prescott. 3d ed. New York: Norton, 1993.

———. *The Faerie Queene*. Ed. A. C. Hamilton. London: Longman, 1977.

———. *The Works of Edmund Spenser: a Variorum Edition*. Eds. Edwin Greenlaw, Charles Grosvenor Osgood, and Frederick Morgan Padelford. 11 vols. Baltimore: Johns Hopkins University Press, 1932–1949.

———. *The Yale Edition of the Shorter Poems of Edmund Spenser*. Eds. William A. Oram, Einar Bjorvand, Ronald Bond, Thomas H. Cain, Alexander Dunlop, and Richard Schell. New Haven: Yale University Press, 1989.

Stallybrass, Peter. "Patriarchal Territories: The Body Enclosed." In *Rewriting the Renaissance: The Discourses of Sexual Difference in Early Modern Europe*, ed. Margaret W. Ferguson, Maureen Quilligan, and Nancy Vickers, 123–142. Chicago, University of Chicago Press, 1986.

Steadman, John M. "The 'Inharmonious Blacksmith': Spenser and the Pythagoras Legend." *PMLA* 79 (1964): 664–665.

Svensson, Lars-Håken. *Silent Art: Rhetorical and Thematic Patterns in Samuel Daniel's Delia*. Lund Studies in English, 57. Lund: C. W. K. Gleerup, 1980.

Sylvester, Richard S., and Davis P. Harding, eds. *Two Early Tudor Lives: The Life and Death of Cardinal Wolsey by George Cavendish: The Life of Sir Thomas More by William Roper*. New Haven: Yale University Press, 1962.

Tasso, Torquato. *Gerusalemme liberata*. Ed. Mario Sansone. Milan: Signorelli, 1973.

———. *Jerusalem Delivered*. Trans. Edward Fairfax. Ed. John Charles Nelson. New York: Capricorn, 1963.

———. *Poesie*. Milan: R. Ricciardi, 1952.

Thiébaux, Marcell. *The Stag of Love: The Chase in Medieval Literature*. Ithaca: Cornell University Press, 1974.

Thomas, Keith. "The Double Standard." *Journal of the History of Ideas*. 20 (1959): 195–216.

Tolkien, J. R. R. "On Fairy Stories." In *Essays Presented to Charles Williams*, ed. C. S. Lewis, 38–89. Grand Rapids, Mich.: Eerdmans, 1966.

Tonkin, Humphrey. "Spenser's Garden of Adonis and Britomart's Quest." *PMLA* 88 (1973): 408–417.

Toulmin, Stephen E. *The Uses of Argument*. Cambridge: Cambridge University Press, 1958.

Tuve, Rosemund. *Allegorical Imagery: Some Medieval Books and Their Posterity*. Princeton: Princeton University Press, 1966.

Umunc, Himmet. "Chrysogone." In *The Spenser Encyclopedia*, ed. A. C. Hamilton, Donald Cheney, W. F. Blisset, David A. Richardson, and William W. Barker, 153. Toronto: University of Toronto Press, 1990.

Vickers, Nancy. "Diana Described: Scattered Woman and Scattered Rhyme." In *Writing and Sexual Difference*, ed. Elizabeth Abel, 95–109. Chicago: University of Chicago Press, 1982.

Virgil. *Eclogues, Georgics, Aeneid, the Minor Poems*. Trans. H. Rushton Fairclough. Rev. ed. (2 vols.). Cambridge, Mass.: Harvard University Press, 1978.

Vitruvius. *On Architecture*. Ed. and trans. Frank Granger. Vol. 1. London: Heinemann, 1931.

Walker, Julia M. "Spenser's Elizabeth Portrait and the Fiction of Dynastic Epic." *Modern Philology* 90 (1992): 172–199.

Waswo, Richard. *Language and Meaning in the Renaissance*. Princeton: Princeton University Press, 1987.

Weller, Barry. "The Rhetoric of Friendship in Montaigne's *Essais*." *New Literary History* 9 (1978): 503–523.

Willbern, David. "Shakespeare's Nothing." In *Representing Shakespeare: New Psycho-analytic Essays*, ed. Murray M. Schwartz and Coppelia Kahn, 244–263. Baltimore: Johns Hopkins University Press, 1980.

Williams, Kathleen. *Spenser's* Faerie Queene: *The World of Glass*. London: Routledge and Kegan Paul, 1966.

Wimsatt, James I. *Allegory and Mirror: Tradition and Structure in Middle English Literature*. New York: Pegasus, 1970.

Wind, Edgar. *Pagan Mysteries in the Renaissance*. 1958. Rev. ed. New York: Norton, 1968.

Wofford, Susanne L. *The Choice of Achilles: The Ideology of Figure in the Epic*. Stanford: Stanford University Press, 1992.

Wölfflin, Heinrich. *Principles of Art History: The Problem of the Development of Style in Later Art*. Trans. M. D. Hottinger. 1932. New York: Dover, 1950.

Woodbridge, Linda. "Palisading the Elizabethan Body Politic." *Texas Studies in Language and Literature* 33 (1991): 327–354.

Woodhouse, A. S. P. "Nature and Grace in *The Faerie Queene*." *ELH* 16 (1949): 194–228.

Woods, Susanne. "Closure in *The Faerie Queene*." *Journal of English and Germanic Philology* 76 (1977): 195–216.

Ziolkowski, Jan. *Alan of Lille's Grammar of Sex: The Meaning of Grammar to a Twelfth-Century Intellectual*. Cambridge, Mass.: Medieval Academy of America, 1985.

Index

Abrams, M. H., 142
Absence: of Amoret, 107, 117–18; and presence, 61, 101–2, 105, 140, 142. *See also* Loss
Absolutes, 142
Actaeon, 29, 33, 38, 150
Adonis, 7–8, 35–48, 49, 152n20, 153n27. *See also* Gardens of Adonis
Æmylia, 118, 121
Agape, 91, 92–94, 97
Alain de Lille, 163n7
Allegory, 3, 66, 143n3, 164n16; Book I, 3–4, 13–14, 15–17, 41; Book III, 5, 6–7, 13–17, 22, 35–48, 56–58, 64, 108, 118, 152n20, 155; Book IV, 10, 73, 87, 90, 96, 98, 107, 117–24, 133, 138, 141; four-fold pattern, 15; moral, 37–38, 123, 164n16
Alpers, Paul J., 36–37, 115, 145n6
Amoret, 59, 130; absence, 107, 117–18; birth, 43; Busirane and, 58–67, 72–74, 85, 118–19, 127, 155–58 passim; chastity of, 66, 69–70, 73, 78, 104, 119; jousts over, 77, 100, 107; in Lust allegory, 117–20, 121, 122, 123–24; rape, 85–86, 165n2; and Scudamore, 8–9, 49, 50, 54, 58, 62–86 passim, 111, 118, 129, 157–63 passim, 168n31; Timias and, 122, 123–24
Anderson, Judith, 107, 115
Androgyny, 8, 29–30, 70, 79, 140, 150n49
Angelica, 151nn6,11
Aphrodite, 52
Apocalypse, 15–16
Archimago, 14, 16
Ariosto: Angelica-Medoro episode, 151nn6,11; Bradamante-Ruggiero combat, 163–64; and Cambina, 96, 162n21; Fiordespina episode, 30–32, 163–64; magic cup, 163n8; mock regret, 126; *Orlando furioso*, 33, 146–47, 148n29; and women, 18–19
Aristotle, 44, 45–46, 92

Artegall, 49, 67, 75; Britomart's combat with, 9, 10, 106–16, 161n9, 163n13; and Britomart's love, 22, 71, 76, 105–16 passim, 150n50; Britomart's quest for, 5, 6–8, 13–33, 71, 84, 105, 106–10; "secret fear," 164n21
Arthur, Prince, 14, 28–29, 56, 74–75, 122–23, 163n11
Attis, 135–36
Augustine of Dacia, 145n11
Authoring. *See* Writing
Autobiography, Scudamore's, 84–86, 128–30

Barfield, Owen, 152n22
Barkan, Leonard, 150n47
Bateson, Gregory, 138
Beginnings/Endings, 90–91
Belphoebe, 151n11; and Lust, 10, 117, 120, 121, 124; and Timias, 36–44, 120
Berger, Harry, Jr.: and Amoret, 156n29; and erotic hunts, 29; and Gardens of Adonis, 37, 38, 40–41, 164n14; and river marriage, 131, 135; and Temple of Venus, 159n15
Bieman, Elizabeth, 149n33
Biology. *See* Body
Birth, of Chrysogone's twins, 43
Blandamour, 77, 78, 89, 95, 100
Boar, 7–8, 35, 36, 44, 47–48, 58
Body, 43, 69–70, 99; erotic, 8, 35, 66; female, 20, 56–58, 65, 101, 102–3, 119–20; fragmentation of, 101, 102–3; Hermaphrodite and, 50–54, 66; as indeterminate, 114; in Lust allegory, 10, 117–20, 123–24; Marinell's, 141; as metaphor, 44, 47–48; and moral allegory, 123; power and, 65, 156n32; prison/lodge, 69–70; social dimension of, 118–20; soul over, 50, 153n3. *See also* Sexuality; Wounding
Bohm, David, 153n5, 157n7
Boldness, 60, 79–80, 158n12
Books, as mirrors, 25

Compositor:	BookMasters, Inc.
Text:	10/13 Palatino
Display:	Palatino
Printer and Binder:	Edwards Brothers, Inc.

BELMONT UNIVERSITY LIBRARY

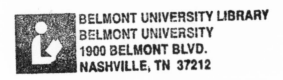

BELMONT UNIVERSITY LIBRARY
BELMONT UNIVERSITY
1900 BELMONT BLVD.
NASHVILLE, TN 37212

DATE DUE			
JUL 16 '00			
GAYLORD			PRINTED IN U.S.A.